Institutional Reform and
Democratic Consolidation in Korea

Edited by Larry Diamond and Doh Chull Shin

Institutional Reform and Democratic Consolidation in Korea

Hoover Institution Press   Stanford University   Stanford, California

The Hoover Institution on War, Revolution and Peace, founded at
Stanford University in 1919 by Herbert Hoover, who went on to become
the thirty-first president of the United States, is an interdisciplinary
research center for advanced study on domestic and international affairs.
The views expressed in its publications are entirely those of the authors
and do not necessarily reflect the views of the staff, officers, or Board of
Overseers of the Hoover Institution.

www-hoover.stanford.edu

Hoover Institution Press Publication No. 461

First printing, 1999

Manufactured in the United States of America

04 03 02 01 00 99   9 8 7 6 5 4 3 2 1

The paper used in this publication meets the minimum requirements of
American National Standard for Information Sciences—Permanence of
Paper for Printed Library Materials, ANSI Z39.48-1984.

Library of Congress Cataloging-in-Publication Data
Institutional reform and democratic consolidation in Korea
edited by Larry Diamond and Doh Chull Shin.
        p.   cm.
    Includes bibliographical references.
    1. Democracy—Korea (South)   2. Korea (South)—Politics and
government—1988–   I. Diamond, Larry Jay.   II. Sin, To-chˆ ŏl.
JQ1729.A15I57   1999
320.95195′09′049—dc21   99-35777
                                                      CIP

Contents

Acknowledgments

M ost chapters in this book were initially presented at a conference, "Institutional Reform and Democratic Consolidation in Korea," held at the Hoover Institution on January 8 and 9, 1998. That conference and the subsequent production of this book were made possible by the generous financial support of the Korea Foundation, which has sponsored several previous conferences and publications in the Hoover Institution's program in Korean studies. The purpose of that initiative is to understand and exchange views on the important changes in the political, economic, and security environment of contemporary Korea, as well as to advance our knowledge of how the Korean experience fits into a comparative analysis of democracy and economic development and reform.

Many people at the Hoover Institution supported and encouraged our work. We would particularly like to thank Associate Director Thomas Henriksen, who helped organize the conference that produced this book and who has led the Hoover Institution's efforts to forge closer collaborative ties with Korean scholars and institutions. We also thank Hoover director John Raisian for his personal support of this project and the entire Korean studies program. We are grateful to Teresa Judd for her help in coordinating the conference, to Marguerite Kramer for her support of the project administration, and to Ann Wood for her always efficient and patient copy editing.

Contributors

MARK ANDREW ABDOLLAHIAN is a vice president at Decision Insights.

LARRY DIAMOND is a senior research fellow at the Hoover Institution and coeditor of the *Journal of Democracy*.

FRANCIS FUKUYAMA is Hirst Professor of Public Policy at the Institute of Public Policy, George Mason University.

HOON JAUNG is an associate professor of political science at Chung-Ang University.

EUN MEE KIM is an associate professor in the Graduate School of International Studies at Ewha Woman's University and an associate professor of sociology at the University of Southern California.

SUNHYUK KIM is an assistant professor of political science at the University of Southern California.

JACEK KUGLER is a director at Decision Insights and Elizabeth Helm Rosecrans Professor of International Relations at Claremont Graduate University.

SOOK-JONG LEE is a research fellow at the Sejong Institute.

YOUNG JO LEE is an associate professor of political science at Kyung-Hee University.

CHAN WOOK PARK is an associate professor of political science at Seoul National University.

HILTON L. ROOT is a senior fellow at the Milken Institute.

KYUNG-RYUNG SEONG is an associate professor of sociology at Hallym University.

DOH CHULL SHIN is Endowed Chair Professor of Korean Politics at the University of Missouri at Columbia.

SEUNG-MOCK YANG is a professor of communication at Seoul National University.

Introduction:
Institutional Reform and
Democratic Consolidation in Korea

Among the dozens of new democracies born during the "third wave" of global democratization,[1] the Republic of Korea (Korea hereafter) is one of the most politically influential and analytically interesting. Korea joined the democratic wave more than a decade after it began in southern Europe in the mid-1970s and after most democratic transitions in Latin America had been completed but before democratization swept through Central and Eastern Europe and parts of the former Soviet Union and sub-Saharan Africa. With the eleventh-largest economy in the world and a gross domestic product larger than nineteen of the twenty-nine states in the Organization for Economic Cooperation and Development (OECD; the exclusive club of industrialized countries), Korea became in 1987 the most powerful democracy in East Asia after Japan. With a peaceful democratic transition driven by a combination of civil society, international pressure, and elite negotiation, followed by almost a decade of relative political stability and continued buoyant economic growth, the country has often been described in the Western

---

1. On this phenomenon, see Samuel Huntington, *The Third Wave: Democratization in the Late Twentieth Century* (Norman: University of Oklahoma Press, 1991), and Larry Diamond, *Developing Democracy: Toward Consolidation* (Baltimore: Johns Hopkins University Press, 1999).

news media and the scholarly community as "an East Asian model of prosperity and democracy."[2]

During 1997, however, the Korean model was shaken to its foundations. The popularity of Kim Young Sam, the first civilian head of government in three decades who had entered as a political reformer with wide public support, collapsed in a series of corruption scandals. Then, in the last two months of 1997, Korea was struck by its worst economic crisis in almost half a century. In November, Korea became a symbol of the Asian financial crisis that shook markets from Hong Kong to Wall Street. When its business conglomerates and merchant banks were unable to pay their huge short-term debts to foreign creditors, Korea had to beg for an international bailout to stave off full-scale bankruptcy. With the largest rescue package ever from the International Monetary Fund (IMF)—$57 billion—the country was quickly transformed from an economic powerhouse, with a gross domestic product larger than ten of the fifteen states in the European Union, into a ward of the international financial community.

Yet economic crisis helped pave the way for a political breakthrough. On December 18, 1997, in its third presidential election since the inauguration of the democratic Sixth Republic, Korea became the first third-wave democracy in East Asia to peacefully transfer power to an opposition party.[3] In that election, the Korean people refused to support the party of a conservative establishment that had ruled their country for decades in collusion with military dictators and massive business conglomerates (*chaebols*). Enraged by a fi-

2. "The Upheaval in South Korea," *New York Times*, December 26, 1995, A14.
3. This does not count the (more ambiguous) frequent changes of government in parliamentary Thailand. But it is worth noting that such a transfer of power to an opposition party has yet to occur in Taiwan and took more than four decades in Japan.

nancial crisis that subjected their country to unprecedented humiliation and devastating economic misery and pain,[4] Koreans elected as their president the country's most determined opposition figure, Kim Dae Jung—a man who had campaigned for the presidency and fallen short three times and who was such an implacable foe of the military that he was nearly put to death by the Chun Doo Hwan regime following the May 1980 Kwangju rebellion.[5]

Undoubtedly Kim Dae Jung's electoral victory represents a major turning point in Korea's journey toward a fully consolidated democracy.[6] It also marks the transition to a new era of democracy in East Asia. Asian democracy has often been equated largely with "rule by a dominant, corporatist party that tolerates a limited opposition but never cedes power."[7] Even if one does not doubt the willingness of a long-dominant party to surrender power if it loses an election, the actual moment represents a qualitative change in the character and vibrancy of democracy. In Korea, however, this remarkable change has coincided with (and was probably made possible by) a profound economic crisis. That crisis has revealed the dark side of the Korean model of democracy and prompted serious debates over whether political democracy can coexist with crony

4. According to Nicholas Kristof ("Many Proud South Koreans Resent Bailout from Abroad," *New York Times*, December 11, 1997, 1), many Koreans view December 3, 1997, the day when the IMF accord was reached, as a day of national humiliation. They also view the aid package as the second national disgrace after the Japanese colonization.

5. Kim was spared the death sentence, it appears, only as a result of U.S. pressure. David I. Steinberg, "The Republic of Korea: Pluralizing Politics," in Larry Diamond, Juan J. Linz, and Seymour Martin Lipset, eds., *Politics in Developing Countries: Comparing Experiences with Democracy* (Boulder, Colo.: Lynne Rienner Publishers, 1995), 383–84.

6. *Dong-A Ilbo*, December 20, 1997.

7. Thomas Carothers, "Democracy," *Foreign Policy* 107 (summer 1997): 10–18. See also Keith B. Richburg, "The Flowering of Democracy," *Washington Post Weekly*, December 22–29, 1997, 16.

capitalism for any extended period of time.[8] Strategically, the economic crisis has occasioned calls for a comprehensive and critical assessment of the Korean democratic experience and for an alternative model of democratic reform for Korea and other dragon states in East Asia.[9]

What specific characteristics define and distinguish the Korean model of democratization to date? What type of institutional reform has been carried out to curtail the power of the deeply entrenched apparatus of military, bureaucratic, and big-business domination? How effective have such reforms been in empowering the Korean mass public and legitimizing nascent democratic rule? Why did the Kim Young Sam government fail to prevent the economic crisis despite signs of troubled economic foundations? What reform measures should the Kim Dae Jung government pursue to resolve the economic crisis and revive the Korean model of prosperity and democracy? What lessons can other new Asian democracies learn from the first decade of Korean democratization? And what do these mixed currents of progress and crisis imply for the consolidation of Korea's new democracy? To discuss these and other important issues of Korean democratization, the Hoover Institution, Stanford University, convened a two-day conference, "Institutional Reform and Democratic Consolidation in Korea," on January 8 and 9, 1998. This volume gathers together revised versions of the papers presented at that conference.

In this introduction, we first offer a chronological overview of the major institutional reforms and political developments in Korea from 1987 to 1998. Then we introduce a multilevel notion of democratic consolidation to guide and sharpen our assessment of Korean

---

8. Francis Fukuyama, "Asian Values and the Asian Crisis," *Commentary*, February 1998, 23–27; A. M. Rosenthal, "Lessons to Be Learned in Asia," *New York Times*, December 26, 1997.

9. Martin Lee, "Testing Asian Values," *New York Times*, January 18, 1998.

democratization for the past decade. Next we discuss a number of theoretical perspectives to promote an adequate understanding of Korea's current problems and its future prospects for becoming a fully consolidated democracy. Finally, we present an overview of the main themes and findings of the individual chapters, which we think offer a wide-ranging and balanced account of where Korean democracy stands now and where it is likely to move in the near future.

Chronology of Major Institutional Reforms

Formally, Korea began its transition to democracy on June 29, 1987, when Roh Tae Woo, the presidential candidate of the ruling Democratic Justice Party (DJP), announced an eight-point pledge, subsequently dubbed the June 29 Declaration of Democratic Reform.[10] This declaration served as the first threshold of Korea's democratic transition from a military dictatorship. In response to seventeen consecutive days of street demonstrations, during which the government fired more than 300,000 tear-gas canisters at protesters, the military government headed by former general Chun Doo Hwan and the ruling DJP formally accepted public demands for democratic reforms and incorporated those demands into Roh's June 29 declaration.

Shortly thereafter, the June 29 declaration was adopted in the National Assembly as a blueprint for amending the Fifth Republic's

10. These reforms are discussed in greater detail in Young-Chul Paik, "Political Reform and Democratic Consolidation," *Korea and World Affairs* 18 (winter 1994): 730–48; Young Whan Kihl, "Political Democracy and Reforms in South Korea," in Sung Chul Yang, ed., *Democracy and Communism* (Seoul: Korean Association of International Studies, 1995), 455–91; the Republic of Korea Ministry of Information, *Reform and Change, Four Years of the New Korea* (Seoul: Korean Overseas Information Service, 1997); and David I. Steinberg, "The Republic of Korea: Pluralizing Politics," in Diamond, Linz, and Lipset, eds., *Politics in Developing Countries*, 369–416.

authoritarian constitution. The institutional reforms it encompassed included (1) a constitutional amendment for direct election of the president by all Koreans aged twenty or older; (2) revising the presidential election law to ensure freedom of candidacy and fair competition; (3) amnesty for longtime democratic dissident Kim Dae Jung and other political prisoners, allowing them to resume political activities; (4) protecting human dignity and promotion of basic rights, including an unprecedented extension of the writ of habeas corpus; (5) restoring freedom of the press by abolishing the repressive Basic Press Law; (6) educational autonomy and local self-government through the popular election of local assemblies and executive heads of local governments; (7) creating a new political climate for dialogue and compromise, especially among competing political parties; and (8) a commitment to enact bold social reforms to build a clean, honest, and more just society.

Building on Roh's June 29 declaration, the National Assembly drafted and approved the new constitutional framework for the democratic Sixth Republic on October 12, 1987. Sixteen days later the new democratic constitution was ratified by 93 percent of the voters in a national referendum. Premised primarily on the principles of presidential democracy—namely, the separation of powers and checks and balances among the various branches of government— the new constitution provided for direct election of the president with a single, nonrenewable five-year term.

As in the past, the president of Korea represents the state and heads the executive branch of government. Under the democratic constitution, however, the president's authority and powers as the head of the government have been curtailed considerably, while those of the legislative and judicial branches have been expanded significantly. Unlike his authoritarian predecessors, the president of the Sixth Republic can no longer dissolve the National Assembly, which is empowered to oversee governmental operations. Nor can he appoint the entire membership of the Constitutional Court, which is authorized by the constitution to pass ultimate judgment on the matters of impeachment and the dissolution of political parties. Although the constitution attempts to redress the historic imbalances among the branches of the government and forbids presidential re-election, the president still enjoys such enormous powers (especially over the national security apparatus) that some consider him to be a kind of civilian dictator. By any measure, the Korean president is much more powerful than the prime minister of Japan.[11]

On February 25, 1988, the Sixth Republic of Korea was born with the inauguration of President Roh Tae Woo, who had been personally chosen as the DJP candidate by the retiring military dictator, Chun Doo Hwan. Roh was elected on December 16, 1987, in the first popular election held in twenty-six years. With only 37 percent of the vote, he prevailed because opposition support was divided between the two most famous Kims of Korean politics, Kim Young Sam and Kim Dae Jung. Although the election was marred by rock throwing and many other incidents of small-scale violence and irregularities, the country achieved the first peaceful transfer of power in recent history.

The agenda of democratic reform did not end with the transition, however. In fact, in many ways it had only begun. Many repressive laws and institutions remained from the authoritarian era, and Korea had yet to acquire many of the institutional foundations and constraints of a liberal democracy.[12] The military and national

11. Andrew Sherry, Shim Jae-Hoon, and Charles S. Lee, "State of Inertia," *Far Eastern Economic Review*, December 11, 1997.

12. On the distinction between liberal and electoral democracy, see Larry Diamond, *Developing Democracy: Toward Consolidation* (Baltimore: Johns Hopkins University Press, 1999), chap. 1. Key components of liberal democracy include strong protection for civil liberties, guaranteed through an independent judiciary that upholds the rule of law; other mechanisms of horizontal accountability to constrain the arbitrary exercise of executive power; substantial scope for autonomous organizations and movements in civil society to articulate and represent a wide range of citizen interests; political equality of all citizens; an open electoral arena; and civilian control over the military.

security establishment remained substantially independent of civilian control. Indeed, many Koreans questioned to what extent Roh Tae Woo, a former general who had attended the Military Academy with Chun Doo Hwan and served as Chun's deputy in the previous military-authoritarian regime, could truly be considered a civilian.

Yet during the Roh Tae Woo administration, a variety of liberalizing reforms were adopted to safeguard political rights and civil liberties among individual citizens as well as civic and political associations. For example, new laws allowing assemblies and demonstrations were enacted in March 1989. A new Constitutional Court was created to prevent any branch of the national and local government from abusing the democratic constitution or human rights. The laws governing judicial proceedings were also modified to make the judicial system more independent of executive control and freer from political interference. The Basic Press Law, one of the most repressive legal tools of the authoritarian Fifth Republic, was formally repealed in November 1987 to ensure freedom of expression and association. Yet it was the Roh government that made freedom of the press de facto by abandoning the various extralegal practices of controlling the news media, such as issuing official guidelines and press cards. The government also liberalized restrictions on foreign travel and bans on the publication and possession of works on communism and North Korea. With these reforms, the Korean political system began a course of political change beyond the procedural realm of electoral politics toward *liberal* democracy.

At the national level, the legislative arena of democracy came into being on April 26, 1988, when 67 percent of Korean voters chose 299 legislators for four-year terms in the 13th National Assembly. Of the total, 224 were elected through the single-member district, plurality system and 75 were allocated to four political parties through proportional representation (initially based on the percentage of seats each party won in the districts). At the local level, two rounds of assembly elections were held, one on March 26, 1991, and one on June 20, 1991, on the basis of the Local Autonomy Law enacted in April 1988.

On May 19, 1992, another significant step was taken to expand the limited practice of representative democracy in Korea when the ruling Democratic Liberal Party (the product of a 1990 merger between the DJP and Kim Young Sam's Reunification Democratic Party as well as Kim Jong Pil's New Democratic Republican Party) selected Kim Young Sam as its presidential candidate through an openly contested nomination process. Terminating the authoritarian practice by which the current party president nominated his successor opened a new age of intraparty democracy.

On February 25, 1993, Kim Young Sam assumed the second presidency of the Sixth Republic, after winning 42 percent of the popular vote the previous December (with Kim Dae Jung once again trailing well behind). Kim Young Sam—the first truly civilian figure to lead a South Korean government since the May 1961 coup brought General Park Chung Hee to power—seemed determined to deepen Korea's nascent democracy. In his inaugural address, President Kim proclaimed as the ultimate goal of his democratic reform effort the birth of a "New Korea" that would be a freer and more mature democratic community. As a first step, Kim formally declared that he would not accept any political funds from any businesses. On February 27, 1993, two days after his inauguration, he formally launched a campaign against political corruption by disclosing his family assets to the public and encouraging other high-ranking government officials to do the same. In May 1993 the National Assembly revised the Public Officials' Ethics Act so as to require that cabinet members, legislators, and other high-ranking government officials register and disclose their assets on a yearly basis. Under the new law, lawmakers and approximately seven thousand government officials, including bureau chiefs, three-star generals, and higher-ups, are required to disclose their own and their immediate family members' assets each year. The same law also set up Public Officials' Ethics Committees in each branch of the national and local government to eliminate corruption and maintain a clean government.

President Kim also moved swiftly to dismantle the deeply entrenched power bases of the previous military authoritarian regimes. Within a few months of his inauguration, he purged the generals and colonels who had been key players in those regimes. He disbanded the Hana Hoe Club, a secret clique in the army whose members had served as pillars of the military dictatorship for thirty years and occupied all the key strategic positions in the military. In January 1994 President Kim successfully persuaded the National Assembly to revise laws on various intelligence agencies to ensure the freely elected government's full authority to formulate and implement new policies. Under the authoritarian Fifth Republic, the executive, legislative, and judicial branches of the government had been legally constrained to share their powers with the military.

The revised laws forced the Agency for National Security Planning (ANSP)—formerly the Korean Central Intelligence Agency— and the Military Security Command, the two most powerful and oppressive institutions of military dictatorship, to "leave politics" and return to their original missions. For the first time in more than three decades, these two and all other security agencies lost their status as "a reserved domain" of Korean politics with exclusive control over national security expenditures, defense strategies, personnel management (promotion), development and procurement of weaponry, and intelligence gathering. Those agencies all became subject to parliamentary oversight and were prohibited from conducting political surveillance over other branches of government, public officials, or private citizens. President Kim also moved to demilitarize the ANSP by appointing a civilian as its director. Those historic measures to demilitarize and downsize the security agencies and to terminate their privileged status established the supremacy of civilian rule, a crucial condition for the emergence of a truly liberal democracy and, we argue, for progress toward the consolidation of Korean democracy.[13]

On August 12, 1993, President Kim Young Sam issued an emergency decree banning anonymous bank accounts and requiring the mandatory use of real names in all financial transactions. This "real-name" financial reform, which was subsequently approved by the National Assembly, aimed to dismantle the structure of political corruption by severing "the collusive links between government and businesses." It also aimed to ensure a rule of law by formally banning underground economic dealings that often involved tax evasion and illicit, speculative investments. By extending to Korean economic life the democratic principles of transparency and accountability, it sought to dismantle the economic foundation of corrupt authoritarian rule.

In March 1994 the National Assembly attempted to strengthen the enforcement of those principles in political life by revising the existing laws on elections, campaign financing, and local autonomy. To ensure freer, cleaner, and more frugal elections, the new Comprehensive Election Law imposed numerous new restrictions on campaigning and spending. As with the Fifth Republic, the initial presidential and parliamentary elections in the Sixth Republic,

---

13. On the concept of civilian supremacy over the military and the contribution that its establishment makes to democratic consolidation, see Huntington, *The Third Wave*, 211–53; Alfred Stepan, *Rethinking Military Politics* (Princeton: Princeton University Press, 1988); Felipe Agüero, *Soldiers, Civilians and Democracy: Post-Franco Spain in Comparative Perspective* (Baltimore: Johns Hopkins University Press, 1995), and "Toward Civilian Supremacy in South America," in Larry Diamond, Marc F. Plattner, Yun-han Chu, and Hung-mao Tien, eds., *Consolidating the Third Wave Democracies: Themes and Perspectives* (Baltimore: Johns Hopkins University Press, 1997), 177–206; Larry Diamond and Marc F. Plattner, eds., *Civil-Military Relations and Democracy* (Baltimore: Johns Hopkins University Press, 1996); and Diamond, *Developing Democracy*, 112–16.

although much freer, were often marred by the age-old practices of vote buying, entertaining, and gift giving. To eradicate such illicit campaign practices, the maximum spending for presidential and parliamentary candidates was lowered from $35 million to $25 million and from $160,000 to $63,000, respectively.

To make political fund-raising and spending "more transparent," the same law required that all parties and candidates use only funds withdrawn from their bank accounts for campaigning and that they submit their account books to the Central Election Management Committee. They are also required to record, on a form provided by the committee, the campaign contributions they receive. If any winning candidate is found to have overspent—even by one-half of the legal spending limit—the election would be declared null and void. The election of a candidate would also be ruled invalid if his or her campaign workers or family members were found to have violated election laws. Moreover, any candidate whose election is ruled invalid would be banned from holding any elective or nonelective public office for ten years.

The new election laws contain other measures to ensure the democratic principles of accountability, fairness, and transparency. Somewhat superficially, the law prohibits campaigning until seventeen days before the scheduled election date to ensure equal opportunity for every candidate and prohibits candidates from door-to-door campaigning and political parties from holding rallies during election campaigns so as to minimize the opportunity to hand out money directly to voters. Furthermore, the new election law reduced the total number of National Assembly seats to be proportionally distributed in the forthcoming 1996 elections to forty-six (after already being reduced to sixty-two in the March 1992 election). The basis for distributing these forty-six nondistrict seats was also changed from the number of district seats each party won to the total percentage of the votes won by each party across all the districts. Those provisions were intended to usher in a new era of "clean and responsive politics" by curbing illegal electioneering and keeping the electoral process transparent and accountable to voters.

The 1994 amendment of the local autonomy law provided for direct election (every four years) of provincial governors, city mayors, and county chiefs. For more than three decades, those executive heads had been appointed by the central government and remained accountable only to its bureaucrats. A new era of devolution of power and grassroots politics was now ushered in. On June 27, 1995, Korean voters took part in the simultaneous election of executive heads and legislators at all the tiers of subnational government for the first time in thirty-four years.

On June 28, 1994, the National Assembly moved to enhance its autonomy from the powerful presidency and to make its operations more democratic and effective. Even in the aftermath of democratic transition in 1988, the legislature had played a marginal and subservient role, passing bills in accordance with the president's guidelines and wishes. The new law of the National Assembly, however, merely provided for the rescheduling of its temporary sessions and the creation of three new standing committees and a training and research institute.

In January 1995, President Kim Young Sam announced his intention to extend the twin principles of transparency and accountability to real estate market transactions. In March the National Assembly enacted the new real-name, real estate registration legislation that President Kim had announced in his New Year's news conference. For years, the price of land and other real estate had been soaring mainly due to unscrupulous speculation practices among the wealthy. As a result, members of the working class, the backbone of Korean industrialization, could not afford to purchase houses. In response, the Kim Young Sam government decided to ease their financial burdens by stabilizing real estate prices. Building on the 1993 real-name financial transaction law, the new law required the use of real names in the registration of all real estate parcels. To date, these two laws, together with the Public Officials' Ethics Act, represent perhaps the most important pieces of anticorruption legislation in any East Asian democracy.[14]

On December 19, 1995, the Kim Young Sam government enacted a special law under which two former presidents and other military leaders were brought to justice. By characterizing the May 18, 1980, mass uprising in Kwangju as a prodemocracy movement, the government supported the passage of the "May 18 Special Law," which authorized the prosecution of those who were responsible for the massacre of hundreds of protesters in Kwangju during May 1980. In parallel fashion, by defining the December 12, 1979, seizure of power as "a couplike military revolt," the law also authorized the prosecution of those who destroyed constitutional order at that time by staging a coup d'état. In April 1997, the Supreme Court upheld lower court rulings sentencing the former president Chun Doo Hwan to life in prison and his successor, Roh Tae Woo, to seventeen years. The Court found Chun and Roh guilty of mutiny, treason, and corruption and Chun guilty of murder as well. In addition, the two former presidents were convicted of bribery and fined heavily: Chun $276 million and Roh $350 million—the amounts they were found to have received while in office. The imprisonment of two former presidents after trials for crimes of the authoritarian past constitutes one of the most far-reaching efforts at retrospective accountability of any third-wave democracy.[15] Some Koreans, however, felt that the lesson of retrospective accountability was muted

14. The only initiative that might match this in scope would be the sweeping new anticorruption provisions and institutions of the 1997 Thai constitution. For details see James R. Klein, "The Constitution of the Kingdom of Thailand, 1997: A Blueprint for Participatory Democracy," Asia Foundation, San Francisco, Working Paper no. 8, March 1998.

15. For the various treatments of authoritarian crimes in other new democracies, see Tina Rosenberg, *The Haunted Land: Facing Europe's Ghosts after Communism* (New York: Random House, 1995).

when Chun and Roh were released on humanitarian grounds at the end of Kim Young Sam's term.

Eight years of Korea's steady progress toward the institutionalization of liberal democracy came to a halt on December 26, 1996, when President Kim Young Sam's ruling party (now renamed the New Korea Party after yet another merger) rammed two important pieces of legislation through the National Assembly in a predawn secret meeting to which opposition lawmakers were not invited. The Law for the Agency for National Security Planning was revised to revive its domestic political role of spying on Korean citizens, which had been abolished in 1994. Specifically, the agency was reauthorized to investigate, arrest, and interrogate people accused of making favorable comments about North Korea or failing to report suspected communist sympathizers. The other piece of legislation, a new labor law, made it easier for companies to dismiss workers, hire replacements for striking workers, and adjust working hours. In contrast to the illiberal national security law, however, the new labor law implemented liberalizing reforms that were long considered necessary to overhaul Korea's highly inflexible labor markets and make the country more competitive in the global economy. That reform was discredited, however, by the undemocratic manner of its adoption and by the postponement of a government promise to allow multiple unions at both the federation and the company level.[16] In an attempt to "fight against communist forces" and "improve international competitiveness," the Kim Young Sam government had fallen back on the undemocratic methods and spirit of the authoritarian past. Intense protests by labor unions, students, and opposition parties, however, soon forced the government to beat a retreat and annul both laws.

16. Byung-Kook Kim and Hyun-Chin Lim, "Labor against Itself: The Structural Dilemmas of State Monism," in Larry Diamond and Byung-Kook Kim, eds., *Consolidating Democracy in South Korea* (Boulder, Colo.: Lynne Rienner Publishers, forthcoming).

On October 31, 1997, the National Assembly made several revisions of a mixed nature to the Comprehensive Election Law it had
passed three years before. The most notable of the revisions, which
the Korean news media criticized as "antidemocratic," were to (1)
permit indoor speaking rallies by political party members or candidates; (2) abolish guilt by association, previously applied to campaign workers who were engaged in illegal practices on behalf of a
candidate; (3) shorten the period in which charges related to campaign violations can be filed; and (4) raise the required monetary de-
posit for a presidential candidate from $333,000 to $556,000. The
most "prodemocratic" revisions were to (1) ban election campaigns
by private organizations such as research institutes; (2) limit "con-
gratulatory" or "condolence" money to $33; and (3) obligate presi-
dential candidates to participate in at least one of three television
debates among themselves.

On December 18, 1997, Kim Dae Jung was elected as the third
president of the Sixth Republic on his fourth attempt at the office,
with 41 percent of the popular vote, in the cleanest and most peaceful presidential race in Korea's history. The country's least expensive
presidential race in a long time, it took Korea across a visible threshold of democratic maturity. Just five years previously, when Kim Dae
Jung contested for the presidency, army generals had openly warned
that they would stage a coup rather than allow the implacable foe of
past military regimes to become the president of their country. This
time there was no such talk. Previously, enormous sums of money
were used by the ruling party in the presidential races to bribe voters. This time, the ruling party distanced itself from such dirty
money politics.[17]

Kim Dae Jung's victory ranks in political significance with the
election of such other courageous democratic dissidents as South

17. Nicholas D. Kristof, "Angry Koreans Elect Longtime Dissident," *New York
Times*, December 19, 1997, A1 & A10.

Africa's Nelson Mandela and Poland's Lech Walesa. Its social implications also parallel in some respects the elevation of Mandela to the highest office of a previously all-white political system. Kim hails from Cholla, the southwestern region of Korea that has long been discriminated against both politically and socially. Kim Dae Jung's victory also contradicts the view that the only kind of viable democracy in East Asia is one based on the enduring dominance of a single party.

On his election, Kim Dae Jung quickly moved to support financial reform bills mandated by the IMF loan deal. He demanded the fundamental restructuring of governmental agencies and major conglomerates controlling over three-quarters of Korea's gross domestic product. At the same time, he began to tame the most powerful labor unions in Asia, which had pushed wages up fivefold in the previous decade, seriously undermining the "miracle" of Korea's export-led growth. In short, Kim Dae Jung's endeavors to restructure crony capitalism and the old way of running politics signaled true change and began to dispel the view that democratically elected governments in Korea could not implement fundamental economic reforms.

In fact, as we have shown, the first decade of democratic rule in Korea produced a large number of political and economic reforms, reshaping the institutions and procedures of military-authoritarian rule into those of representative democracy. Laws were passed to promote free and fair electoral competition at all government levels. Three free and competitive presidential elections were conducted, the third of which produced a historic rotation of power. Three rounds of parliamentary elections also enabled the people to choose their representatives to the National Assembly. In local communities, popularly elected governors and legislators have taken the place of appointees of the central government.

Korea thus has fully restored civilian rule by extricating the military from power. Also Korea has fully established the other minimal architecture of procedural democracy. Accordingly, Korean democracy today meets the criteria of a robust procedural democracy or polyarchy specified by Dahl and other scholars:[18] to wit, a political regime practicing free and fair elections, universal adult suffrage, multiparty competition, civil liberties, and a free press. It is also an increasingly *liberal* democracy, one of only six countries in Asia that is rated "free" by Freedom House.[19]

The Notion of Democratic Consolidation

In Korea today, there is general agreement that electoral politics has become the only possible game in town. The successful establishment of electoral democracy, however, cannot be equated with the consolidation of Korean democracy. As many theorists point out,[20] democratic consolidation involves more than a structure of governance featuring the periodic participation of the mass public in free and competitive elections. To become consolidated, democracy must achieve deep, broad, and lasting legitimacy at three levels: political elites, politically significant parties and organizations, and the mass public. At each level, actors must manifest both a norma-

18. Robert A. Dahl, *Polyarchy* (New Haven: Yale University Press, 1971); Larry Diamond, "Consolidating Democracy in the Americas," *Annals of the American Academy of Political and Social Science* 550 (March 1997): 12–41.

19. For the 1999 Freedom House ratings of political rights and civil liberties, see Adrian Karatnycky, "The 1998 Freedom House Survey: The Decline of Illiberal Democracy," *Journal of Democracy* 10, no. 1 (January 1999): 112–25.

20. Juan Linz and Alfred Stepan, *Problems of Democratic Transition and Consolidation: Southern Europe, South America, and Post-Communist Europe* (Baltimore: Johns Hopkins University Press, 1996); Diamond, *Developing Democracy*; and Doh Chull Shin, "On the Third Wave of Democratization," *World Politics* 47 (October 1994): 135–70. For a skeptical view about consolidation as a concept, which nevertheless voices some similar theoretical considerations, see Guillermo O'Donnell, "Illusions about Consolidation," *Journal of Democracy* 7 (April 1996): 34–51.

tive commitment to democracy as the best form of government (or at least better than any imaginable alternative) and a behavioral commitment to comply with the specific rules and procedures of the constitutional system. Often this requires (or may be facilitated by) some redistribution of political and socioeconomic resources, but at bottom democratic consolidation involves political leadership and institution building.[21]

In new democracies, like the one in Korea, where in the past the military ruled for decades, holding competitive elections and reestablishing representative institutions alone cannot bring about significant changes in the redistribution of political power and other valued resources. Nor can the formal (electoral) institutions of democracy be expected to ensure adequate protection for human rights or the political incorporation of previously marginalized groups. As Terry Karl suggests, to treat competitive elections as a sufficient condition for democracy is to commit the "fallacy of electoralism" and thereby neglect many of the institutional arenas in which reform may be needed to make democracy meaningful, even in strictly political terms.

We therefore ask in this volume, what other specific institutional changes and reforms, besides the institutionalization of electoral competition and participation and the reforms that have already been adopted, are needed to consolidate democracy in Korea? As O'Donnell emphasizes, any meaningful assessment of democratic change must include the informal practices of political exchange and the cultural norms that may undermine the performance of formal democratic institutions—whether or not we accept democratic consolidation as a useful concept.[22] As Linz and Stepan and Diamond note, democratic consolidation also involves the strengthening of state and

---

21. Diamond, *Developing Democracy*, chap. 3; see also Linz and Stepan, *Problems of Democratic Transition and Consolidation*, chap. 1.
22. O'Donnell, "Illusions about Consolidation."

judicial institutions, the restructuring of political institutions in the direction of greater accountability and responsibility, and the invigoration of a previously inhibited civil and political society.

In the present volume, therefore, the consolidation of Korean democracy is considered to be a dynamic process at the micro- and macrolevels as well as in the private and public spheres of Korean political life. At the microlevel of individual citizens, democratic consolidation involves an increasing commitment to the ideals and procedural norms of democratic politics, which may be fostered by or manifested in greater participation in public affairs and requires a certain (peaceful, law-abiding, respectful) *style* of participation. At the macrolevel, democracy is consolidated when political leaders, parties, and organizations (including those in civil society that act in the political or policy arena) manifest a sufficiently clear and unequivocal commitment to the rules of the democratic game (both written and unwritten) so that their competitors come to have confidence in their future compliance and restraint. That situation, which encompasses the cultural and behavioral equilibrium Dahl called a "system of mutual security,"[23] may be fostered by visionary and accommodating leadership. More often, however, it is constructed by mutually suspicious and even ignoble leaders—ordinary politicians—who see that all their interests will collectively be better served if they commit to mutual limits on state authority through the "coordinating mechanism" of a constitution.[24]

This is why the constitutional order is profoundly important to the quality and stability of democracy and thus why consolidation requires both appropriate institutional designs and an independent

23. Dahl, *Polyarchy*, 36–37.
24. Barry R. Weingast, "The Political Foundations of Democracy and the Rule of Law," *American Political Science Review* 91, no. 2 (1997): 251.

judiciary capable of enforcing the constitution and the rule of law. All these dynamics, in turn, heavily affect how the mass public views democracy and whether it will become deeply and intrinsically committed to its legitimacy. Democratic consolidation will advance to the extent that the political institutions of democracy are deepened and improved to become more open, responsive, accountable, and respectful of the law and to the extent that democracy is *seen* by the mass public to be delivering the political goods it promises: freedom, justice, transparency, participation, and a predictable, stable, constitutional order.

Our notion of democratic consolidation as a multilevel and multidimensional phenomenon guided the organization of the Hoover conference and the present volume, which begins with an assessment of democratization at the macrolevel of political society and the state apparatus. From political parties and elections, we turn to the workings of the national legislature, then to the Kim Young Sam government (1993–98), and finally to local government. Later, business conglomerates, the news media, and civil society are, in turn, examined to determine the extent to which democratization has penetrated economic and civil society. Finally, we analyze the microlevel of Koreans' commitment to democratic ideals and practices, their perceptions of the extent of democratic progress, and the larger role of political culture.

Facilitating Conditions

The transition from authoritarian military rule, holding free and fair elections, and installing a new electoral democracy encompass well-defined, single tasks. In sharp contrast, the consolidation phase is confronted with a multitude of diverse and pressing institutional and policy challenges: corruption, the crimes of the authoritarian

past, lawlessness, feeble judicial systems, ineffectual bureaucratic institutions, a fragmented political party system, deep-seated regional
or ethnic divisions, growing social inequality, and now a profound
economic crisis.

The conditions that favor democratic transition do not necessarily promote democratic consolidation; conditions such as negotiated pacts may actually hinder the consolidation process.[25] What
would contribute to the deepening and consolidation of Korean
democracy? Changes in elite behavior, political culture, civil society, institutional structure, and economic performance may all play
a role. By briefly examining these (and summarizing some of the
findings from this book in a more overarching, thematic fashion), we
can observe Korea's progress toward democratic consolidation.

Accommodation among Political Elites

Political elites in new democracies hold strategic positions in key
government and nongovernmental organizations and can shape the
trajectory and pace of democratic consolidation more powerfully
than the masses. Yet elite groups differ significantly in the extent to
which they are united on the worth of the democratic institutions
they have established and on the need to abide by the rules of the
political game. If a democratic transition has come about partially
or entirely through negotiation, rather than imposition or revolution
from below, some degree of elite accommodation will already have
occurred. Deep differences over political values and institutional
preferences, however, typically remain among key elite groups. Democratic consolidation is advanced when all politically significant
elites become "consensually unified" around the basic procedures
and norms by which politics will be played, and when this unity becomes embedded in mutually respectful, cross-cutting patterns of

---

25. Evlyne Huber, Dietrich Rueschemeyer, and John D. Stephens, "The Paradoxes of Contemporary Democracy," *Comparative Politics* 29 (April 1993): 330.

face-to-face interaction.[26] Such a consensually unified elite may be produced rapidly by key "settlements" (pacts) or agreements, or it may emerge through a more incremental, transformative process. No such broad and definitive elite settlement has occurred in Korea, although the June 1987 agreement between the Chun regime and the democratic opposition on direct presidential elections and other reforms certainly counts as a partial elite settlement. Rather, elite consensual unity has emerged incrementally in Korea. In fact, judging by the harshness and unpredictability with which politics are waged and power is exercised in Korea, and the methods that are used to forge alliances and win support, it would be difficult to argue that Korea's political elite is as yet fully "consensually unified."

Popular Commitment to Democracy

If democratic consolidation is at the least a process of legitimation, then it must involve some changes in political culture.[27] Unlike the transition stage, in which the masses may not be actively involved or their attitudes and values heavily weighed, the practice of democracy after the transition involves the participation of a

26. See Michael G. Burton and John Higley, "Elite Settlements," *American Sociological Review* 52 (1987): 295–307; John Higley and Michael Burton, "The Elite Variable in Democratic Transitions and Breakdowns," *American Sociological Review* 54 (1989): 17–32; and Michael G. Burton, Richard Gunther, and John Higley, "Introduction: Elite Transformations and Democratic Regimes," in Higley and Gunther, eds., *Elites and Democratic Consolidation in Latin America and Southern Europe* (Cambridge: Cambridge University Press, 1992), 1–37; and John Higley, Tong-yi Huang, and Tse-min Lin, "Elite Settlements in Taiwan," *Journal of Democracy* 9, no. 2 (1998): 148–63.

27. See in particular Diamond, *Developing Democracy*, chap. 5, and the literature cited therein. For comparative evidence on South Korea, see Doh C. Shin, *Mass Politics and Culture in Democratizing Korea* (Cambridge: Cambridge University Press, 1999); Doh C. Shin and Huoyan Shyu, "Political Ambivalence in South Korea and Taiwan," *Journal of Democracy* 8 (July 1997): 109–24; and Richard Rose and Doh C. Shin, *Qualities of Incomplete Democracies: Russia, the Czech Republic and Korea Compared*, Studies in Public Policy No. 302 (Glasgow: University of Strathclyde, 1998).

multitude of new and inexperienced political actors. Elite accommodation and conciliation may make strategic contributions to the normalization of politics and the consolidation of democracy, but they are not sufficient.[28] Citizens must become sufficiently convinced of the superiority of democracy over any alternative form of government that they are willing to defend it and continue to support it even through times of hardship and crisis.[29] When this democratic support and legitimacy is manifested by large majorities of the population (at least two-thirds) consistently across repeated surveys and different types of measures, we may judge that democracy is consolidated at the level of public norms. As we will see, the values and judgments of the Korean public, while strongly sympathetic to democracy in some respects, are as yet too conflicted, ambiguous, and unstable to signal the consolidation of democracy.

Engagement in Civic Life

A growing body of theory and evidence suggests that a vigorous civil society is instrumental, if not vital, to the consolidation of new democracies.[30] A dense network of civil society organizations, move-

28. It is in equating the achievement of elite consensual unity with democratic consolidation that Higley and Burton and their coauthors go astray theoretically in our view. For an extended critique, see Diamond, *Developing Democracy*, chap. 3.

29. For a seminal empirical study of the dynamics of popular support for democracy after the transitions from communism, and of the role of comparative judgments about alternative regimes in shaping this support, see Richard Rose, William Mishler, and Christian Haerpfer, *Democracy and Its Alternatives: Understanding Post-Communist Societies* (Oxford: Polity Press, 1998).

30. Larry Diamond, "Rethinking Civil Society: Toward Democratic Consolidation," *Journal of Democracy* 5, no. 3 (1994): 4–17, and *Developing Democracy*, chap. 5; Robert D. Putnam, *Making Democracy Work: Civic Traditions in Modern Italy* (Princeton: Princeton University Press, 1993); Michael W. Foley and Bob Edwards, "The Paradox of Civil Society," *Journal of Democracy* 7 (July 1997): 38–52; Philippe C. Schmitter, "Civil Society East and West," Aleksander Smolar, "From Opposition to Atomization," and E. Gyimah-Boadi, "Civil Society in Africa," in Diamond et al., *Consolidating the Third Wave Democracies*, 239–92.

ments, and networks can perform many functions for the consolidation of democracy. Citizen associations independent of the state not only prevent the state from dominating the rest of society, and check the potential abuse of power, but also facilitate a broader distribution of public benefits. Certainly they provide additional channels, beyond political parties, through which citizens articulate their needs and interests to candidates for office and elected representatives, and with which they hold public officials accountable. Acting as public laboratories in which citizens can learn the art of self-rule, those voluntary groups and associations make it possible for electoral or procedural democracies to be transformed into ones of higher quality. Civil society organizations can foster social trust and cooperation, expand the participants' sense of self, and even allow dilemmas of collective actions to be resolved.[31] Not least important for the concern of this volume, the institutions of civil society can generate powerful momentum for institutional reforms to remove authoritarian enclaves, expand citizen rights, tame corrupt practices, widen the political arena, and so deepen the quality of democracy. In Korea, civil society organizations have clearly made important contributions to both the transition and the improvement and consolidation of democracy. But they have not as yet evolved the depth of organization or elicited the breadth of sustained popular involvement that could enable them to realize their full potential. In particular, civil society organizations are only now beginning to coalesce around the broad and demanding challenge of developing a mass political culture of democracy through various civic education initiatives.

31. For a seminal articulation of these dynamics, see Putnam, *Making Democracy Work*, and also "Bowling Alone: America's Declining Social Capital," *Journal of Democracy* 6, no. 1 (1995): 65–78.

Choice of Political Institutions

"The core of the consolidation dilemma," Philippe Schmitter notes, "lies in coming up with a set of institutions that politicians can agree on and that citizens are willing to support."[32] A crucial issue for democratic consolidation in Korea is whether the constitutional framework of the Sixth Republic commands the consensual support and loyalty of both elites and the mass public. The current constitution combines in the presidency considerable powers with a direct mandate from the electorate. This system of a relatively strong presidential democracy was derived from the traditions of authoritarian rule and culture with little concern for the harsh realities of Korea's highly fragmented political parties, based on personal and regional ties. Consequently, during its first decade, Korea's Sixth Republic has oftentimes been plagued by a predicament that Mainwaring characterizes as "a difficult combination of presidentialism with multipartyism."[33]

The separation of the presidency and the National Assembly, and the resultant legislative stalemates—known in Korea as *yeoso yadae* (small government party, large opposition party)—have often frustrated both politicians and citizens. They account in part for the ideologically strange partnership between Kim Dae Jung and Kim Jong Pil; the preelection agreement between the two parties to work to convert the constitution to a prime ministerial system (which Kim Jong Pil would then lead, as a reward for his electoral partnership with Kim Dae Jung); and the intensive, ultimately successful efforts in 1998 by the new Kim Dae Jung administration to use the inducements and threats of executive power (in particular, the prosecutorial power of the public procurator's office) to win a sufficient number

32. Philippe C. Schmitter, "The Consolidation of Democracy and the Representation of Social Group," *American Behavioral Scientists*, 1992, 425.

33. Scott Mainwaring, "Presidentialism, Multipartyism, and Democracy: The Difficult Combination," *Comparative Political Studies* 26 (1993): 198–227.

of defections from the plurality party in the National Assembly, the Grand National Party (the renamed former ruling party), in order to achieve a National Assembly majority for his National Council of New Politics, in alliance with Kim Jong Pil's United Liberal Democrats. Although President Kim Dae Jung's coalition now has its legislative majority, the solution is a temporary and purely political one. Democratic consolidation would certainly be advanced by (if not absolutely dependent on) institutional reform.

Juan Linz and many other theorists argue for the general superiority of parliamentary democracy on both logical and empirical grounds. The mutual dependence of executive and legislature in such a system creates a series of incentives and decision rules that facilitate the minimization of legislative impasses, the removal of inefficient government, and the expansion of mass participation in the political process.[34] The dynamics of mutual dependence enable a parliamentary system to accommodate a legislature with a fragmented multiparty system, which Przeworski and his associates find a "kiss of death" for presidential democracy.[35] Although a recent study of Third World democracies has found "no evidence that [this] constitutional type has had any significant bearing on the success of Third World experiments in democracy between 1930 and 1995,"[36] we think a strong case could be made that parliamentary democracy would fit better the political circumstances and vulnerabilities of Korea today, even if it represented a dramatic change in the country's political and institutional culture. In any case, this huge

34. Alfred Stepan and Cindy Skach, "Constitutional Frameworks and Democratic Consolidation: Parliamentarianism versus Presidentialism," *World Politics*, 1993, 17.

35. Adam Przeworski, Michael Alvarez, Jose Antonio Cheibub, and Fernando Limongi, "What Makes Democracy Endure?" *Journal of Democracy*, 1996, 46.

36. Timothy J. Power and Mark J. Gasjiorowski, "Institutional Design and Democratic Consolidation in the Third World," *Comparative Political Studies* 30 (April 1997): 144.

institutional issue will have to be resolved one way or another before
democracy can be consolidated.

Economic Performance

Korea's quest for democratic stability is greatly advantaged by its
relative wealth. Numerous studies find a strong relationship between
economic development and democracy, particularly between development and the likelihood that democracy will endure.[37] In fact,
Przeworski and his colleagues find that, between 1950 and 1990, no
democracy ever broke down with a level of per capita income any-
where near that of Korea's today.[38] Moreover, recent evidence suggests that political performance is at least as important, if not more
so, for the accumulation of political legitimacy in a new democracy
as is economic performance.[39] This is why it is important for Korea
to improve its democratic institutions and rule of law—so that citizens will perceive that their democracy is actually delivering the
transparency, order, responsiveness, and accountability that democracy promises.

Still, even in a rich country (and Korea is not quite that), prolonged economic crisis and stagnation can breed democratic disaf-
fection, if not breakdown. Certainly progress toward democratic
consolidation threatens to be stalled, if not reversed, unless Korea's

37. This literature is reviewed in Larry Diamond, "Economic Development
and Democracy Reconsidered," *American Behavioral Scientist* 35 (March/June,
1992): 450–99.

38. Przeworski et al., "What Makes Democracies Endure?" 41. Even allowing
for inflation, Korea's 1997 annual per capita income, in purchasing power parity,
is about twice as high as the threshold of income "impregnability"—$6,055 in
1985 purchasing power parity dollars—identified by Przeworski et al. For the Korean figure, see World Bank, *World Development Report 1998/99* (Oxford and New
York: Oxford University Press, 1999), table 1, 191.

39. For empirical evidence, see Rose et al., *Democracy and Its Alternatives*,
chaps. 7–9, and Diamond, *Developing Democracy*, chap. 5.

democratic system shows that it is capable of finding solutions to the systemic economic crisis it entered in November 1997 in ways that are perceived to share the pain and promote a fair distribution of opportunities and rewards. In this regard, Korea faces a distinctive challenge, for its economic "miracle" was forged under a pair of military authoritarian regimes, and survey evidence shows that the public continues to look back on the first of those rulers, Park Chung Hee, with considerable nostalgia. It is always dangerous in the social sciences to take the past as a guarantee of the future and, in this case, to assume that it is impossible for democracy to break down in a country as economically developed as Korea. We believe that Korea *will* find solutions to its economic crisis, and indeed in its first year in office the Kim Dae Jung administration began to implement the kind of far-reaching reforms of the *chaebols* and financial institutions that are necessary to rekindle economic investment and growth and avoid a new financial meltdown. But such economic reforms must continue and go further if Korea is to find a favorable economic and social context for consolidating its democratic institutions.

The Chapters

By definition, all democracies hold elections in which political parties compete for power freely and openly. But democracies vary greatly in the extent to which political parties and the party system are institutionalized. This variation has important implications for the speed and likelihood of democratic consolidation and for the type of democracy that will be consolidated. In chapter 2, Hoon Jaung assesses the institutionalization of political parties and the party system in Korea with a focus on three criteria: representativeness, governability, and stability. In the extent to which elections enable all major interests in society to be fully represented by political parties and in the National Assembly, Jaung finds the current electoral system far from satisfactory. Under the current system, small parties and labor organizations have little chance of representation in the formal process of democratic governance. The current electoral system is also deficient in producing an effective government—especially by making it difficult for the president's party to control the National Assembly. Finally, political parties suffer from a high degree of instability as evidenced by their frequent splits, mergers, and dissolutions. In view of these findings, Jaung recommends a two-ballot electoral system, one ballot for single-member district seats and the other for a proportional representation (PR) party list, with significantly more seats being allocated through PR than the current forty-six (about 15 percent of the total National Assembly). He also appeals for concurrent presidential and legislative elections to increase the prospects that the president's party will have a National Assembly majority, a runoff presidential election in close races, and various initiatives to strengthen political parties institutionally.

In chapter 3, Chan Wook Park analyzes the functioning of the National Assembly and the degree to which it has been democratized and institutionalized since the transition. Looking at change and continuity in the assembly's relationship with the executive branch headed by the president, Park sees some progress toward institutionalization, mainly due to the restoration of its investigative and related powers that had been curtailed under the past authoritarian regime. In functioning, however, the National Assembly is neither autonomous nor capable of managing internal conflicts according to the rules of the democratic game. The highly centralized structure and tight party discipline within the National Assembly have prevented it from becoming an autonomous and democratic body capable of exerting a strong policy influence on the executive branch. To strengthen the National Assembly's policy influence, Park suggests a number of institutional reforms, including year-round assembly sessions; procedures to strengthen the political neutrality of the assembly speaker; transfer of the audit and inspection board from presidential to legislative supervision; and strengthening the legislative staff and information services.

Young Jo Lee reviews in chapter 4 the dramatic course of reform during the administration of Kim Young Sam, who began with over 90 percent public approval and finished with 90 percent disapproval. In examining the relationships among Kim's political, economic, and other reform measures, and the contrasts between the early, successful political reforms and the later failures in socioeconomic reform, Lee unravels the mysterious process by which the first civilian president of the Sixth Republic became a "heroic failure."[40] Lee underscores the importance here of political process. By issuing decrees, the Kim government was able initially to carry out a variety of anticorruption measures and other political reforms targeted at the individual political elites of the past military regimes. Social and economic reforms, however, involved a wider variety of programs, whose goals collided, and a multitude of key players, who were pitted against one another. Relying solely on the powers of the state apparatus, the government could not bring about lasting changes in these sectors. As a stepchild—born out of an abrupt and unpacted transition and an extension of the ruling political party of the past authoritarian regime—the Kim Young Sam administration lacked the institutional and moral bases to create a reform coalition, and Kim himself lacked the political dexterity to do so. The Korean people judged their first civilian president on the basis of his failures to build the democratic community that he promised at the start of his term, and by the national financial collapse that marred the end of his term. Nonetheless, Lee gives President Kim credit for deepening electoral democracy and restoring the supremacy of civilian rule in Korea.

40. Nicholas Kristof, "Seoul's Departing President a Heroic Failure," *New York Times*, December 22, 1997, A6.

In chapter 5, Kyoung-Ryung Seong shifts our focus from the central government by analyzing the democratic reforms that have taken place at the local level. Assuming that local self-rule is essential to the deepening and consolidation of a new democracy, Seong examines the system of local autonomy that was launched in 1991. He finds that, although the system allows for direct election of local leaders, it denies them the authority and resources necessary for genuine self-rule at the grassroots level. Local government heads and legislative councils, for example, are not authorized to make their own ordinances independent of national laws and presidential decrees. For this reason, Seong characterizes the current system of local autonomy as "a variant of authoritarian central control of the past with a democratic facade" and calls for its restructuring in the direction of federalism. Yet for all the structural, cultural, and political constraints the system faces, Seong acknowledges that it has worked to improve the quality of local governance.

In the vast literature on democratic transition and consolidation, one of the most neglected subjects is the mass media. Seung-Mock Yang addresses this lacuna in chapter 6 by analyzing how democratic regime change has affected Korea's news media. Yang shows that the news media no longer play the role of "voluntary servant" that they did under military regimes. With the growing trust of the public and their unprecedented power, the media have recently begun to define the public agenda and even shape public opinion. Competing for a relatively small market, however, the media have increasingly become subservient to market forces and engaged in the practices of commercialism and sensationalism. The invisible hand of capitalism has become the Korean news media's new master, replacing the visible hand of the authoritarian government.

At the core of the economic crisis that has gripped Korea since November 1997 are the huge business conglomerates, the *chaebols*. Yet the dangers and vulnerabilities for the entire economy inherent in the crony capitalism of the *chaebol* structures and practices were

not revealed all of a sudden by the financial crisis; they had been
known for some time and targeted by reformers in and outside the
country. In chapter 7, Eun Mee Kim reviews and critically assesses
the *chaebol* reform policies of the Kim Young Sam administration
and compares them with those of the new Kim Dae Jung administration. She shows that although Kim Young Sam put a high pre-
mium on injecting democracy and transparency into the market,
just as he was seeking to do in politics, his *chaebol* reform policies
failed because of contradictions between two sets of goals and because of the political turmoil and incapacity that befell the Kim administration. In forcing more coherent structures and more
transparent, financially responsible practices on the *chaebols*, Kim
Dae Jung began to succeed where his predecessor had failed, in part
because of the economic crisis—with its attendant international
pressure—that followed from the latter's failure, and in part because
his reputation as an outsider and lack of collusive ties to the economic elite gave him more scope to press for real reform.

The process of economic reform has only begun, however. As
Abdollahian, Beier, Kugler, and Root show in chapter 8, Korea will
remain vulnerable to renewed economic crisis unless it can address
more vigorously the fundamental structural flaws that hamper its
economic competitiveness and the integrity of its financial system.
These flaws include the overextension of the *chaebols* far beyond
their core productive competencies; the lack of ownership and management accountability to minority shareholders as well as workers;
the collusive financial links between government and business that
have led to economically irrational patterns of credit allocation; the
extraordinary rigidity of Korea's labor market, which discourages
new investment and renders Korean exports increasingly uncom-
petitive; and the undercapitalization of Korea's stricken banks. In
fact, the authors show that, after a year of economic reform under
President Kim Dae Jung, industrial concentration has sharply increased, with just five *chaebols* dominating. Kim Dae Jung has so far

been more successful at imposing macroeconomic austerity than negotiating the complex package of needed structural reforms. This is precisely because austerity measures can be centrally imposed, whereas diverse structural reforms require mobilizing a political consensus among conflicting interests—something that is difficult to achieve with Korea's weak and ineffective political institutions.

The authors therefore propose a grand bargain of structural reform, which international financial institutions might help broker among the *chaebols*, the banks, labor, and government. The skills, information, and decision-making authority to run the financial system must be transferred from the government to market-based institutions, "forcing domestic banks to take full responsibility for the loans they authorize" while subjecting banks to more effective, independent inspection. Korea's financial system needs to be made more transparent and competitive, with "open bond, equity, and insurance markets." The *chaebols* must be cut back to their core specialties by restricting their cross-shareholding and cross-guarantees of loans, and the rights of small shareholders must be protected with more diversified management and corporate boards and greater corporate transparency. Finally, companies of all kinds must be given more flexibility to lay off workers when economic conditions require it. The authors suggest that real structural reforms may only be possible on these various fronts if they are all pursued simultaneously, so that each sector gives up and at the same time gets some of its objectives. Such a "package deal" would allow "for a higher level of liberalization than has been attained so far" by mobilizing a broad political consensus.

Doh Chull Shin analyzes in chapter 9 a core dimension of the consolidation puzzle, the evolution of popular support for democracy during the Kim Young Sam government. Assuming that democratic political culture is a multilevel phenomenon, Shin explores the extent to which Korean public opinion surveys in this period evidenced change in the direction of greater democratic legitimacy and related values. His findings reveal that the overall support of the Korean people for democracy has not broadened, deepened, or stabilized appreciably in this period, despite the institutional reforms that Kim Young Sam, as the first civilian president of the Sixth Republic, vigorously implemented during his term. Instead, Koreans' support for democracy (while higher than in some other third-wave democracies) tends to remain superficial, fragmented, and mixed with authoritarian habits. Based on these findings, Shin concludes that Korea is not likely to form a truly democratic nation in a single generation.

Norms and attitudes are not the only elements of political culture. Also important is how the mass public perceives the country's democratic system, and how it compares the new system with previous regimes. These perceptions, which may have an important impact on the dynamics of popular support for democracy, are analyzed by Sook-Jong Lee in chapter 10 with evidence from national sample surveys conducted in 1995, 1996, and 1997. These three surveys consistently show the Korean people believe their current political system to be significantly more democratic than the one in which they lived ten years ago. Moreover, Koreans are optimistic about democracy. Although they see their system as far from fully democratic, they expect it to become appreciably more democratic in the next decade. In addition, the surveys reveal that Koreans' perceptions of democracy are significantly affected by the region in which they live and their perceptions of economic performance. Although the data underscore the degree to which regional identity colors political perceptions and alignments in Korea, they also show that the effect of region largely melts away when Koreans state their expectations for the level of democracy in the future, a hopeful sign. At the same time, the degree to which favorable perceptions of democracy are linked to positive perceptions of national economic conditions underscores the importance for democratic consolidation in Korea of restoring the economy to good health.

In chapter 11, Sunhyuk Kim examines the actual involvement of Koreans in the democratization process by focusing on civil society. Beginning in March 1984, labor unions, religious groups, and student associations were rapidly resurrected and formed an alliance against the Chun Doo Hwan military regime. This grand coalition of various civic groups, and their successful mobilization of many Koreans from all walks of life in a series of prodemocracy rallies, forced the Chun regime to accept the popular demand for democratic regime change. During the posttransition period, Kim shows, civic groups have deepened electoral democracy by monitoring electoral irregularities and expanding citizen participation. They have also pressured the existing government to expand democratic reforms and have prevented it from reverting to authoritarianism. On the basis of these findings, Kim concludes that it is civic mobilization, not elite interactions, that has made the most important contribution to democratic change in Korea.

In the final chapter, Francis Fukuyama explores the prospects for democratic consolidation in Korea from a cultural perspective that emphasizes its linkage to the cultural factors of social trust and political activism. Fukuyama observes a relatively low radius of trust among the Korean people, which he characterizes as the root cause of their propensity for social conflict and political corruption. But he notes that these problems of particularism and corruption are likely to be lessened in the future if the current economic crisis can create a strong sense of national solidarity among the contending parties and strengthen their commitment to more democratic and accountable government. Fukuyama also observes that Koreans, as compared with their peers in East Asia, tend to place greater emphasis on individual rights and are more willing to assert their own interests against various forms of authority. These cultural values of individualism and antiauthoritarianism, he notes, are likely to help

Korea stay on the path to the further democratization that consolidated democracies in Europe took many decades ago to achieve. This path involves the development of interest groups, the broadening of mass political participation, and the emergence of a multiparty system based on societal interests, not personalities.

Toward Consolidation?

The twelve chapters of this book show that Korea has been one of the more vigorous members in the family of third-wave democracies. Several waves of institutional and legal reforms have been carried out in order to establish the necessary institutions and procedures of representative democracy and to rectify the wrongs of the authoritarian past. Although not all these reforms have been equally successful and much remains to be done, Korea has firmly institutionalized the two most important principles of procedural democracy, free and fair electoral competition and civilian supremacy over the military. For Korea and for East Asia, the presidential election victory in 1997 of a lifelong democratic dissident and opposition leader who was almost put to death by the military and his assumption of office without incident represent a particular milestone on the path to democratic maturity.

Yet for all the reforms it has pursued and adopted during its first decade of democracy, Korea remains far from a consolidated, liberal democracy. *Behaviorally*, the mass public tends to shy away from democracy in action. *Normatively*, citizens are committed to the ideals of democracy but show some growing ambivalence about whether democracy is the best system for Korea in this troubled time. Elites remain more divided than united, even over the basic structure of democratic governance, including the preferred form of government for the country. Although the ruling coalition, headed by President Kim Dae Jung and Prime Minister Kim Jong Pil, is committed to switching to a parliamentary system by 2001, the leadership of the opposition Grand National Party opposes the change in the belief that the continuing threat from the communist North requires a strong president. Members of Kim Dae Jung's own party are also raising more explicit doubts as the date by which he would voluntarily surrender real executive power approaches.

At the level of *elite behavior*, governmental and nongovernmental forces alike often appear unwilling to abide by all the rules (written and unwritten) of the democratic game, including those of accountability and transparency. As revealed in a series of major scandals involving the two democratically elected former presidents, Roh Tae Woo and Kim Young Sam, the formal norms of accountability and constitutionalism remain overpowered by the informal norms of clientelism, cronyism, and personalism.[41] Both elected officials and their representative institutions are yet to be dissociated from the various legacies of the authoritarian past. The Agency for National Security Planning's clandestine operation to smear Kim Dae Jung's presidential campaign in December 1997 vividly testifies to the fact that Korea is yet to become a *Rechsstaat*, a state subject to law.

Substantively, Korea remains far from a fully liberal state even after a decade of democratic rule, although it is one of the most pluralistic nations in Asia. Citizens in the South, for example, are still not free to visit, without governmental permission, North Korea's home page on the Internet or to own its books and magazines. Even those who try to listen to North Korean radio broadcasts continue to be imprisoned under the National Security Law that was

41. Steven Mufson, "Rebuilding South Korea's House of Cards," *Washington Post*, December 27, 1997, A1 and A20.

promulgated in 1948.[42] According to Minkahyup, a human rights group in Korea, there were 478 political prisoners in Korean jails when Kim Dae Jung took office.[43] This number is not known to have been reduced to any significant degree. Under the democratic Sixth Republic, as in the authoritarian past, tolerance of communism remains "an unaffordable luxury" among ordinary citizens, despite their president's "sunshine" policy toward North Korea.

What can and should be done to deepen, liberalize, and consolidate democracy in Korea? Along with responding to the economic crisis, this is the most serious challenge the Kim Dae Jung government now faces.[44] If Korea does not switch to a parliamentary system, one simple but effective reform of presidentialism would be to amend the election laws to provide for simultaneous election of the president and the National Assembly, and perhaps of all local and provincial offices as well. Simultaneous elections would establish a democratic system of mutual dependence among various representative institutions and minimize the legislative impasses resulting from the frequent occurrence of *yeoso yadae*. It would also strengthen the role of political parties in the electoral and legislative processes.[45] Proposals in this volume by Jaung, to restructure and strengthen the PR component of the system for electing assembly members, and by Seong, to strengthen the autonomy of local governments, also merit close attention. Electing as much as half of the National Assembly from PR lists in multiseat regional districts would

42. According to Freedom House, hundreds of Koreans are arrested each year for allegedly pro–North Korean statements, contacts, and other nonviolent activities under this law. *Freedom in the World: The Annual Survey of Political Rights and Civil Liberties, 1997–1998* (New York: Freedom House, 1998), 317.

43. Nicholas Kristof, "Seoul Leader, Ex-Inmate Himself, Is Slow to Free Political Prisoners," *New York Times*, March 10, 1998, A10.

44. This and other challenges are discussed in Jong-Yil Ra, "Political Tasks Facing Kim Dae-Jung Administration," *Korea Focus* 6 (January–February 1998), 1–7.

45. For a comparative perspective, see Peter C. Ordeshook, "Institutions and Incentives," *Journal of Democracy* 6, no. 2 (1995): 46–60.

not only strengthen the potential for more ideological politics and more coherent parties. It would also enable parties to win some seats in regions where they might now have little if any chance to win a plurality in a single-member district. This is one mechanism by which the predominance of regional identity in electoral politics might be softened.

The Kim government should continue its effort to restructure the business conglomerates that have served as pillars of crony capitalism and have stifled the invigoration of other civil society organizations. In the first year of his presidency, the vigor with which Kim Dae Jung pursued a fundamental restructuring of the *chaebols* represented a real source of hope for Korea's economic and political future. However, as the authors of chapter 8 show, these efforts are not sufficient in scope. The *chaebols* need to develop more diversified and transparent ownership structures, and the national economy also needs both a more flexible labor market and a more vigorously competitive and open financial system. These three fundamental reforms may only be achieved together, through a grand bargain, if they are to be achieved at all. Although Korea's judiciary is generally considered independent, reform of the larger system of justice should explore how the power of prosecution could be insulated from partisan political interference and manipulation. The current government should also revise the age-old National Security Law that has been a political and legal instrument for silencing opposition against the government and allow Koreans to exercise their political rights and civil liberties to a greater extent. However, citizens must learn that democracy is the government for their entire nation and free themselves from "regional feudalism."[46] This will require both institutional incentives to transcend regionalism in voting behavior and more comprehensive, coherent efforts at civic

46. For this communitarian perspective on democratization, see James G. March and Johan P. Olsen, *Democratic Governance* (New York: Free Press, 1995).

education not only in the schools but by civil society organizations through a diverse range of activities. At this writing, the principal federation of Korean civil society organizations is beginning to address this challenge.

The consolidation of democracy in Korea will no doubt be advanced by generational change as well. In all likelihood, Kim Dae Jung will be the last president of the political generation that led the struggles for and against Korea's developmental authoritarian state. Even if the septuagenarian Kim Jong Pil should assume power as an executive prime minister in a new system, he would likely be a transitional figure. With the exit from the political stage of these last two of the "three Kims," and the emergence of a new generation of political party leaders, there is the chance that the intense pulls of political regionalism will attenuate and the agenda for political and economic reform will gather momentum. In this respect, ironically, Kim Dae Jung—once derided as a dangerous leftist—may now be laying the foundation for deeper and more sustainable reform by opening Korea more fully to the economic and social forces of globalization. His ambitious agenda for economic, political, and social reform coincides with and is reinforced by a renewed flourishing of Korean civil society. If, through a process of dialogue and negotiation with business and labor, Kim Dae Jung can succeed in restructuring and opening up the economy, while buffering the pain for the roughly two million Koreans who will have to cope with unemployment during this wrenching transition, he will not only rekindle economic growth but also alter the political and economic culture of Korea in ways that will diffusely benefit the consolidation of its maturing but still awkward democracy.

Electoral Politics
and Political Parties

$\mathbf{S}$ince the historic transition to democracy in 1987, Korean citizens and political elite have endeavored to consolidate the new democracy. Yet the journey toward a consolidated democracy seems, so far, to have produced mixed results. On the one hand is a positive view of the progress of Korean democracy, emphasizing the lack of any significant attempt to return to an authoritarian regime and the consolidation of electoral democracy with regular and competitive elections. On the other hand, many Koreans endorse a pessimistic assessment, stressing that Koreans have not as yet devised a satisfactory institutional framework that coordinates their competing interests under democratic principles. Given this mixed evaluation, this chapter assumes that Korean democracy is now somewhere between a Schumpeterian electoral democracy and a consolidated democracy. It sees that Korean democracy is still faced with the challenge of further progress toward democratic consolidation. That is, democratic institutions need to be reformed further because democratic consolidation requires widespread acceptance, legitimation,

The author is grateful for the valuable comments by the editors of this volume, Larry Diamond and Doh C. Shin.

and habituation of democratic norms and institutions behaviorally, attitudinally, and constitutionally.[1]

This chapter deals with the question of institutional reform with particular attention to political parties and the election system. It has been widely accepted that parties and the election system are critical elements in the course of democratic consolidation.[2] Only when parties and the election system reflect citizens' demands to the government properly can democratic institutions obtain legitimation and effectiveness. Only when parties and the election system stabilize political competition among conflicting interests can democratic norms and order be habituated among elites and the public.

First, I will assess the performance of political parties and the election system in linking citizens' demands and governmental policies in democratic Korea. How effective and coherent are parties and elections in aggregating and representing social demands? How stabilized are they as an institutional framework within which competing demands can negotiate and compete with one another? An evaluation of the institutional performance of the election system and the parties would show the strengths and weaknesses of the current parties and election system.

Such an evaluation enables us to discuss the direction and strategy of institutional reform in the election system and the parties. For the election system and the parties to provide enhanced representativeness and governability in Korean democracy, do we need changes in procedures and rules for elections and parties? If we bring in legal and procedural changes, should they be designed for more representativeness or more governability? Or is it necessary that the perceptions and attitudes of the elites and the masses toward the election system and the parties be reformed?

1. Juan Linz and Alfred Stepan, "Consolidating New Democracies," *Journal of Democracy* 7 (April 1996): 14–33.

2. Seymour Martin Lipset, "The Social Requisites of Democracy Revisited," *American Sociological Review* 59 (February 1994): 1–22.

Second, in addition to the content and direction of institutional reform, various conditions for implementing reform packages need to be examined. The task of implementing reform packages tends to be constrained by both facilitating and obstructing factors. Thus we need to explore which contextual and structural factors support electoral and party reform and which economic and political factors preclude reforming election system and parties. By examining these conditions, we expect to have a more practical prospect for institutional reform and eventually for democratic consolidation in democratic Korea.

The performance of the election system and the parties should be evaluated in terms of their quintessential roles in democratic politics. Classics on electoral and party politics have emphasized that their essential roles consist of (1) aggregating social demands and translating them into governmental policies and (2) providing the elected government with stability and coherence for governance.[3] Whereas the first involves the democratic *responsiveness* of representative institutions to civil demands, the second is about the *effectiveness* of representative government. Thus the aggregation and translation of social demands refers to representation that involves the election system and the parties in reflecting citizens' demands and interests in the process of electoral competition. For this role, the parties and the election system are evaluated by how exactly social demands and conflicts are reflected, which we call *representativeness*. Election systems and parties are also supposed to provide government with "sufficient concentration and autonomy of power to choose and implement policies."[4] Because governments in competitive democracies are elected through electoral competition

---

3. Maurice Duverger, *Political Parties* (London: Methuen, 1954), and Giovanni Sartori, *Comparative Constitutional Engineering* (London: Macmillan, 1994).

4. Larry Diamond, "Three Paradoxes of Democracy," in Larry Diamond and Marc Plattner, eds., *The Global Resurgence of Democracy* (Baltimore: Johns Hopkins University Press, 1993), 100.

among political parties, the election system and the parties should provide the stability and coherence necessary for managing government effectively, which we call *governability*. For instance, if too many social demands are translated into government, there will be problems of overload. Hence, electoral competition by parties should reduce and channel social demands to a manageable level.[5]

Both representativeness and governability are criteria that are employed for election systems and parties in democratic governments in general. However, one additional criterion is needed for new democracies. Studies of democratic consolidation in new democracies have underscored the significance of stabilizing electoral behavior and the party system. They stress that democratic consolidation requires stable democratic rules and institutions in which conflicting interests negotiate and compete.[6] When democratic rules and institutions are stabilized in terms of the attitudes and behaviors of the political elites and the masses, democratic consolidation is accomplished. In this vein, case studies of democratic consolidation in various countries have attempted to measure the stabilization of electoral politics and political parties.[7]

5. Diamond points out that representativeness and governability constitute one of the key paradoxes of democracy that most new democracies inevitably face in the course of democratic consolidation. According to him, the other two sets of paradoxes of democracy consist of the tension between consent and conflict and between conflict and consensus. For more, see Larry Diamond, *Developing Democracy: Toward Consolidation* (Baltimore: Johns Hopkins University Press, 1999).

6. Scott Mainwaring and Timothy Scully, *Building Democratic Institutions: Party Systems in Latin America* (Stanford: Stanford University Press, 1995), 6–8; Leonardo Morlino, "Political Parties and Democratic Consolidation in Southern Europe," in Richard Gunther, Nikiforos Diamandouros, and Hans-Jurgen Puhle, eds., *The Politics of Democratic Consolidation: Southern Europe in Comparative Perspective* (Baltimore: Johns Hopkins University Press, 1995), 316.

7. Scott Mainwaring, "Brazil: Weak Parties, Feckless Democracy," in Scott Mainwaring and Timothy Scully, *Building Democratic Institutions*, and Leonardo Morlino, "Political Parties and Democratic Consolidation in Southern Europe," in Gunther, Diamandouros, and Puhle, *The Politics of Democratic Consolidation*.

The Election System and Political Parties
in Democratic Korea

Representativeness

The first criterion for representativeness is the proportionality of the election system. *Proportionality* is the congruence of parties' seat shares and their vote shares. That is, it measures how the election system translates the voters' decision into government through the number of seats in parliament. Of the various attempts to measure proportionality, we will use the index developed by Rose.[8] In this index, the absolute values of all vote-seat differences are added and then divided by two and that value is subtracted from one hundred. Table 1 shows the proportionality of the election system in Korea since the democratic transition in 1987.

As we see in table 1, the proportionality index has ranged between 88 and 90, while the average proportionality index in the three parliamentary elections is 89, which is low compared with those in advanced democracies. According to Rose's study, which explores the proportionality of election systems in twenty-four western democracies in 1982, the five highest proportionality indexes in proportional representation (PR) democracies were 99 (Austria), 98 (West Germany), 97 (Denmark, Ireland, Netherlands). Among seventeen PR democracies in Rose's study, fifteen had proportionality indexes higher than 90. For non-PR democracies, the index was 94 for the United States, 91 for Japan, 88 for Canada, and 87 for Australia.[9] The average index for seven non-PR democracies was 86.2. Given these, the proportionality index of the Korean election system is slightly higher than those in

---

8. Richard Rose, "Electoral System: A Question of Degree or of Principle?" in Arend Lijphart and Bernard Grofman, eds., *Choosing Electoral Systems: Issues and Alternatives* (New York: Praeger, 1984).

9. Ibid., 75.

TABLE 1   Proportionality of Korean Election System, 1988–1996

Party	1988 Parliamentary Election*			
	DJP	RDP	PPD	NDRP
Share of vote (%)	33.9	23.8	19.2	15.5
Share of seats (%)	41.8	19.7	23.4	11.7
proportionality index = 90				

Party	1992 Parliamentary Election**				
	DLP	DP	RNP	NPP	PP
Share of vote (%)	38.5	29.2	17.4	1.8	1.5
Share of seats (%)	48.9	31.6	10.1		
proportionality index = 89.5					

Party	1996 Parliamentary Election***				
	NKP	NCNP	DP	ULD	Indep.
Share of vote (%)	34.4	25.3	10.9	16.5	13
Share of seats (%)	46	26	5	16	5
proportionality index = 88.4					

*DJP: Democratic Justice Party, RDP: Reunification Democratic Party, NDRP: New Republican Democratic Party, PPD: Party for Peace and Democracy

**DLP: Democratic Liberal Party, DP: Democratic Party, RNP: Reunification National Party, NPP: New Political Party, PP: People's Party, NCNP: National Congress for New Politics

***NKP: New Korea Party, ULD: United Liberal Democrats, Indep: Independents.

SOURCE: National Election Commission, *Korean National Election Data* (Seoul: National Election Commission, various issues).

non-PR countries and lower than those in PR countries. Considering that the Korean election system is a hybrid, combining a first-past-the-post system (253 seats) and the PR system (46 seats), the proportionality of the Korean election system is moderate.

The second indicator of representativeness are the institutional barriers to electoral strength. On the basis of this criterion, representativeness in Korean democracy is in serious trouble. First, the electoral threshold for small parties is not generous. For a party to qualify for PR seat allocation, it needs at least five seats won from the first-past-the-post (FPTP) system or 5 percent of the vote. Although Germany and France maintain an electoral threshold of 5 percent, electoral thresholds in Sweden, Spain and Israel range from 4 percent to 1 percent. Minorities in Korean politics thus have to surmount a high hurdle in order to be represented politically.[10] Not since 1987 has a small party passed the electoral threshold. Second, labor organizations have not been allowed to participate in electoral competition. Electoral laws prohibit labor organizations from donating political funds or forming political organizations.[11] Thus industrial workers have no institutional channel to translate their collective interests into the political system. The absence of workers' parties has allowed conservative parties to dominate party politics in electoral competition as well as in governmental power. Conservative parties, which are either renovations of the governing party or opposition parties from the authoritarian era, advocate economic distribution based on competition rather than on social protection and are reluctant to show any association with labor interests. As a result, the political and economic interests of industrial workers are not reflected by political parties. This distorted reflection of social reality seriously undermines the representativeness of party politics.

The third criterion for representativeness is the congruence between legislative seats and voting population that measures the equality of the vote among the electorate. Employing the Webster

10. According to Lijphart's study, the size of the electoral threshold has the strongest impact on the proportionality of an election system. See Arend Lijphart, *Electoral Systems and Party Systems: A Study of Twenty-Seven Democracies 1945–1990* (New York: Oxford University Press, 1994), 108–9.

11. In April 1998 the newly elected Kim Dae Jung government eliminated these institutional constraints for industrial workers by revising the election laws.

index, one study indicated a great disparity in the value of vote between urban and rural areas.[12] Since the democratic transition, the Webster index for big cities has ranged from 77 to 86 percent, indicating significant underrepresentation among urban voters. In comparison, the Webster index for rural areas has been around 150 percent, which means rural voters have been largely overrepresented. This disparity results, in part, from the historical legacy of the authoritarian era, when the regime relied heavily on mobilized support from rural areas. In any case, the unequal vote between the urban and rural areas is another sign of representation problems in the election system.

The fourth criterion is the evenness of the distribution of electoral support for political parties across regions. Because regionalism has been a dominant factor in party competition in democratic Korea, measuring those regional distributions will indicate the representativeness of political parties. When parties are evenly supported throughout a region they are more likely to be representative. To measure the evenness of support, we use the index of regional voting, which is the percentage point difference between the share of the vote of a party in its regional home base and its share of the vote outside the home base.[13]

Using that index, we see that regional representativeness of electoral support for parties is notably low (see table 2). Most political parties obtain highly concentrated support from their home regions while commanding meager support from outside. The most promi-

12. Gap-Yun Lee, "Reforming Congressional Electoral System" (in Korean), *Korean Journal of Legislative Studies* (spring 1996): 96–97.

13. The calculation of regional voting index is the same one that Robert Alford used in measuring the extent of class voting in western democracies. Robert Alford, *Party and Society: The Anglo-American Democracies* (Chicago: Rand McNally & Company, 1963), 78.

nent case is the party of the Honam (or Cholla) region, the National Congress for New Politics (NCNP), which obtained 95 percent of the Honam's vote while drawing only 30 percent of votes outside Honam in the 1997 presidential election. The same problem applies to other parties, although the concentration is not as strong.

In sum, the democratic representativeness of the election system and political parties is low in democratic Korea. Although the first criterion—proportionality of the election system—shows moderate representativeness, the other criteria indicate the low representativeness of the election system and party politics.

TABLE 2 The Regional Voting Index in Presidential Elections

	*The 1988 Presidential Election**		
	DJP	*RDP*	*PPD*
Home Region (share of votes)	49	37	80
Outside Home Region (average share of votes)	40	17	10
Regional Voting Index	9	20	70 ✓
National Average Share of Votes	37	28	27

	*The 1997 Presidential Election***	
	NCNP	*GNP*
Home Region (share of votes)	95	61
Outside Home Region (average share of votes)	30	26
Regional Voting Index	65	35
National Average Share of Votes	40	38

*DJP: Democratic Justice Party, RDP: Reunification Democratic Party, PPD: Party for Peace and Democracy

**NCNP: National Congress for New Politics, GNP: Grand National Party

SOURCE: National Election Commission, *Korean National Election Data* (Seoul: National Election Commission, various issues).

Governability

The first criterion for governability is an undivided government. Unfortunately, divided government has been a normal phenomenon in democratic Korea. Although the size of the minority has varied from time to time, elections have continued to result in divided control of the presidency and the parliament. In the 1988 and the 1992 parliamentary elections, President Roh's Democratic Justice Party failed to obtain a majority, while having 41.8 percent and 49.8 percent of the seats, respectively. In the 1996 parliamentary election, President Kim Young Sam's party also failed to gain a parliamentary majority, obtaining 46 percent of the seats. And the 1997 presidential election brought about divided government again as the new president Kim Dae Jung's party (NCNP) and his coalition partner (the United Liberal Democrats) together controlled only 43 percent of the seats.

Divided government results from the interaction of several factors, the first of which is electing the president by a simple plurality. That plurality rule risks the problem of minority government faced with a parliament controlled by opposition parties. In fact, the winning candidates, Roh in 1987, Kim Young Sam in 1992, and Kim Dae Jung in 1997 obtained only 37, 41, and 40 percent of the vote, respectively. Because the president is elected by a simple plurality, the president's party's share of the legislative seats tends to be lower than 50 percent. Because the presidential and parliamentary elections are not simultaneous, due to the different terms of the two branches, the president's party cannot expect significant coattail effects in parliamentary election. The second factor, the fragmentation of regionalism, is also responsible for divided government. Regional conflict, the most dominant factor in political competition in democratic Korea, consists of rivalry among three or four major regions. Thus, presidential elections have been dominated by three or four regional parties with solid regional bases.

The second criterion for governability is the effective number of parties. In general, if there are too many parties in a political system, it is likely to have governability problems. In democratic Korea, the issue of the number of parties is closely related to the problem of divided government, as discussed above. To discover the effective number of parties in democratic Korea, let us employ the formula developed by Laakso and Taagepera[14] that calculates the effective number of parties by squaring each party's share of seats, adding all of these squares, and dividing 1.00 by this number. Using this formula, the effective number of parties was 3.6 in the 1988 parliamentary election, 2.9 in the 1992 election, and 3.0 in the 1996 election; the average number of parties was 3.2. That number is not problematic if we look at the consolidation process in southern European democracies. In Italy and Spain, party politics began to stabilize and get on the track of democratic consolidation with about three effective parties. According to Morlino, Italian democracy began to stabilize following the 1948 election in which the number of parties started to settle at around 3.5. In Spain, democracy began to consolidate when the number of parties stabilized at between 2.5 and 3.0.[15]

If we examine the cases of stable presidential democracies, however, the number of 3.2 looks inauspicious. According to Mainwaring's study, stable presidential democracies tend to have few effective parties. Among the thirty-one presidential democracies around the world, only four can be classified as stable. And their effective number of parties are about two — 1.9 for the United States, 2.1 for Colombia, 2.2 for Costa Rica, and 2.8 for Venezuela, suggesting that presidential democracy is more likely to have long-term stability with a two-party system. Thus, although the number of parties in Korea is not too large to obstruct democratic governability

14. Markku Laakso and Rein Taagepera, "'Effective' Number of Parties: A Measure with Application to West Europe," *Comparative Political Studies* 12 (April 1979): 3–27.

15. Morlino, "Political Parties and Democratic Consolidation in Southern Europe," 326–27.

seriously, it does not form an optimal match with presidentialism. In other words, the number of parties is not a determining factor for governability but should be considered in conjunction with other factors, especially presidentialism, which we will turn to later.

Another way of measuring the degree of aggregation of the party system is the fractionalization among political parties. Rae's widely used index of fractionalization, which measures the likelihood that any two members of a parliament will belong to different parties, squares each party's share of seats, adds them, and subtracts the sum from one. According to Rae's index, the seat fractionalization among parties was .72 in 1988, .65 in 1992, and .69 in 1996 in democratic Korea. The average index was .69. Once again, this score of seat fractionalization is remarkably higher than those in stable presidential democracies except Chile (see table 3).

In sum, the numbers of parties and seat fragmentation in democratic Korea appear problematic when compared with stable presidential democracies. If compared to democratic consolidation experiences in Italy and Spain, however, they do not look so gloomy. That is, the number of parties and fragmentation do not cause serious governability problems by themselves. Rather, the governability of elections and parties is deeply interwoven with presidentialism in Korea.

What is critical is the president's party's share of seats in parliament rather than the number or fractionalization of parties. Note that the president's party's average share of seats is about 50 percent or more in most stable presidential democracies (see table 3). In democratic Korea, too, the governability problem was not serious when the president's party's share of seats was about or more than 50 percent (e.g., 1992 and 1996). The deadlock between the parliament and the presidency became troublesome in 1988 and 1997, when the president's party's share was substantially short of the par-

TABLE 3   Stable Presidential Democracies Compared with Korea, Italy, and Spain

Stable Presidential Democracies	Elections	Mean Party System Fragmentation	Mean Number of Effective Parties	Mean Share of Legislative Seats Controlled by President's Party
The Philippines	1953–1969	.436	1.85	63.1%
United States	1968–1986	.475	1.9	45.8%
Colombia	1974–1986	.521	2.09	52.2%
Costa Rica	1974–1986	.592	2.45	50.9%
Uruguay	1942–1973	.595	2.47	49.3%
Venezuela	1973–1988	.620	2.63	49.9%
Chile	1946–1973	.796	4.90	30.2%
Korea	1988–1996	.69	3.2	45.6%
Italy	1946–1994	.766	—	n.a.
Spain	1977–1993	.728	—	n.a.

n.a.: not applicable

SOURCE: Scott Mainwaring, "Presidentialism, Multipartyism, and Democracy: The Difficult Combination," *Comparative Political Studies* 26 (April 1993):213; Morlino, "Political Parties and Democratic Consolidation," 324.

liamentary majority.[16] Unfortunately, such a situation of divided government has and will continue to happen in Korean democracy as a result of various political and institutional causes.

Stability

A third measure of political institutions is stability: whether political institutions provide effective enough rules to regulate competition among political forces. Only when political institutions

16. The effective numbers of parties were about the same across the different situations.

develop lasting bases of support and attachment, and when the elites and the public at large become habituated to them, does a new democracy progress toward democratic consolidation. A common criterion for stability in new democracies is electoral volatility among political parties. Various studies have investigated electoral volatility in new democracies to evaluate the progress toward democratic consolidation.[17] It is not, however, easy to measure electoral volatility in democratic Korea. The reasons are twofold: (1) Not enough elections have been held to trace the trend of electoral volatility after the transition. There were only three parliamentary elections and three presidential elections from 1987 to 1997. (2) There have been frequent mergers and splits among the major political parties. This high degree of instability makes it difficult to measure electoral volatility among political parties.

Given these constraints on measurement, let us examine the electoral volatility in Korea and compare it with those in other new democracies. Electoral volatility is calculated by adding the absolute value of all changes in the percentages of votes cast for each party since the previous election and dividing them by two.[18] Because election numbers are few, both parliamentary elections and presidential elections are included without any distinction.

If we rely only on electoral volatility, the party system in democratic Korea had achieved considerable stability by the 1992 presidential election. As happened in Italy in 1953 and Spain in 1986, electoral volatility in Korea began to decrease substantially following the 1992 presidential election (see table 4). To see this as a critical election in building democratic stability, let us consider the electoral volatility in other unconsolidated democracies. For instance in Brazil, which is no-

17. Morlino, "Political Parties and Democratic Consolidation," and Mainwaring, "Brazil: Weak Parties, Feckless Democracy."

18. Mogens Pedersen, "The Dynamics of European Party Systems: Changing Patterns of Electoral Volatility," *European Journal of Political Research* 7 (July 1979): 1–26.

TABLE 4 Electoral Volatility in Democratic Korea, Italy, and Spain (in percent)

	Korea	*Italy*	*Spain*
1946		42.9	
1948		22.8	
1953		13.3	
1958		4.5	
1963		7.9	
1968		3.4	
1972		4.9	
1976		8.2	
1979		5.3	10.8
1982			42.3
1983		8.5	
1986			11.9
1987		8.4	
1988	11.0		
1989			8.8
1992	22.4	16.2	
1992a	4.6		
1993			10.6
1994		41.9	
1996	8.0		
1997	7.0		

SOURCE: Morlino, "Political Parties and Democratic Consolidation in Southern Europe," 318. Electoral volatility in Korea is calculated from the data in various issues of *Korean National Election Data* (Seoul: Korean Election Management Commission). In Korea 1992a indicates the presidential election while 1992 refers to the parliamentary election in the same year.

torious for the underdevelopment of party politics, electoral volatility was 42.5 between 1982 and 1986 and 38.6 between 1986 and 1990.[19] However, if we recall that the major political parties are still plagued by incessant mergers and splits, the reduction of electoral volatility may not be a reliable sign of increasing stability (see figure 1).

19. Mainwaring, "Brazil: Weak Parties, Feckless Democracy," 374.

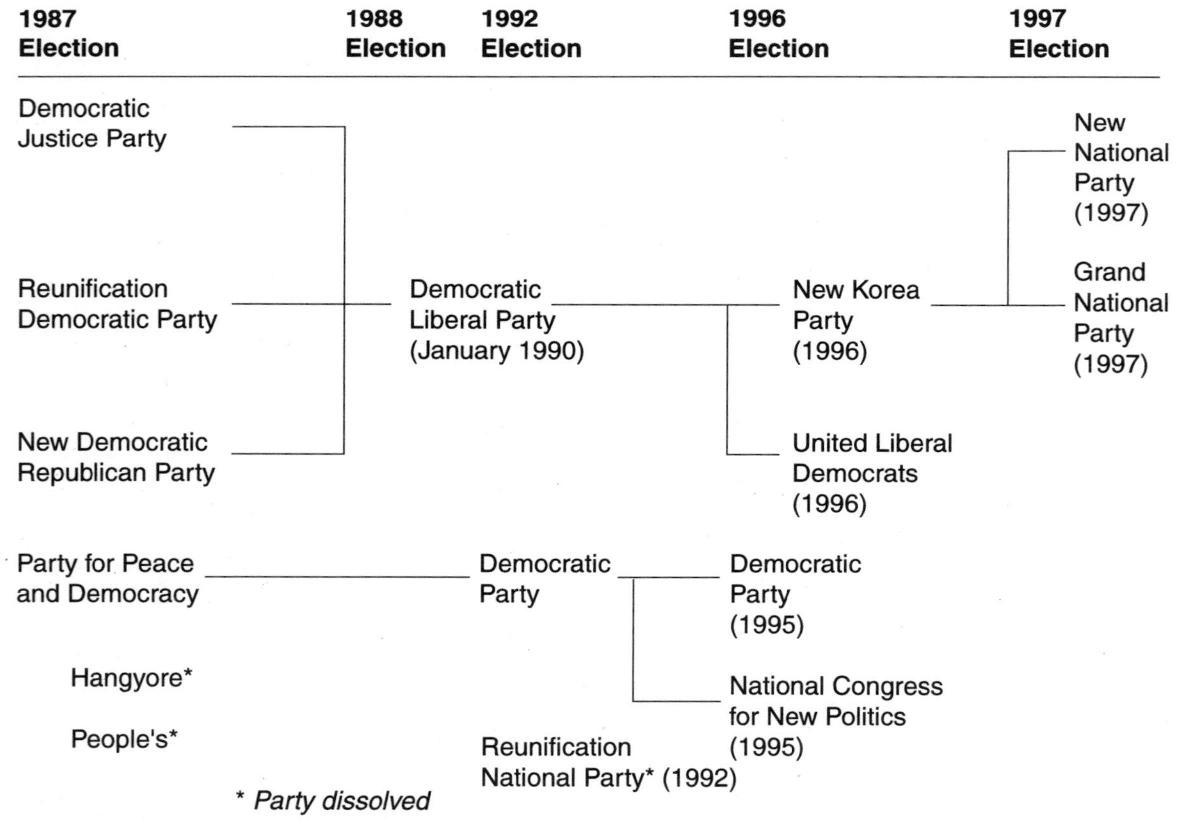

1987 Election	1988 Election	1992 Election	1996 Election	1997 Election

Democratic
Justice Party

Reunification
Democratic Party
    Democratic
    Liberal Party
    (January 1990)
        New Korea
        Party
        (1996)
                New
                National
                Party
                (1997)

New Democratic
Republican Party
        United Liberal
        Democrats
        (1996)
                Grand
                National
                Party
                (1997)

Party for Peace
and Democracy
    Democratic
    Party
        Democratic
        Party
        (1995)

Hangyore*

People's*
    Reunification
    National Party* (1992)
        National Congress
        for New Politics
        (1995)

* *Party dissolved*

FIGURE 1 Mergers and Splits among Political Parties in Democratic Korea

SOURCE: Compiled from *Chosun Daily*, 1987–1996.

The other measurement of institutional stability—the institutionalization of party organizations indicates that Korean democracy still has a ways to go.[20] Political parties have, thus far, failed to strengthen their notoriously weak party organizations. In the democratic era, political parties still suffer from the lack of adaptability, complexity, and coherence that Samuel Huntington regards as key elements of the institutionalization of political organizations.[21] The inability of Korean parties to adapt to changing environments has not changed at all; political parties can still not adjust to environmental changes and internal crisis. Recurrent splits, mergers, and dissolutions clearly attest to their weak adaptive capacity. Since the democratic transition, every major political party has experienced at least one merger or split. For instance, Roh Tae Woo's Democratic Justice Party (DJP) merged with two opposition parties in 1990 to solve the problem of minority government and changed into the Democratic Liberal Party (DLP). The DLP became the New Korea Party (NKP) as President Kim Young Sam was reinforcing his control over the party. The NKP, once again, merged with the DP (Democratic Party) and changed its name to the Grand National Party in the course of the 1997 presidential campaign.

The level of complexity of Korean political parties is also low. Although there has been some proliferation of party subunits at the national, provincial, and local levels, these nominal organizations do not play substantial roles in such crucial functions as setting campaign strategy and raising campaign funds. These key functions have

20. The discussion of the institutionalization of political parties is largely drawn from Hoon Jaung, "A New Democracy at a Crossroad: Democratization, Party System, and Economic Growth in South Korea," paper presented at the "International Conference on Democratization, Party System, and Economic Growth in Seven Asia and South-East Asian Countries," organized by the United Nations University, Kuala Lumpur, February 19–20, 1997.

21. Samuel Huntington, *Political Order in Changing Societies* (New Haven: Yale University Press, 1968), 12–22.

been managed by top-level party leaders and their close aides. The situation is similar in functional subunits of party organizations.

In sum, political parties in democratic Korea are not highly institutionalized in terms of age, adaptability, and organizational complexity. Instead, they are still suffering from the symptoms of inchoate and fluid political organizations that are common among political parties in many postauthoritarian regimes.

Our examination reveals that the election system and the parties in democratic Korea have performed relatively weakly in terms of governability, representativeness, and stability. Although governability has fluctuated occasionally from medium to low, representativeness and stability have been consistently low.

The Direction of Institutional Reform

The poor performance of political institutions, as examined above, calls for the reform of political institutions. When the current political institutions were chosen in the process of democratic transition, they reflected the hope and vision of many Koreans as well as the power relations among political elites.[22] Yet it is now clear that those initial choices need to be reformed. As structural changes in political institutions are neither desirable nor plausible at this stage, we need to concentrate on reforming political institutions while maintaining their basic structure.

To explore the direction and strategy of institutional reform, let us begin with the current political institutions, which provide only medium-to-low governability and low representativeness (see figure 2).

22. In explaining the initial institutional choice in Eastern European democracies, Geddes argues that the power relation among political elites exerts the most significant influence on the institutional choice. See Barbara Geddes, "Initiation of New Democratic Institutions in Eastern Europe and Latin America," in Arend Lijphart and Carlos Waisman, eds., *Institutional Design in New Democracies: Eastern Europe and Latin America* (Boulder, Colo.: Westview Press, 1996), 23–27.

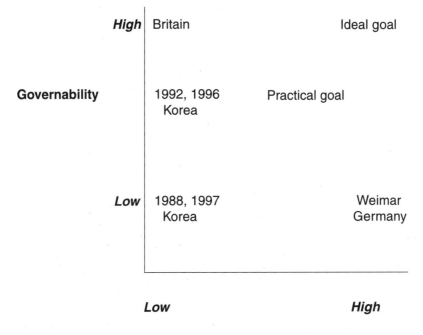

FIGURE 2 Conceptual Map of Governability and Representativeness

The 1988 parliamentary election and the 1997 presidential election resulted in low representativeness and low governability, whereas the 1992 and the 1996 parliamentary elections resulted in medium governability and low representativeness. That is, we can put the results of the 1988 and 1997 election at the lower left corner of the figure and the results of the 1992 and 1996 election at the midleft side. In this conceptual map, the ideal location for most democracies should be the upper right corner (ideal goal). In the real world, however, no political system can maximize both governability and representativeness. Thus, a more practical goal for new democracies should be somewhere around the center of our conceptual map, which denotes medium-to-medium-high governability combined with medium-to-medium-high representativeness. In fact, the desirable location for each new democracy varies according to its historical experience, structure of social conflict, and cultural idiosyncrasy. Yet the general direction should be around the center of the figure, marked as practical goal, because representativeness and governability are both to some extent necessary for the sustenance of democracy and for democratic consolidation.

Electoral Reform

If we assume that the center of the conceptual map is a practical goal for democratic Korea, we can suggest some reform packages to get there. For an election system, probably the most practical alternative is a double-ballot system in which voters cast two ballots — one for single-member district (SMD) seats and the other for a proportional representation (PR) list.[23] In fact, such a system is not unfamiliar to Korean politics, for the current election system is a combination of SMD and PR. The current system, however, is problematic at least in two senses. First, the share of PR seats is too small — only 46 out of 299 — to maintain a desirable level of representativeness. Second, the allocation of PR seats is based on the share of the votes that each party gains in the SMD. Because SMD voting is largely determined by candidates and constituency-specific factors, the current PR element can not fulfill its original purpose.

The double-ballot system can be introduced by increasing the share of the PR seats and providing the voters with a second ballot for PR list. Such a change would improve the representativeness of the election system without seriously hampering governability. The increased number of PR seats would improve the proportionality of the election system (the PR system in general enhances proportionality), and the increased PR seats would allow minor political forces,

23. Chan-Wook Park also proposed the introduction of the double-ballot system. See Park, " Reforming the Election System for Parliament," *National Strategy* 3 (1997): 249–78.

including workers, to attain parliamentary seats, which in turn would widen political representation.

The problem with the double-ballot system is that it may reduce governability by increasing the number of parties and by enhancing the likelihood of a minority government. The governability of the double-ballot system, however, largely depends on the share of PR seats and the electoral threshold in PR allocation: the bigger the share of PR seats, the greater the number of parties; the lower the electoral threshold, the greater the number of parties. Thus, the issue is to what extent should the PR seats be increased and at what level should the electoral threshold be set. As recent cases of conversion to the double-ballot system indicate, electoral reform varies according to a number of factors, including the structure of the previous system and the relative strength of reformists and antireformists. The 1993 electoral reform in New Zealand followed the German model: allowing half the seats for the PR list and setting the electoral threshold at 5 percent.[24] In contrast, Italy and Japan allowed more seats for SMD and set their electoral threshold at lower than 5 percent.[25] In other words, there is no specific formula for a double-ballot system. Its contents should be decided by negotiation when a substantial force for reform emerges in democratic Korea.

Another problem in electoral reform is how to elect the president. If a double-ballot system is introduced in the current system, the likelihood of a minority president would increase somewhat. One way to bolster governability is to reform the presidential election by introducing concurrent elections for the presidency and the

24. Jack Vowles, "The Politics of Electoral Reform in New Zealand," *International Political Science Review* 16 (January 1995): 95–116.

25. Thomas Lancaster, "The Origins of Double Ballot Electoral Systems: Some Comparative Observations," paper presented at the XVII World Congress of the International Political Science Association. Seoul, Korea, August 17–21, 1997.

parliament, which would enhance the coattail effect for the winning presidential candidate and thereby reduce the likelihood of divided government. Another way to reform the presidential election
would be to introduce a runoff election. Under the current plurality rule, winning candidates have had about 40 percent or less of the
vote, which has resulted in weak mandates. Yet simple runoff elections may stimulate fragmentation in the presidential race, as has
been the case in several Latin American countries.[26] A more realistic reform is a compromise in which there is a runoff election only
if the shortfall of the runner-up from a majority of votes is less than
double the leading candidate's shortfall from a majority.[27] If the
front-runner does not meet this condition or wins a first-round majority, there is no runoff.

Party Reform

The other major element of institutional reform is party reform.
Whereas electoral reform involves fine-tuning the rules of political
competition to enhance governability and representativeness, party
reform focuses on improving the quality of intermediary organizations between citizens and government. In this sense, party reform
consists of three main areas: improving the institutionalization of
party organizations, enhancing the linkage between society and the
political parties, and strengthening the relationship between parties
and the government.

Enhancing the institutionalization of political parties means
eliminating the pervasive personalism in party organizations. Korean political parties have been dominated by charismatic leaders
who have monopolized almost every major function, dominating
candidate selection, party finance, campaign strategy, and so forth.

26. Matthew Shugart and John Carey, *Presidents and Assemblies: Constitutional Design and Electoral Dynamics* (New York: Cambridge University Press,
1992), 210–12.
27. Ibid., 218.

That omnipresent personalism has undermined the adaptability, complexity, and cohesion of party organizations. Even in the age of democratization, the dominance of personalism over political parties has not changed substantially. The rise of so-called delegative democracy has only served to reinforce the personalism in party politics. As O'Donnell persuasively argues, presidentialism in new democracies tends to strengthen individuality rather than institutional accountability. The delegative president is likely to rely on direct support from voters rather than being constrained by institutional checks and balances.[28] As a result, presidents tend to favor weak and undisciplined political parties and see them as mere ornaments of democratic legitimacy. This phenomenon of delegative president and the consequent weakening of political parties is happening not only in democratic Korea but also in several new democracies in Latin America.[29]

In other words, the institutionalization of party organizations should involve diluting the concentrated powers of party leaders and distributing them across functional and hierarchical subunits. Party reform (like the reform efforts in America in the 1970s) should decentralize the decision-making process within parties. Specifically, nominees for public offices should be decided on by a great number of party members or the electorate. Developing and coordinating the policy direction of parties should be participated in not only by party leaders and their aides but also by delegates of party members and various specialists. Also, party finance should rely on various sources, including individual donations as well as corporate donations. When these changes occur political parties no longer depend on personal leaders but on institutionalized procedures and rules.

28. Guillermo O'Donnell, "Delegative Democracy," *Journal of Democracy* 5 (January 1994): 55–69.
29. Scott Mainwaring, "Presidentialism in Latin America," *Latin American Research Review* 25 (1990): 157–79.

Another aspect of party reform is enhancing the linkage between the society and political parties. (I discussed this reform in relation to the double-ballot system.) Now I explore reforming the linkage by concentrating on the political parties. For political parties to build stable roots in civil society, first they should provide a consistent and stable identity whereby voters can develop a stable identification. As discussed above, such stabilization requires diluting charismatic leaders' personal dominance. Second, political parties should be more responsive to the political and economic demands of voters. Only when a political party aptly reflects the political and economic demands of a segment of voters can voters develop a stable identification with a party.

The final aspect of party reform is strengthening the relationship between parties and the government. Such a reform consists of two changes. First, once a party has won governmental power, it should be able to fill key positions within the government with its own members or at least with those who understand and are convinced about the party's policy orientation. Second, the governing party should be able to direct government bodies toward its policy orientation.[30] For these changes to occur, both the recruitment pattern and the power structure within political parties have to change. Political parties should recruit activists who understand the political and economic issues, and these activists should have more say in the internal decision-making process within the parties.

Conclusion: The Future of Institutional Reform

The election system and political parties in democratic Korea have not developed impressively. The representativeness, govern-

---

30. Richard Katz, "Party Government: A Rationalistic Conception," in Francis Castles and Rudolf Wildenmann, eds., *The Future of Party Government*, vol.1. (New York: Walter de Gruyter, 1986), 43.

ability, and stability of parties and electoral politics have been far short of expectations. Thus various reforms in parties and the election system are mandatory. To conclude, let us examine several structural and contextual factors that are sure to influence the future of institutional reform.

Let us begin with facilitating factors. As various cases of institutional reform around the world indicate, "the window for reform"[31] becomes wider when the political system is in crisis. For instance, electoral reforms in Italy and Japan evolved when those countries were suffering massive economic and political crises. In Italy, an economic crisis in the early 1990s, the uncovering of widespread political corruption, and a separatist movement by the Northern League converted the long and widespread dissatisfaction with the unstable and irresponsible political system into a reform movement.[32] In Japan, a series of political scandals, including Recruit and Sagawa, and the consequent political crisis gave rise to enormous pressure for political reform. Combined with grievances over the decades-long Liberal Democratic Party dominance, the pressure culminated in a referendum for electoral reform and the consequent adoption of the double-ballot electoral system.[33]

In this sense, the window for institutional reform appears to be wide open in democratic Korea. First, economic conditions provide immense pressure for reform. Although the Korean economy has shown a mixed performance, with recurrent ups and downs since the democratic transition, it rapidly plummeted in the final phase of Kim Young Sam's administration. After one of the top conglomerate

31. For the concept of "the window for reform," see John Keeler, "Opening the Window for Reform: Mandates, Crises, and Extraordinary Policy-Making," *Comparative Political Studies* 25 (January 1993): 433–86.

32. Leonardo Morlino and Marco Tarchi, "The Dissatisfied Society: The Roots of Political Change in Italy," *European Journal of Political Research* 30 (July 1996): 41–65.

33. Rei Shiratori, "The Politics of Electoral Reform in Japan," *International Political Science Review* 16 (January 1995): 79–94.

groups went bankrupt, several more followed suit. In addition, there was serious turmoil in the financial markets culminating in the borrowing of stand-by funds from the International Monetary Fund. This grave economic crisis will strengthen pressure for political reform because many Koreans believe that the crisis resulted not only from economic but also from political reasons. They have complained that pervasive political corruption and irresponsible political institutions are mainly responsible for the economic crisis.

The crisis is not limited to the economic sphere. Political crisis looms large, too. Not only political and economic governance but also the effectiveness of the whole representative system in the democratic regime are being questioned. The inconsistent and inept handling of critical matters by Kim Young Sam's government resulted in grave doubts about economic governance by a democratic government. The unsuccessful management of key economic issues, such as the premature introduction of new labor laws in 1996 and financial market chaos in 1997, also led to increasing doubts.

Furthermore, a series of political corruption scandals rocked the democratic government. First, a number of former ministers, generals, and high-rank bureaucrats were accused of political corruption as President Kim Young Sam launched the clean government campaign in 1993. Following a series of corruption scandals, even the former president, Roh Tae Woo, was indicted for having a huge slush fund. The dirty money scandal also hurt Kim Young Sam's administration. Although the president himself was reportedly not involved, his son was charged with receiving illegal money and abusing his influence. Even though the corruption scandals have not developed into a *mani pulite* (clean hands) investigation for the whole political system, as in Italy, those indictments confirmed the suspicions of the public and aggravated public dissatisfaction with the political system.

Another aspect of the political crisis is the public distrust of the political system as a whole. Various surveys indicate that the Korean public has an unfavorable estimation of the performance of the political system. For instance, about three-fourths of the respondents in a 1995 survey believed that people's opinions were not well represented in the political system. Also the public does not believe that the political system guarantees citizens' basic rights.[34] This distrust and dissatisfaction on the part of the public represents a widespread political crisis. In sum, severe crises in the political and economic sphere may provide the impetus for a reform movement in Korean democracy.

However, political and historical factors also constrain the success of a reform movement in democratic Korea. Successful reform requires reformists mobilizing public dissatisfaction with the status quo and coordinating a reform movement, a force that is unlikely to emerge in the current political circumstances. As discussed above, the current institutional framework has relatively high barriers for any new political force, no matter whether it consists of industrial workers, environmentalists, or others.

There is a remote possibility that a reformist force might arise from within the system. Ever since the democratic negotiation in 1987, both former authoritarian elites and leaders of the democratic movement have dominated electoral and party politics. Alternating governmental power between them, they have never allowed a new political force to enter their realm, maintaining their dominance by various institutional and political devices. Regional dominance by charismatic leaders, the single-member district system, and pervasive personalism within political parties have served together to maintain exclusive control over electoral and party politics and to be as antireform as the circumstances allow.

34. For more about this, see Peter McDonough and Doh Chull Shin, "Conservative Democratization and the Transition to Mass Politics in Korea," in Sung Chul Yang, ed., *Democracy and Communism* (Seoul: Korean Association of International Studies).

In addition to the problem of the rise of reformists, there are ob-structing factors that are specific to electoral and party reform. With the double-ballot system, comes the dilemma of the collective good. Although the increase in representativeness of the double-ballot sys-tem is good for electoral politics as a whole, it does not give any tan-gible or immediate benefits to extant political forces within the system. Because the extant political parties are strongly supported by their regional bases, they do not see any substantial incentives in in-creased representativeness.

There are also factors obstructing party reform beginning with the existence of a strong state. Although there has been some dissi-pation of state power, the traditionally strong state has remained largely intact in the age of democratization. The state still maintains the upper hand over the National Assembly as well as governing par-ties, witness the introduction of new labor laws in 1996. Although the governing New Korea Party wanted to be somewhat flexible to-ward the interests of workers, it was simply overwhelmed by the gov-ernment. As both the president and the labor ministry were concerned with administrative efficiency, they pushed the govern-ing party to pass the law. This case illustrates, as do cases in Latin America, that a strong state greatly forecloses the task of building de-mocratically responsible parties.[35]

Whereas the strong state hinders the linkage between parties and the government, the changing nature of political campaigns ob-structs the reform of democratizing party organizations. In most ad-vanced democracies, the mass media play an increasing role in election campaigns. The 1997 presidential election indicates that media politics has now become a significant factor in Korean elec-tions. The three major candidates had several television debates that were watched by millions of voters. Also it was estimated that politi-cal advertising on television and radio substantially affected voters'

35. Mainwaring, "Brazil: Weak Parties and Feckless Democracy," 396–97.

choices. Such an increasing media impact is likely to strengthen the influence of party leaders, for as election campaigns rely more on media than on party organizations, the relative significance of party organizations will decrease. Media-centered campaigns will thus reinforce the role of presidential candidates by emphasizing the personal attraction of the candidate rather than the policy positions of the parties.

In short, the success of the institutional reform of the election system and political parties will be largely determined by the relative strengths of obstructing and facilitating factors. It will also take a considerable amount of time and patience for Korean politicians and citizens to implement institutional reforms and to see substantial results. It should be emphasized, however, that the quality of Korean democracy and the progress toward a consolidated democracy crucially depend on such institutional reform.

Legislative-Executive Relations and Legislative Reform

The institutionalization of a legislature, which links the state and society, lies at the heart of democratic consolidation. An institutionalized legislature maintains autonomy in its relations with other institutional structures, such as the executive branch. It puts *esprit de corps* above partisan cleavages to produce legislative outputs through coordination. It has elaborate rules and procedures and a highly differentiated internal organization, together with staff and other types of resources available to it. In all probability, an institutionalized legislature has the capability of exerting a significant influence on public policy, for effectively responding to societal demands, and hence for enhancing legitimacy and integration of the regime.[1]

Along with the transition of the Fifth Republic's authoritarianism to the present Sixth Republic's democracy in Korea, the

---

1. Samuel P. Huntington, *Political Order in Changing Societies* (New Haven: Yale University Press, 1968), pp. 8–23; Gerhard Loewenberg and Samuel C. Patterson, *Comparing Legislatures* (Boston: Little, Brown, 1979), pp. 7–42; Samuel C. Patterson, "Legislative Institutions and Institutionalism in the United States," *Journal of Legislative Studies* 1 (1995): 10–29; Gary W. Copeland and Samuel C. Patterson, eds., *Parliaments in the Modern World* (Ann Arbor: University of Michigan Press, 1994), pp. 5–7; Lawrence D. Longley, "Parliaments as Changing Institutions and as Agents of Regime Change," *Journal of Legislative Studies* 2 (1996): 22–44; and Nelson W. Polsby, "The Institutionalization of the United States House of Representatives," *American Political Science Review* 62 (1968): 144–68.

constitutional status of the National Assembly has been heightened. The elections for the National Assembly have become increasingly regularized, free, and fair. The national legislature, which underwent three dissolutions and two more curtailments of its term, will most likely not suffer another abrupt collapse in the near future. This reflects a remarkable success in the democratic transition that has taken place over the past decade. Yet the current legislative politics also reveals consolidation's weaknesses and limitations. As far as its formal rules and internal organization are concerned, the legislature shows a semblance of institutionalization. In its interactions with external forces, however, the legislature is hardly autonomous. Internal conflict is not managed in an orderly manner. The National Assembly has yet to establish itself as an effective player. Overall, the legislature remains uninstitutionalized.[2]

For the Korean National Assembly to serve as the agent of democratic consolidation, it needs reform, beginning with building up its autonomy. With the exception of the short-lived Second Republic, Korea has adopted a presidential system for most of its contemporary history. The autonomy of the legislature is determined mainly by its political standing vis-à-vis the president, the apex of the executive branch. In brief, any major effort for reforming Korean legislative politics needs to focus on legislative-executive relations.

The goal of this chapter is to discuss the conditions, patterns, and reform issues of legislative-executive relations in Korea. To analyze how the conditions and patterns of legislative-executive relations have changed or continued to exist amid the democratization process, I compare the thirteenth through fifteenth assemblies of the current Sixth Republic with the eleventh and twelfth assemblies of the military-dominated authoritarian Fifth Republic. Fur-

---

2. Chan Wook Park, "The National Assembly in the Consolidation Process of Korean Democracy," *Asian Journal of Political Science* 5 (1997): 96–113.

thermore, I explore important measures for reforming legislative-executive relations.

Conditions of Legislative-Executive Relations

Constitutional/Legal Provisions

The constitutional and legal framework is an important category defining and shaping the character and pattern of legislative-executive relations. When one examines legislative-executive relations, it is helpful to begin by looking into the relevant constitutional and other legal provisions.

Each of the Fifth and Sixth Republic constitutions provided a presidential system based on separation of powers and on checks and balances among different governing branches. For example, the National Assembly was authorized to give its consent or approval to presidential actions, such as nominating the prime minister, making treaties, declaring war, and granting a general amnesty.

A comparison of the Fifth and Sixth Republic constitutions shows a contrast between the authoritarian and democratic regimes. Stronger presidential power was given under the Fifth Republic constitution than under the Sixth Republic. The Fifth Republic constitution was imposed by the military leadership, whereas the Sixth Republic constitution was negotiated among political parties. On the basis of its substantive content as well as its adoption procedure, the Fifth Republic constitution was not democratic, for the president was clearly predominant over the National Assembly. The president had the right to dissolve the National Assembly whenever he considered it necessary for the nation's security or other interests. In case of serious turmoil, the president could exercise emergency measures covering a whole range of national affairs. The total number of days during which the National Assembly was in session in a year was limited to 150. The Sixth Republic's constitution in contrast, allows the National Assembly a stronger position than before. The National Assembly cannot be dissolved by the president. There is no limit to the total annual number of its session days. Besides the existing power to investigate specific matters when necessary, the National Assembly now may inspect all aspects of executive operations during every annual regular session.

Still, the present constitution does not make the president and National Assembly equal in power and authority. Unlike the United States prototype of presidentialism, the Korean type tips the power toward the president. Several constitutional constraints on the national legislature keep it from extending its regular or special sessions, deliberating the national budget, and so on. During periods of serious turmoil, the president can bypass the National Assembly, although these powers are more limited in the constitutional text than they were previously.

Together with the nation's constitution, there exist several formal rules and regulations to organize the National Assembly and have it conduct internal business and formulate decisions. Of these rules, the National Assembly law is the most important. After the law was initially promulgated in the Constituent Assembly, it has been revised twenty-nine times, either partially or on a full scale.

The twentieth revision initiated under the military authoritarian leadership in 1981 set the tone for the eleventh assembly (April 1981 to April 1985) and the twelfth assembly (April 1985 to May 1988) of the Fifth Republic. Under the pretext of boosting the efficiency and productivity of the legislative institution, the National Assembly law limited members' opportunities for making speeches and participating in debates and kept strict controls on the proceedings. In a nutshell, the National Assembly law of the authoritarian Fifth Republic significantly constrained legislative autonomy.

In contrast, the revisions of the National Assembly law since the late 1980s were intended to build a strong and internally democratic legislature. Two major revisions deserve special mention. The twenty-third revision of 1988, effective in the thirteenth assembly (May 1988 to May 1992), marked a restoration of the legislature's powers that had been curtailed under the authoritarian dictatorship. For example, a procedure of investigative hearing was introduced to exercise an effective check over the executive branch. The twenty-seventh revision, carried out in the fourteenth assembly (May 1992 to May 1996), further opened up the possibility of the democratic and effective management of legislative proceedings. This revision, which touched on wide-ranging organizational and operational aspects of the National Assembly, aimed to routinize all kinds of legislative proceedings, to galvanize debates and deliberation, and to strengthen the committee system and professional staff organization. However, talks are ongoing about further reform.

Party/Electoral Factors

Apart from the legal framework, several other categories of factors have a significant bearing on legislative-executive relations. Political party and electoral variables constitute one such category. Political parties are a key force in organizing legislative members' activities within and outside the National Assembly. A party's political status within the legislature, its internal discipline, and its relations with other parties affect the ways its members interact with the president, cabinet ministers, and executive agencies. Since reelection is the prerequisite for a successful legislative career, it is important to understand how members' electoral incentives affect legislative-executive relations.

The president's party often emphasizes that a stable legislative majority is needed to secure governability. In effect, however, a wide majority controlled by the ruling party reduces the extent of legislative autonomy. The stronger the ruling party is in the legislature, the less it feels necessary to compromise with the opposition. The ruling party can easily translate its preferences into decisions in the legislature by imposing strong party discipline on its members and by imposing the principle of majority rule on the opposition parties. As would be expected, given the authoritarian nature of the Fifth Republic, its eleventh assembly was the most subservient to the president among the assemblies under study here. During that time, the ruling Democratic Justice Party commanded 55 percent of the legislative seats and was not effectively checked by the tame opposition parties.

In the thirteenth assembly election, after the transition to democracy, the president's party failed to gain a majority for the first time in Korea's constitutional history, with the National Assembly split among four parties. This "divided government," in the American parlance, generated an opportunity for developing the politics of coalition building. Given the strength of the opposition, the legislature could be put up on an independent standing. In early 1990, however, the ruling party, having found it both time-consuming and difficult to build working majorities and make compromises, merged with two opposition parties to form the Democratic Liberal Party, which commanded a more than two-thirds majority. In the second half of the thirteenth assembly, the ruling party rammed through controversial bills supported by the president, thus critically undermining the autonomy of the National Assembly.

In the elections for both the fourteenth and the fifteenth assemblies (in March 1992 and April 1996, respectively), the president's party was not able to obtain a majority of legislative seats. But after the election, the ruling party drew in some opposition members and independents and eventually manufactured a majority. The ruling party's betrayal of the electoral mandate hindered the National Assembly from being an autonomous institution.

If it were not for strong party discipline, the president could not depend on his party to realize his will in the National Assembly. The

Korean ruling party is highly centralized with strong internal discipline. Party leaders strictly control their rank-and-file members. At every stage of decision making, legislative members follow instructions from above.[3] Even the speaker, ostensibly the supreme leader of the National Assembly, is not immune from party discipline, which is why the speaker is unable to run the legislature in an impartial manner and keep up its autonomy.

Strong electoral incentives exist for members to obey their leaders' directives. For a member to be reelected, he or she must first obtain a party nomination from the party leadership, making a member's loyalty to his party's top leaders an important issue. Also, the candidate needs the party's financial and organizational support, crucial for electoral campaigns and for constituency representational activities after the election.[4]

Even during the democratic Sixth Republic period, the National Assembly has not significantly changed, in that strong party discipline is still embedded in the legislative process. Members in both majority and minority camps risk expulsion if they defy party lines on major issues. Strong party discipline, especially that of the ruling party, reins in members and restricts the autonomy of the National Assembly. The fluidity of Korean political parties, which is particularly evident at this phase of democratic consolidation, makes it difficult to coordinate among them, which keeps the National Assembly from acting as a unified body when dealing with external forces.

Not only ever-shifting parties but intense partisan conflicts devastate cross-party accommodation and cooperation in the National

3. Chong Lim Kim, "The Unwritten Rules of the Game in the National Assembly of the Fifth Republic," *Asian Perspective* 12 (1988): 5–34.

4. Chan Wook Park, "Legislators and Their Constituents in South Korea: The Patterns of District Representation," *Asian Survey* 28 (1988): 1049–65; and his "Constituency Representation in Korea: Sources and Consequences," *Legislative Studies Quarterly* 13 (1988): 225–42.

Assembly. Numerous fierce skirmishes were waged on the floor of the National Assembly that resulted in legislative deadlock or domination by one party.[5] Most of the energy was consumed in the twelfth assembly of the Fifth Republic in arguing over whether to rewrite the constitution. Likewise, the second half of the thirteenth assembly was characterized by standoffs and stalemates over major issues of partisan interests. In the regular session of 1994, the members of the fourteenth assembly were unable to deliberate the budget proposal because of arguments over whether or not to prosecute those involved in the military takeover in 1979. As long as legislative politics is conducted in such a fashion, there can be no fruitful legislative check over the executive branch.

Legislative Organizational Features

I now turn to the organizational features of the National Assembly that affect its control over the executive branch, including the number of sessional days, the proportion of experienced members, the importance of committees, and the availability of professional staff, all of which have significant implications for the National Assembly's deliberative capacity. Members' working days in the chamber of the National Assembly are constrained by the constitution and the National Assembly law. The sessions of the National Assembly are not year-round but meet either in regular or special sessions. The regular session opens annually on September 10 (September 20 during the Fifth Republic period) or the next day if the tenth is a holiday. A special session may be convened at the re-

5. Chan Wook Park, "Partisan Conflict and *Immobilisme* in the Korean National Assembly: Conditions, Processes, and Outcomes," *Asian Perspective* 17 (1993): 5–37; and Jang-seok Kang, "Conflict Management in Divisive Legislatures" Ph. D. diss., University of Hawaii, 1988.

quest of the president or at least one-fourth (formerly, one-third) of the total membership. The regular session may not last more than one hundred (formerly, ninety) days; a special session may not last longer then thirty days. Officially, the eleventh assembly of the authoritarian Fifth Republic averaged 144 sessional days a year, including regular and special sessions. This figure is misleading, however, because the plenary session only averaged thirty-six days a year, meaning that three-fourths of the total time was spent on committee work, intermittent recesses, or interparty disagreement over the legislative agenda. In the democratic Sixth Republic, the thirteenth assembly met on average 165 days a year, and the plenary session, 41 days.[6] Thus, the National Assembly falls far short of being a constantly deliberating body.

Because contemporary policy issues are complex and technical in nature, the executive branch, teeming with policy specialists and technocrats, enjoys a decisive edge over a generalist legislature. This deficiency can be compensated for, however, by the presence of career politicians in the legislature. Indeed, legislatures with a significant policy influence are characterized by a low rate of turnover, as measured by the percentage of freshmen members.[7] Thus we see that first-term members in the eleventh assembly constituted 79 percent of the total membership, for the military leaders barred old politicians from engaging in politics. Career politicians thus became a rare breed in that assembly. After the political ban was lifted, the percentage of first-term members in the twelfth assembly went down drastically, to 39 percent. Because the democratic opening of the

6. The Secretariat of the Korean National Assembly, *Ŭijŏng charyojip* (Compiled materials on the National Assembly) (Seoul: Chŏng-mun sa, 1995), pp. 133–38.

7. Michael L. Mezey, *Comparative Legislatures* (Durham, N.C.: Duke University Press, 1979), pp. 249–51.

Sixth Republic ushered in new political aspirants, the percentage in the thirteenth assembly rose again, to 55 percent. That number decreased to 41 percent for the fourteenth assembly and then showed a slight increase for the present fifteenth assembly (46 percent).[8]

The character of the committee system is related to the legislature's autonomy relative to the executive. When committees have the power to scrutinize executive proposals, the legislature is highly likely to amend, delay, or even reject those proposals.[9] Committees' deliberative capacities are maximized if they are organized in parallel to existing executive departments or agencies, specialized according to their exclusive jurisdictions, permanently established, composed of members with the relevant policy interests and expertise, small enough for lively debates among the members, and given extensive powers of agenda control, amendment, and evidence taking.[10]

At the beginning of the 1960s the National Assembly law placed committees center stage throughout policy deliberations in the national legislature. Before a legislative proposal or any matter for deliberation is formally introduced to the National Assembly, it must first be referred to an appropriate committee. A committee may make amendments to a legislative proposal, which are usually upheld by the plenary session. A committee may also hold public hearings, request explanations from high-level executive officials, and question them about the matters of importance.

8. The Secretariat of the Korean National Assembly, *Ŭijŏng charyojip*, p. 47.
9. Loewenberg and Patterson, *Comparing Legislatures*, pp. 263–68.
10. Philip Norton, "The Legislative Powers of Parliament," in Cees Flinterman et al., eds., *The Evolving Role of Parliaments in Europe* (Antwerpen: MAKLU Uitgevers, 1994), pp. 15–32; John D. Lees and Malcolm Shaw, *Committees in Legislatures* (Durham, N.C.: Duke University Press, 1979); Ingar Mattson and Kaare Strøm, "Parliamentary Committees," in Herbert Döring, ed., *Parliaments and Majority Rule in Western Europe* (New York: St. Martin's Press, 1995), pp. 488–527; and Kaare Strøm, "Parliamentary Committees: A Global and European Perspective," *Journal of Legislative Studies* 4 (1998).

When the committee system of the authoritarian Fifth Republic's assemblies is compared with that of the democratic Sixth Republic's, differences emerge in some detailed aspects of committee organization and operation, such as the number of committees, the frequency of their off-session meetings, and the opportunities for speech making in committees.

The committee system has yet to take a firm hold in the deliberative process. First, committees do not meet regularly. In the eleventh through fourteenth assemblies, the meeting days of a full committee and its *ad hoc* subcommittees numbered at most thirty-seven a year.[11] Second, committees are party dominated rather than autonomous, meaning that committee appointments are controlled by parties and the committee deliberations are liable to become partisan skirmishes. A sense of identity is missing in the committees. Expertise is not appreciated, and reviews of legislation are on the whole hastily conducted.[12]

Quality legislative functioning cannot be achieved without the aid of able staff, for the legislature as a whole, as well as its committees and its individual members. Thus the Korean National Assembly has been steadily upgrading its support organization and personnel. In the middle of the fourteenth assembly, for instance, the Office of Legislation and Budget was created within the Secretariat of the National Assembly, indicating a trend toward more committees and staff personnel to assist members' in their legislative activities. However, staff resources are still not adequate; the average number of professional staff per committee, excluding administrative, clerical, and other minor staff, remains at around six in the fourteenth assembly.

11. The Secretariat of the Korean National Assembly, *Ŭijŏng charyojip*, pp. 275–95; and the Secretariat of the Korean National Assembly, *Che Sipsadae Kukhoe kyŏnggwa pogosŏ* (Report on the proceedings of the fourteenth National Assembly) (Seoul, 1997), pp. 57–8.

12. Chan Wook Park, "The Organization and Workings of Committees in the Korean National Assembly," *Journal of Legislative Studies* 4 (1998): 206–24.

Patterns of Legislative-Executive Relations

Lawmaking

The legislature interacts with the executive branch to make laws, deliberate budgets, conduct legislative oversight, and so forth. To investigate the patterns of legislative-executive relations in the Fifth and Sixth Republics, we will look first at lawmaking.[13]

Both the members of the National Assembly and the executive branch can introduce legislative bills. The executive branch's proposals are called *government bills*. The average number of bills introduced a year was 122 in the eleventh assembly and 126 in the twelfth assembly. But those numbers almost doubled in the democratic Sixth Republic: An average of 235 bills was introduced each year during the thirteenth assembly; the comparable figure for the fourteenth assembly was 225.[14] This sharp increase in legislative workload may result from proliferating popular demands for gov-

13. Examples of previous research on legislative-executive relations in Korea include the following: Chong Lim Kim, "The Keystone of Korean Democracy: Conflict and Cooperation in Legislative-Executive Relations," in *Proceedings of the Seminar on Political Conflicts in Korea* (Seoul: Graduate School of Policy Studies, Korea University, 1988), pp. 33–54; Young-Chul Paik, "Legislative Institutionalization and Political Instability in the Modernization Process," Ph.D. diss., University of Hawaii, 1985; Chong Lim Kim and Seong-Tong Pai, *Legislative Process in Korea* (Seoul: Seoul National University Press, 1981); Chong Lim Kim et al., *The Legislative Connection: The Politics of Representation in Kenya, Korea, and Turkey* (Durham, N.C.: Duke University Press, 1984); Young O. Yoon, "Policy-Making Activities of the South Korean National Assembly," *Journal of Northeast Asian Studies* 10 (1986): 29–48; Myungsoon Shin, "Change and Continuity of Parliamentary Politics in Democratizing Korea," paper presented at the Conference on Democratic Institutions in East Asia, Durham, N.C., November 7–9, 1996; Chan Wook Park, "Korea, South" in George Thomas Kurian, *World Encyclopedia of Parliaments and Legislatures*, vol. 1 (Washington, D.C.: Congressional Quarterly, 1998), pp. 393–401.

14. The Secretariat of the Korean National Assembly, *Ŭijŏng charyojip*, p. 386; and the Secretariat of the Korean National Assembly, *Che Sipsadae Kukhoe kyŏnggwa pogosŏ*, p. 171.

ernment action and appropriate laws in a newly emerging democratic regime. But an increase in the sheer load of legislation does not necessarily mean that the National Assembly has strengthened its legislative influence on the executive branch.

The portion of member bills among the total introduced bills is sometimes used to indicate legislative initiatives taken by legislative members relative to the executive branch. Overall, throughout the history of the National Assembly, government bills have outnumbered member bills.[15] The question is whether members' legislative initiatives have become more visible in the democratic era than they were in the authoritarian era. The numbers show that the portion of member bills was 41.3 percent in the eleventh assembly and 55.7 percent in the twelfth assembly. The comparable figure in the thirteenth assembly was 60.7 percent and 35.5 percent in the fourteenth assembly.[16] Thus the regime's democratization had no consistent effect on the pattern of members' legislative initiatives.

It is also the case that the executive branch drafts legislative proposals to a greater extent than suggested by the figures above. In every session, some bills prepared by the executive branch are formally proposed and sponsored by the ruling party's legislative members. In the fourteenth assembly these included such reform measures as public officials' ethics law, election law, and the like. This assembly even passed a special law, drafted by the executive branch, to prosecute those involved in the military coup d'état and brutal crackdown of the Kwangju uprising, including two former presidents. Most of these bills were initiated and prepared by presidential aides and then delivered to ruling party members for their formal introduction.

15. The Secretariat of the Korean National Assembly, *Ŭijŏng charyojip*, pp. 376–77.

16. See note 14.

The extent to which a legislature exercises influence over the executive branch is affected by its capacity to determine the legislative agenda. As far as government bills are concerned, the National Assembly is fundamentally unable to control the agenda for reviewing them. A long-established pattern has most government bills being introduced in the fall regular session. For instance, in 1993, about 82 percent of the total government bills were proposed during that session,[17] meaning that the government controls much of the legislative agenda.

The success rate of government bills can also indicate legislative influence over the executive branch. As one would expect, the passage rate of government bills was a bit lower under democratic rule (lowest in the thirteenth assembly). Still, even in this democratic legislature, approximately 87 percent of government bills were adopted, pointing to heavy executive dominance of the lawmaking process and continuation of that dominance into the democratic era.[18]

The legislature's modifications to government bills are another way to measure its influence on the executive branch.[19] In the National Assembly, bill amendments consist mostly of changes in a bill's title, improvements in wordings and legal formalities, and other minor adjustments, leaving the backbone of most executive proposals intact. Moreover, the National Assembly does not allot enough time to add significant amendments to a bill; committee and floor procedures for legislation proceed too hastily. The average time between a bill's introduction and its final passage was seventy-four days in the eleventh assembly, eighty in the twelfth, forty-five in the thir-

17. The Committee on Institutional Improvements, Korean National Assembly, *Purok* (Appendix: Materials for examination by specific topic for discussion) (Seoul, 1994), p. 269.

18. The Secretariat of the Korean National Assembly, *Ŭijŏng charyojip*, pp. 376–77, 387; and the Secretariat of the Korean National Assembly, *Che Sipsadae Kukhoe Kyŏnggwa Pogosŏ*, p. 171.

19. Jean Blondel, "Legislative Behavior: Some Steps towards a Cross-National Measurement," *Government and Opposition* 5 (1969–70): 67–85.

teenth, and sixty-one in the fourteenth.[20] The actual time given to the deliberation of a bill in committee and plenary meetings is likely to be tiny: from a few hours to several minutes. The National Assembly is used to terminating deliberation in a hurry and deciding on a number of bills in clusters at the end of the session. All this suggests that a heavier load of legislative work in the democratic era has caused it to be handled more cursorily than in the authoritarian era.

The National Assembly's inability to reject government bills is seen vividly when the president's party rams through a bill with a snap vote, dubbed *nalch'igi t'onggwa* (snatching the passage of a proposal). If a bill important to the president is strongly opposed by the minority, the president's majority party will often ignore the legal framework for passing bills. The speaker or other presiding officer loyal to the president curtails questions and debates even when objections are raised. Then the bill is railroaded through with floor votes by the majority party. Such practices have not disappeared in the democratic era except, briefly, in the first half of the thirteenth assembly. In the fifteenth assembly two controversial bills—one concerning labor rights and the other the National Security Planning Agency—were favored by the president but objected to by the opposition parties. In the early morning hours of December 26, 1996, the legislative members of the ruling New Korea Party sneaked into the National Assembly building and rushed the bills through to obey the presidential directive.

The president's use of the veto power (or threat of using it) demonstrates the dynamics of conflict and cooperation between the president and the legislative branch. In the authoritarian Fifth Republic, the president never found it necessary to wield his veto power. In the current Sixth Republic, the presidential veto was used only during the first half of the thirteenth assembly (when it was exercised

20. The Committee on Institutional Improvements, Korean National Assembly, *Purok*, p. 94.

seven times). At that time, the combined opposition majority passed some important legislative bills through the legislature against the president's will. The lack of presidential vetos in the Fifth Republic and during the most of the Sixth Republic does not exemplify much cooperation between the president and the legislature. Rather, it implies that the legislature is docilely subordinate to the executive. If the legislature has autonomy and is willing to express its own views and concerns, conflict can legitimately develop according to the constitutional design. How to manage such conflict is another question. In the unassertive National Assembly conflict is generated not from legislative-executive relations but from interparty relations.

Fiscal Control

Government budget proposals should be approved by the National Assembly before their execution. Thus the National Assembly receives the proposed budget from the executive branch in the plenary session and then sets committee review procedures in operation. Each standing committee examines the portion of the budget that concerns that committee's jurisdictional counterpart in the executive branch. The special committee on budget and accounts then examines the overall budget. After a modified budget proposal has been adopted by the special committee on budget and accounts, it is reported to the plenary session for final approval.

The modifications able to be made by the National Assembly to the original budget proposal are strictly bounded. In both the Fifth and the Sixth Republics changes amounted to just 1 percent of the original proposal, with the single exception of the budget for the fiscal year 1990.[21] The legislature is such a passive reviewing body that

21. The Secretariat of the Korean National Assembly, *Ŭijŏng charyojip*, p. 397; and the Secretariat of the Korean National Assembly, *Che Sipsadae Kukhoe kyŏnggwa pogosŏ*, p. 168.

its budgetary power cannot be a decisive source of leverage in its dealing with executive agencies.

There has been no discernible changes in the pattern of the National Assembly's budget review process between the authoritarian and democratic eras. First, the time schedule remains much the same and thus hardly conducive to a thoroughgoing review. A standing committee's preliminary review lasts five or six days; the overall review of the budget and accounts committee is conducted within at most two weeks. Second, there is a significant constitutional constraint on the legislature's deliberations. If the legislature wants to increase the amount of any item of expenditure or create a new item in the budget, it must obtain the consent of the executive branch in advance. Third, the National Assembly law itself is also restrictive in this regard. To amend the budget proposal in the plenary session requires the support of at least fifty members. Furthermore, the budget for the National Security Planning Agency (formerly the Central Intelligence Agency) is only subject to the preliminary review by the intelligence committee in a closed session, thus bypassing a comprehensive review by the budget and accounts committee. Last but not least, the budget and accounts committee is a temporary committee that changes membership every year and does not deal with fiscal matters on a continuous basis.

Legislative members are well aware that the National Assembly exercises little control over the budget. Those members, in both the ruling and the opposing camps, lobby the government to make funds available to their district projects during the summer, when the finance and economy board is preparing the budget proposal to be submitted to the legislature![22]

22. *Chosun Ilbo*, November 2, 1996.

Legislative Oversight

Legislative oversight refers to those activities that review the decision making and policy implementation of the executive branch and hold the executive branch accountable for its policy actions. Under such oversight, the legislature must obtain information on government operations and investigate possible irregularities, policy failures, and abuses of power.[23] The Korean constitution provides the National Assembly with various means of legislative oversight, including inspection, investigation, and interpellation.

At the outset of the annual regular session, the National Assembly sets aside a period of twenty days or less for conducting inspections of government operations. Each standing committee oversees the government ministries or agencies under its jurisdiction. The National Assembly lost this inspection power during the authoritarian Fourth and Fifth Republics and regained it after democratic transition.

Supervising the executive branch, however, is hampered by shortcomings and drawbacks in the organization of inspection activities, in the behavior patterns of members as inspectors, and in the agencies' attitudes toward the inspection. Too many agencies are chosen by the committees for inspection every year, and too many witnesses are summoned. As a result, members are pressed by a tight schedule, some agencies are subject to overlapping inspections, and some witnesses are questioned superficially. Members' inappropriate behavior patterns include obsessing about exposing irregularities, seeking their own visibility, emphasizing partisan or district interests, neglecting to check that past agency problems have been corrected, demanding that irrelevant documents be submitted in

23. Bert A. Rockman, "Legislative-Executive Relations and Legislative Oversight," in Gerhard Loewenberg, Samuel C. Patterson, and Malcolm E. Jewell, eds., *Handbook of Legislative Research* (Cambridge, Mass.: Harvard University Press, 1985), pp. 519–72.

unreasonably large quantities, and conducting inspections even when drunk. In addition, agencies often do not conscientiously respond to members' requests for information and documents.

The legislature is also empowered to investigate specific matters with a standing or a special committee. That right was not annihilated but was never exercised in the authoritarian Fifth Republic. In the first half of the thirteenth assembly of the democratic Sixth Republic, however, it launched a series of probes into the brutal crackdown of the Kwangju uprising, egregious abuses of power, and wrongdoing under the rule of President Chun. The former president had to testify before a hearing panel organized jointly by two special investigative committees.

National Assembly investigations depend on the changing political climate. During most of the fourteenth assembly, when President Kim Young Sam was highly popular and had a good grip on the ruling party, no cases were under investigation. When public opinion and the political situation are not pressing for a legislative investigation, the National Assembly is unlikely to carry one out.

In early 1997, the Hanbo financial scandal, together with the controversial passage of two bills in late 1996, caused presidential popularity to plummet. Thus the political parties agreed to appoint a temporary special committee to investigate. The committee held a series of hearings involving not only senior politicians, an incumbent cabinet minister, and a presidential aide but also the president's second son concerning influence peddling and bribery. Such investigative activities, which were never attempted in the authoritarian era, suggest that the legislature can defy the president when the political tide is strongly against him.

Despite the investigative hearings serving as a forum for executive accountability, the hearings did not dispel public suspicion about the matters under investigation. Legislative members had difficulty taking evidence and getting access to documents. Members were unskilled at handling witnesses, who evaded and perjured themselves. Such plenary sessions may require the presence of the prime minister, ministers, or other government representatives for interpellation, a procedure through which a legislative body calls the government to account.

In the democratic Sixth Republic, both ordinary people and legislative members enjoy much greater freedom of speech than in the previous authoritarian regime. On paper, the constitution of the Fifth Republic guaranteed legislative members parliamentary privileges and immunities, such as the exemption of legal accountability for opinions officially expressed in the legislature. In reality, however, unwritten taboos, called *sŏngyŏk*, are not to be spoken of in the legislature. Such taboos include critical remarks about the existing constitutional order, about the behavior of the president and his extended family, and about the president's major policies.[24] In the twelfth assembly, an opposition member was arrested because of a speech criticizing President Chun's authoritarian regime. To dodge the controversy concerning the member's privileges and immunities, the prosecution indicted him for distributing materials containing antistate remarks to reporters before his speech in the legislature. By contrast, in the Sixth Republic, because members are not prohibited from dealing with any topics in the legislature, interpellation time may come to serve as a forum for executive accountability.

Despite members' enlarged freedom of speech, it is hard to say that floor interpellation serves its intended purposes. Legislative members rarely raise concise and genuine questions. Some members, forgetting their proper role of lawmaking, ask a cabinet minister if he or she has any intention of making such-and-such a law. There is doubt about whether members' questions will ensure executive accountability or contribute to the information base on which members exert a policy influence. Cabinet ministers do not seem to provide sincere answers to the questions raised. Interpellation thus

24. Kim, "The Unwritten Rules," p. 19.

remains tedious, unmoving, and no more than a blunt warning against executive mismanagement.

Building an Autonomous Legislature

In the authoritarian era, the National Assembly was a handmaid of the executive. With the democratic transition, the legislature has restored the constitutional powers lost under the authoritarian regime, and legislative autonomy seemed possible at the beginning of the Sixth Republic. But the legislature has become a weak body. Change is short, but continuity is long for legislative-executive relations in Korea. The National Assembly leaves much to be desired.

How can the legislature exercise meaningful checks over the executive? What specific measures will advance legislative autonomy and sustain it? Some important measures would be to

- Introduce a year-round sessional system, which would be conducive to frequent sittings of the National Assembly, its full review of legislative matters, and the dispersal of legislative workload.
- Transfer the audit and inspection board from presidential control to the National Assembly. The legislature would thus be able to examine public expenditures and keep a watchful eye on government operations.
- Make the speakership politically neutral. The president should not be involved in selecting the leaders of the National Assembly, especially the speaker. The speaker and his or her deputies should withdraw from their party after being elected by a secret ballot in the legislature. This would make the speaker able to preside over and manage the affairs of the National Assembly independent of partisan pressure. Their terms need to be extended to four years instead of the current two years.

- Render committees strong. Members should be discouraged from changing committees in the middle of their term. Limited concurrent membership of standing committees may be considered to accommodate members' committee preferences. The budget and accounts committee should be converted into a standing committee for thoroughgoing review of fiscal matters. All committees need to be induced to hold public hearings frequently. Confirmatory hearings should be held so that the National Assembly can check presidential appointments of high-ranking officials.

- Prop up legislative investigation. Currently, legislative investigation may be initiated by a third of the membership, but it must be approved by a simple majority before the investigation can begin. Such an initiation should be directly translated into action without majority approval. Similarly, the majority requirement applied to a committee engaged in legislative investigation should be eased when it summons a witness, sends for documentation, or files a complaint against a perjurer.

- Step up specialized staff service. Strong efforts need to be made to expand the information system and staff service that back up members in their policy activities.

Legislative reform needs to be approached from a broad perspective, incorporating party and electoral factors. Parties should be policy-oriented, responsible, and internally democratic actors in both the electoral and the legislative arenas. The current electoral system, combining the single-member plurality district system and nominal proportional representation, serves only to strengthen the personality-dominated and region-based nature of existing political parties. As an alternative, I recommend a mixed two-ballot system in which the single-member plurality district system and proportional representation have equal weight. Compared with the current system, the proposed system will be conducive to party competition based more on policy programs and less on regional cleavages. To discourage legislative members' midterm changes of party affiliation and make them responsible to the electorate, district representatives as well as at-large representatives must give up their legislative seats when they leave their parties. The modified electoral system should be accompanied by safeguards against concentrations of power and control in parties' top leaders. Ordinary members should be given an opportunity to nominate candidates for legislative elections. This would provide incentives for members to respond to their rank-and-file supporters rather than to their party's top leadership and to use their own discretion in legislative voting. Also, a legislative party group should be able to serve as a forum for free and open discussion among its members before it decides on policy positions.

Last but not least, citizens have an important role in successful legislative reform. On their shoulders fall passing judgment on parties and candidates according to the merits of their policy positions and programs. For the reform measures to get through the National Assembly, citizens as individuals or in groups need to keep a watchful eye on what legislative members do and, if necessary, apply pressure to them.

The Rise and Fall
of Kim Young Sam's
Embedded Reformism

The most salient feature of Korean democratization in 1987–88 was its continuity with the authoritarian past. Except for the electoral regime becoming more open and competitive, the political system remained virtually the same. Although democratization usually involves some degree of redistribution of power, in the Korean case there was little noticeable change. The state apparatuses, the personnel that filled them, and state-society relations remained virtually intact from the authoritarian years. By the time Roh Tae Woo completed his term as president, five years after the transition, Korean democracy remained, at best, "conversations among gentlemen."[1]

The significance of the reforms of Kim Young Sam's administration (1993–98) lay in the fact that they were the first serious efforts to expand and deepen the hard-won democracy. To the extent that the initial transition was incomplete, the Kim Young Sam reforms had to be sweeping and across the board.

The reforms of the Kim Young Sam government had several distinct characteristics. The initiative and momentum of the reforms

---

1. The expression is from Alexander Wilde, "Conversations among Gentlemen: Oligarchical Democracy in Colombia," in *The Breakdown of Democratic Regimes: Latin America,* ed. Juan Linz and Alfred Stepan (Baltimore: Johns Hopkins University Press, 1978).

were provided mainly by the new president himself—to the point that his program was dubbed "reform authoritarianism." The intended reforms were far-reaching and broad in scope. They aimed to sweep away all the authoritarian legacies and to replace them with new democratic institutions in all aspects of Korean life: politics, economy, and society. And the reforms were swiftly executed: all the reforms were packed into the first four years of President Kim's tenure.

In addition to initiative, scope, and speed, the Kim Young Sam reforms had one additional feature: early success and subsequent failure. In the early stage, the reforms looked tremendously successful. However, by the time President Kim entered the second half of his term, the vigorously implemented reforms had begun to lose steam. By early 1997, the reform package, which had once enjoyed overwhelming popular support, was completely discredited and Kim's personal popularity had collapsed. Indeed, the president became so unpopular that all the presidential hopefuls tried to disassociate themselves from him.

Given the extremely low popular regard for Kim Young Sam's reforms, is it fair to characterize them as unqualified failures? I argue for a more balanced view. At least in the early phase, his reforms, particularly those in the political realm, were successful. Then why did he fail in the later stage? What explains the earlier success and the later failure? Why was he more successful in political reforms than in nonpolitical reforms? This chapter tries to answer these questions.

There are many reasons for the ultimate failure of President Kim Young Sam's reforms. I believe that the most important one lies in the model of reform that was embraced. I call that model *embedded reformism* because of the way it was packed, implemented, and legitimated and because it was shaped by a fundamental continuity in personnel, practices, and institutions from the authoritarian past. The reforms were born in response to prevalent authoritarian legacies, implemented in an authoritarian way, and justified in the time-honored instrumental terms. Both the earlier successes and the later failures are attributable to the authoritarian character of the reform process.

In the following pages, I analyze both the context and the text of President Kim Young Sam's reform efforts. Both historically specific conditions and the content and implementation of the reform program are dynamically linked, which helps explain the reforms' performance. The political, economic, and social context in which the reforms were undertaken shaped the scope, level, sequence, and methods of the initial reform measures, which in turn shaped the context for later reform measures.

The Context of Kim Young Sam's Reforms

Reforma Nonpactada and Strong Authoritarian Legacies

A major factor in democratic reform and consolidation is a sharp, clear break from the authoritarian past. In this regard, many emphasize the importance of the way in which the democratic transition occurred.[2] When the authoritarian regime collapsed and was replaced by a democratic one, authoritarian legacies are fewer and political reform is consequently easier. Where the authoritarian regime initiated and dominated the transition process, its legacies are more likely to be powerful and reform more difficult to achieve.

Obviously, the Korean case is neither replacement nor transformation, the two ideal-typical modes of democratic transition.[3] The process was not characterized by a clear-cut rupture, as in Portugal

2. For example, see Guillermo O'Donnell, "Challenges to Democratization in Brazil," *World Policy Journal* (spring 1988): 281–86; O'Donnell, "Transitions, Continuities, and Paradoxes," in *Issues in Democratic Consolidation*, ed. Scott Mainwaring, Guillermo O'Donnell, and J. Samuel Valenzuela (Notre Dame, Ind.: University of Notre Dame Press, 1992).

3. Samuel Huntington, "Will More Countries Become Democratic?" *Political Science Quarterly* 99, no. 2 (summer 1984): 193–218.

and Argentina, where authoritarian regimes were replaced by democratic ones. Nor was democratization primarily initiated by the authoritarian regime itself, as in Spain and Brazil, whose transitions involved a prolonged and gradual process of taming, negotiating, and pact making.

One feature of Korean democratization was the speed with which new democratic procedures were adopted by the authoritarian regime, which was being pressured from below. On June 29, 1987, Roh Tae Woo, the presidential candidate of the ruling Democratic Justice Party (DJP), declared that he would accept the opposition's demand for direct election of the president. Following Roh's concession, a new constitution, political parties, and election laws were quickly drawn up. In November 1987, Roh was elected president by the first direct popular vote in sixteen years and was sworn into office in February 1988. Two months later, a National Assembly election was held under the new election laws.

The lack of a pact and the rapidity of the process had serious implications for the nature of Korea's new democracy and its prospects for consolidation in the succeeding years. The urgency of establishing electoral democracy precluded many other important potential reform issues on the agenda. Contributing to this was the abrupt acceptance by the regime of the opposition demands, which at that point were only modestly articulated. To borrow the parlance of discourse analysis, the power bloc captured the critical vocabulary of civil society—that is, democratization—and limited its meaning to formalities, thus neutralizing its latent power. The result was that the electoral regime democratized but the administrative features of the authoritarian regime persisted. The state, whether understood as the summation of government organs and personnel or as a political apparatus of class domination, was little changed.

Although its banner-carrier had won the presidency, the ruling DJP suffered a resounding defeat in the National Assembly election of February 1988, winning less than half the seats. This left the Roh administration in the unenviable situation of *yosoyadae* (small government and large opposition). At the helm of a minority ruling party, Roh had difficulty governing and was forced to give in to various opposition demands. To rectify this weakness, the DJP merged in February 1990 with two of the opposition parties, Kim Young Sam's Reunified Democratic Party (RDP) and Kim Jong Pil's New Democratic Republican Party (NDRP), to form the Democratic Liberal Party (DLP).

The DLP was a coalition of heterogeneous conservative forces drawn together by anti-Honam regionalism (that is, opposition to the two southern Cholla provinces that constitute the home base of Kim Dae Jung). The three-party merger gave the Roh administration the political wherewithal it needed to govern effectively but also signaled the closure of reformism and the retrenchment of conservatism.

A Weak Political Society and a Fragmented Civil Society

Exclusionary authoritarian regimes try to crush civil as well as political society.[4] The virtual elimination of political opposition, however, may paradoxically contribute to an authoritarian regime's undoing, as the resultant vacuum is filled by apparently non-political groups and movements working in seemingly innocuous issue areas: consumer societies, neighborhood organizations, base communities, and so on. These "substitute arenas and actors" eventually spill over into the political ones, contributing to redemocratization.[5] Korea was no exception to this pattern. Although the more

4. The political society refers to the arena in which the polity arranges itself for political contestation over the public power and the state apparatus. Key institutions are elections and political parties. The civil society refers to the arena in which the social movements and the civic organizations arrange themselves to promote particularistic and/or general societal interests. A similar conceptualization is found in Alfred Stepan, *Rethinking Military Politics: Brazil and the Southern Cone* (Princeton, N.J.: Princeton University Press, 1988), chap. 1.

5. Manuel Antonio Garreton, "Political Process in an Authoritarian Regime: The Dynamics of Institutionalization and Opposition in Chile, 1973–1980," in

conventional political and civic organizations were tame and pliable, new issues and movements mushroomed toward the end of the authoritarian period.[6]

The newborn civil society, however, quickly lost its vigor after formal democratization, as in many other new democracies.[7] Once they lost the common enemy that had tied them together, the civic organizations and movements retrogressed to a dispersed and parochial state. Besides, as described above, democratization itself was attained by a compromise at the elite level. The civil society was again kept out of the political arena and left to decay by "exclusionary democratization."[8]

In general, reforms can progress when the social forces are either very strong and encompassing or very weak.[9] Since encompassing organizations receive a large share of national collective goods (and bads), they cannot get away with narrowly self-interested behavior. Therefore, they have little incentive to "free ride."[10] Thus, the government can elicit voluntary cooperation from the social forces.

Military Rule in Chile: Dictatorship and Opposition, ed. J. Samuel Valenzuela and Arturo Valenzuela (Baltimore and London: Johns Hopkins Press, 1986). This is a rather universal pattern, not limited to Chile. For similar experiences in Brazil, see Alfred Stepan, ed., *Democratizing Brazil: Problems of Transition and Consolidation* (New York and Oxford: Oxford University Press, 1989), part III, Democratizing Pressures from Below.

6. See chapter 11, this volume.

7. See ibid. For the Chilean experience, see Philip Oxhorn, "Where Did All the Protesters Go? Popular Mobilization and the Transition to Democracy in Chile," *Latin American Perspectives* 21, no. 3 (summer): 49–68.

8. Ho-keun Song, "Exclusionary Democratization and the Postponed Double Transition," in *Korean Society and Democracy: Assessments and Prospects of Ten Years of Korean Democratization* (in Korean). ed. Jang-jip Choi and Hyun-chin Lim (Seoul: Nanam Publishing House, 1997).

9. Adam Przeworski, *Democracy and the Market: Political and Economic Reforms in Eastern Europe and Latin America* (Cambridge and New York: Cambridge University Press, 1991), p. 180.

10. Mancur Olson Jr., *The Rise and Decline of Nations* (New Haven and London: Yale University Press, 1982).

Conversely, when the social forces are weak and fragmented, they cannot effectively challenge the reforms. The most dangerous situation for a reformer comes when social forces are strong enough to block reforms but not strong enough to generate the voluntary cooperation that can aid the adoption of the reform process.[11]

Thus, there can be two ideal-typical reform strategies: *pactismo*, or reform by pact, which seeks the broadest possible support from unions, parties, and other organizations; and *decretismo*, or reform by decree, which bypasses other political and social forces, rendering their opposition ineffective. In posttransition Korea, which lacked strong, centralized, and encompassing organizations, *decretismo* was a likelier reform strategy.

In Korea's new political society, open and competitive elections were taking root. But the party system was far from institutionalized.[12] Political parties were dominated by clientelist leaders who controlled party finance, drawn largely from contributions by businessmen, and nominated candidates for public offices. Korean political parties were in a state of flux, made and unmade overnight by the whims and fates of their leaders. Bosses could break up political parties and enter into new marriages of convenience, only to go through another round of divorce and remarriage. With electoral politics gaining importance as a result of democratization, the cycle of party mergers and breakups accelerated.

Korean political parties were unable to offer differentiated programs or to develop a network of organizational links to interest groups in the civil society. A few charismatic personalities dominated the party machines, and the masses remained outside the party system.

Lacking any class, ideological, or religious base, Korean parties fed on regionalism, the single most important cleavage in Korean

---

11. Przeworski, *Democracy and the Market*, pp. 180–81.
12. For details, see chapter 2, this volume.

society. Although condemning regionalism as a national plague, all major political parties mobilized votes along regional fault lines and nurtured regional networks of support. Under such conditions, it was virtually impossible to base reform politics on the party system. Political parties and their leaders were more likely to be objects of reform rather than subjects.

The Rise and Fall of Kim Young Sam's Reforms

In such a historical context, it was almost inevitable that the president would assume the initiative for reform. Table 1 summarizes the major reform measures taken by Kim Young Sam since he assumed the presidency on February 25, 1993. As we see from the table, his five-year term was a period of presidential activism. Having promised during his campaign to cure the "Korean disease" and construct a "new Korea," President Kim Young Sam first launched an anticorruption drive. He announced that he would not take even a cent of political funding. He also disclosed his family's wealth to the public, forcing elected officials and high-ranking bureaucrats to follow suit. A requirement for public officials to disclose their family's wealth was later enacted into law. In the course of this anticorruption campaign, many old guards of authoritarianism who played instrumental roles in Kim's own election were purged. President Kim also tightened the laws on political funds and campaign finances in order to control political corruption.

The purification drive was backed up by a set of economic reforms that directly challenged the sources of corruption. Six months into office, President Kim issued an extraordinary presidential decree forbidding holding financial accounts in false names (the "real-name" financial reform). A year later he also outlawed holding real estate in false names.

At the same time, President Kim embarked on reform of the military, purging senior officers closely linked to former military strongmen Chun Doo Hwan and Roh Tae Woo. Contrary to the advice of

TABLE 1 Reforms under Kim Young Sam's Administration and Their Outcomes

	Political Arena	Economic Arena	Social Arena
FIRST STAGE (March 1993 to February 1994)	• Registration of wealth of public figures • Purge of public figures • Military reform • Anticorruption*	• Financial real-name system* • Deregulation/financial Autonomy/privatization*** • National competitiveness* • Chaebol reforms/fair competition**	• Consciousness reform/burden sharing** • Restoration of national history • "Upstream" purification** • Anticorruption*
SECOND STAGE (March 1994 to December 1995)	• Unified electoral codes** • Local elections • Decentralization* • Administrative reform*** • Rectification of history	• Globalization* • Real Estate real-name system • Structural reform of the primary sector* • Support for small and medium enterprises*	• Educational reforms*** • Judiciary reform*** • Unemployment insurance • Welfare reforms*** • Informatization** • Environmental reforms**
THIRD STAGE (January 1996 to February 1998)	• Party system reform*** • Political system reform***	• Integrated taxation on financial assets** • Tax reform** • Labor reform***	• Quality-of-life reforms**

NOTES: *Implemented but poor outcome

**Poorly implemented or retrogressed

***Attempted but failed or distorted by the interested parties

transitions theorists not "to take or even to circumscribe too closely
the movements of the transitional regime's queen [the military],"[13]
President Kim dethroned the queen. On grounds of corruption and
incompetence, he discharged, reassigned, or postponed promotion
of generals and colonels who belonged to the Hanahoe (Society of
One). Hanahoe, an unofficial fraternity of military officers organized by Chun Doo Hwan, had been a major pillar of authoritarian
rule before 1993.

A year and a half later, in 1995, in the name of "rectification of
history," several former military elites, including the two former presidents, Chun Doo Hwan and Roh Tae Woo, were tried and jailed
for military insubordination, subversion of the constitutional order,
and corruption. The military coup d'état of 1979 was neither for-
gotten nor forgiven.

In a major initiative for political decentralization, President Kim
also reinstituted the provincial and local elections thirty-two years after
they had been suspended by the military coup of 1961 (see chapter 5).
He also appointed a commission to seek ways to improve administrative efficiency, culminating in the restructuring of government.

The reforms of Kim Young Sam's administration also reached
into the economic and social arenas. In 1993 the government announced the Five Year New Economy Plan, which aimed to reduce
the state presence in the economy through deregulation, financial
reform, and privatization. The government also tried to reverse and
reduce the ever-increasing economic concentration in big business
groups through stricter application of the fair competition laws (see
chapter 7). It also attempted to revamp the education, legal, and labor systems.

---

13. Guillermo O'Donnell and Philippe C. Schmitter, *Transitions from Authoritarian Rule: Tentative Conclusions about Uncertain Democracies* (Baltimore
and London: Johns Hopkins University Press, 1986), p. 69.

In sum, the reform initiatives taken by the Kim Young Sam government were far-reaching and even heroic. Each of the reform measures was virtually unprecedented and could have removed obstacles that had long obstructed Korea's developing into an advanced country.

The reform efforts began to falter, however, as President Kim entered into the second half of his term. Although relatively successful in political reforms, the government failed to achieve the desired economic and social reforms. The government reported solid progress, but the actual results were far from satisfactory. Those reforms could succeed only when cooperation or at least acquiescence was forthcoming from the negatively affected groups who needed consultation and persuasion, not authoritarian dictum.

According to the government, out of 1,790 deregulation items 1,759 were implemented as of March 31, 1996.[14] These numbers are deceptive, however, because they included obsolete regulations that needed to be removed. Key regulations were retained; a new broad umbrella regulation absorbed and replaced a large number of old minor ones.

The financial reform involved five goals: free interest rates, reduction of "policy credit" and other state interventions, inducement of specialization and enlargement of the financial institutions, liberalization of foreign exchange and capital markets, and increased monitoring to ensure fair competition. According to the government, as of the end of 1995, 54.6 percent of the 172 reform targets had been achieved, while 34.9 percent were in the midst of implementation.[15] However, few real changes had been made by the time the financial and currency crises broke out in late 1997.

---

14. Ministry of Finance and Economy (MOFE), *White Papers on Economy* (Seoul, 1996), p. 140.
15. MOFE, *White Paper*, pp. 168–69.

The privatization plan selected 68 of 133 public enterprises for sale in 1994–98.[16] But it was only partially implemented. *Chaebol* reforms were also left incomplete, partly because of the *chaebols'* political clout based on close relationships with the bureaucrats, media, and politicians and partly because of the *chaebols'* preponderance in the economy. Given the frequency of elections, the government had constantly to worry about short-term economic performance, which depended on the performance of the *chaebol* firms.

Similarly, overhauling the educational, legal, and labor systems was not possible without active support from the interested parties. The president could set the agenda, but its successful implementation required the cooperation of the very political actors who were selected as the targets of reform.

Moreover, popular support for Kim, which had once topped 90 percent,[17] began to taper off. One year after his inauguration, it fell to slightly more than 60 percent, and, at this point the citizens who assessed his reforms negatively outnumbered those who saw them positively.[18] Six months later, satisfaction with the reforms had fallen to slightly more than 30 percent.[19] Two years into office, the approval rating for the civilian government surged back to 66 percent and popular satisfaction also increased but with a wide variance depending on the reform issues. The real-name systems and anticorruption campaigns got high points, while the political reforms and daily life–related reforms got low evaluations. By April 1996 public approval of President Kim's performance had fallen dramatically, and it continued to plummet in subsequent months (see figure 1).

The support for the ruling DLP displayed a similar trend but with lower levels of initial support (see figure 2). More ominously for the

16. Economic Planning Board, *White Paper on Economy* (Seoul, 1994), p. 190.
17. Gallup Korea poll, May 11–12, 1993.
18. *Joongang Ilbo*, February 24, 1994.
19. *Joongang Ilbo*, September 22, 1994.

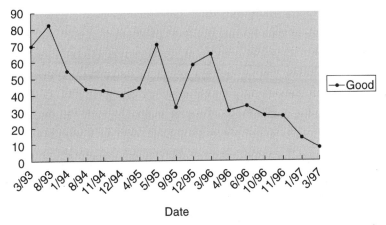

FIGURE 1 Rating President Kim's Performance (in percent)
SOURCE: Gallup Korea.

DLP, its anti-Honam regional coalition disintegrated. In the course of the early phase of reforms, the old guard within the DLP suffered the brunt of purification and anticorruption drives. Right before the local election of 1995, Kim Jong Pil and his followers broke away from the DLP to form the United Liberal Democrats (ULD).

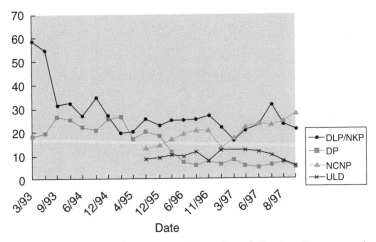

FIGURE 2 Popular Support for Political Parties (in percent)
SOURCE: Gallup Korea.

In the local elections of June 29, 1995, the DLP suffered a devastating defeat, with regionalism determining the performance of the political parties. The Democratic Party, supported by Honam native Kim Dae Jung, won all the seats in the Honam region and a landslide in Seoul. Kim Jong Pil's ULD swept his native Chungchong region. The DLP won a landslide in Kim Young Sam's native Pusan-Kyungnam region. In the Taegu-Kyungpuk region, which had produced the bulk of political leaders during the authoritarian period, the independents performed well, winning the mayorship of Taegu.

It looked like the DLP would lose the upcoming National Assembly election in 1996. Because another electoral defeat would make it virtually impossible to continue the reform program, a serious debate occurred within the DLP over amending the already implemented reforms. Two were at issue: the real-name financial account system and the pardon and reinstatement of the purged public figures. Although the idea was to broaden the reform coalition by moderating the reforms, it risked undermining the reform efforts. Besides, the DLP and the Kim Young Sam government, both of which relied heavily for their legitimacy on the success of reforms, feared that adulterated reforms would further alienate the public.

Indeed, nationwide polls at the time indicated that the public expected further reforms. In a Gallup Korea poll of July 29, 1995, commissioned by the Ministry of Public Information, 89 percent responded that the reforms needed strengthening. Respondents listed as the most important reform achievements the real-name financial account system (46.6 percent), eradication of corruption (22 percent), the purge of corrupt legislators and officials (20 percent), the real-name real estate system (14 percent), and registration and public disclosure of the wealth of public officials (11 percent). Although the conservatives in the DLP argued for revising the real-name system, the public viewed it as the single most important reform accomplishment.

The DJP old-guard faction of the DLP also demanded an amnesty for those purged in the course of earlier reforms, most of whom were from the Taegu-Kyungpuk region. To mend fences with that old guard, on August 15, 1995, Kim Young Sam pardoned and reinstated several purged former officials from Taegu-Kyungpuk in the name of "national reconciliation." But the public response was divided.[20]

Confronted with the dilemma of deepening reforms while mending the reform coalition, Kim Young Sam bet his political fate on deepened reforms. In November 1995, he pressed criminal charges against Roh Tae Woo and Chun Doo Hwan for corruption and insubordination in the name of "rectification of history." The measure was very popular, with nine out of ten citizens supporting it.[21] But it further alienated the DJP faction within the DLP and the residents of Taegu-Kyungpuk, the native place of the two former presidents.

In the National Assembly election of April 11, 1996, the successor party to the ruling DLP, the New Korea Party (NKP), performed better than expected, though it lost eight seats and failed to win a majority. Around this time, however, President Kim's popularity plunged irrevocably (see figure 1), and he was no longer in a position to provide the needed initiative for reforms. Reforms virtually stopped after the "rectification of history."

In the course of the rectification of history, the opposition National Congress for New Politics (NCNP, which absorbed the old Democratic Party) raised two issues that directly challenged President Kim. One charged that President Kim had taken political funds from the former presidents (more than 70 percent of the adult citizens believed that he had).[22] The other concerned President Kim's campaign expenses in the 1992 presidential election (again, a

---

20. *Joongang Ilbo*, August 12, 1995.
21. A Seoul Research poll cited in *Joongang Ilbo*, November 12, 1995.
22. Gallup Korea poll, October 27, 1995.

majority of the citizens believed that he had violated the ceiling set by the election laws).

The coup de grâce was delivered when President Kim's personal confidants and son were implicated in a scandal involving illegal loans to the bankrupt Hanbo Steel Corporation. President Kim's weakened position meant that he could no longer carry out reforms. Having assumed a puritanical reform stance and having eschewed the construction of a broad reform coalition, his success depended on maintaining a large and committed popular following. The loan scandal, however, undermined his moral authority to engineer political reforms and to claim to speak for the nation's moral good. In a sense, he was brought down by his own moral crusade.

The day of reckoning came in December 1996. President Kim had the deadlocked labor reform bill passed in the old-fashioned way: by the ruling party assemblymen alone in a secret session held after midnight. The new law provoked strong protests from the opposition parties and the labor organizations and was revoked and amended in January to be more palatable to organized labor. This episode was another proof that President Kim's autocratic way was no longer effective.

Why did the reform program collapse so abruptly? Why could it not maintain its vigor? The following section tries to answer these questions.

Problems with Kim Young Sam's Reform Politics

As the first civilian president since 1961, President Kim Young Sam enjoyed substantial support and legitimacy. This initial political strength and the concentration of political power provided by the existing authoritarian features of the state and party system enabled the forceful implementation of reforms, despite many obstacles and difficulties. Yet, as noted above, around halfway through his term, President Kim's reform program faced a crisis. The governing coalition was reduced, and popular support for reform began to erode sharply.

The reduction of the governing coalition and of popular support did not necessarily doom reform, for some forces commonly abandon the ship of reform in midcourse. In fact, the defection of those who suffered direct damage from the reforms showed that the earlier reforms were effective, and the reform agenda changed as the result of the successful earlier reforms. Indeed, the national survey data attested to this. The public expected reforms to move from the high plane of politics to the more mundane level of daily life. When these reforms were not forthcoming as quickly as expected, the public became critical of the government even while holding its past reform performance in high regard.

Seen from this light, Kim Young Sam's reform politics suffered a "crisis of success." Successful early reforms caused the supporting coalition to shrink, a problem that became salient to several problems reform efforts faced.

The Heterogeneity of the Reform Coalition

That Kim Young Sam's government was born in the womb of Roh Tae Woo's administration, which was the extension of military authoritarian rule, was one of the greatest obstacles to Kim Young Sam's reform politics. The compromise with the heirs to authoritarianism helped establish a grand electoral coalition (the anti-Honam coalition), but it aroused suspicion about the nature of the regime. More important, it also built heterogeneity into the ruling bloc, causing internal friction. Last but not least, the Faustian deal made President Kim's moral crusade suspect.

Whenever he put forward a new reform measure, President Kim had to deal more with the internal dissenters in his political party than with the external opponents. When he adjusted the level of reform for effective implementation, he was seen to be serving the parochial interests of his faction. Indiscriminate reform threatened to fragment the fragile governing coalition. President Kim thus had to walk a tightrope between implementing reforms and maintaining his reform coalition.

The 1990 three-party merger that created the DLP was for Kim a "Trojan horse" by which he could undermine the obstinate citadel of authoritarianism from inside. But at the same time it turned out to be his "original sin," raising doubts at every turn about the ulterior motive behind his reform efforts. In the eyes of his opponents, President Kim was "a Machiavellian prince" who had "sacrificed his *de facto* allies in defense of his personal interests."[23]

Thus, for example, his decision to press criminal charges of mutiny and subversion on former presidents Chun and Roh should have won unqualified support from the opposition. But instead it was perceived as a stratagem to distance himself from the growing public outrage over the wrongdoings committed by the former rulers and to gloss over the public suspicion that the secret political funds illegally collected by President Roh had flowed into Kim Young Sam's own presidential campaign coffers. Kim Young Sam called the prosecution of Chun and Roh an act of "rectifying history"; his opponents called it merely a betrayal of personal trust.

The Problem of the Blitzkrieg Strategy

A fundamental choice for any reformer is the pace of the reform process, between what Huntington calls the "blitzkrieg" approach and the "Fabian" approach: whether to strike rapidly and across a broad front or to unfold the reform program in a piecemeal and incremental fashion. Blitzkrieg reform catches the opponents off guard and takes maximum advantage of the broad coalition for re-

---

23. Byung-Kook Kim, "The Politics of Reform in Confucian Korea: Dilemma, Choice and Crisis," *Korean Journal of Area Studies* 11 (1997): 112–13.

form that frequently exists in its early days. But it also risks rallying the opposition.[24]

To maximize the strengths and minimize the risks involved in the two approaches, Huntington suggests combining Fabian strategy and blitzkrieg tactics. "To achieve his goals the reformer should separate and isolate one issue from another, but, having done this, he should, when the time is ripe, dispose of each issue as rapidly as possible, removing it from the political agenda before his opponents are able to mobilize their forces."[25]

The manner in which Kim Young Sam implemented the reforms was characterized by a combination of blitzkrieg strategy and blitzkrieg tactics. Given the nature of some reform issues, the blitzkrieg tactics seemed almost inevitable; the problem was the blitzkrieg strategy. One reform issue was hardly settled when another was put on the reform agenda. Even when the reform issues did not overlap temporally, the interval between reforms was extremely short, which had the unintended effect of uniting the opponents of different reforms in a common cause.

Also, the dizzying speed of reforms and their imposition mainly by presidential initiative opened the way for criticism of "civilian authoritarianism" by reform opponents and the general public. President Kim resorted to blitzkrieg tactics because of the strong presence of the authoritarian legacies and because some reforms, such as the real-name financial system, could only be implemented in a surprise attack. The problem lay in the lack of efforts to isolate the opponents by publicizing and justifying the necessity of such surprises.

The compressed reform schedule also escalated the public expectations to an insatiable level. The extraordinary initial popular

---

24. Samuel P. Huntington, *Political Order in Changing Societies* (New Haven and London: Yale University Press, 1968), pp. 344–62.

25. Huntington, *Political Order*, p. 346.

support for reform of more than 90 percent was one sign that popular expectations were too high. With such high expectations, not only the opponents but the supporters were bound to be dissatisfied in the end. Under such circumstances, the one-front war against the standpatters became a two-front war: the reformer had to deal with the ever-increasing popular demands as well.

The Problem of Instrumental Legitimation

As with other reforming governments, the Kim Young Sam administration could not rely on the legitimacy of existing institutions, for reform is an admission that the existing institutions are flawed. Thus, a reforming government must rely more on other (instrumental and electoral) forms of legitimation.

First and foremost, Kim Young Sam's administration justified the reform measures in particular and the regime in general on the promises of a better future. It promised "clean politics, prospering economy, and healthy society." When the government showed it meant what it had said by purging the established elites of the ruling bloc, the public gave its overwhelming support to the reform and the regime.

The quick success, however, raised public expectations to a level that could not possibly be satisfied. Besides, as the earlier successes were routinized and taken for granted, more successes were needed to maintain the same level of support. Sooner or later, instrumental legitimation was bound to collapse.

Another problem was that whatever reforms the government accomplished, the public also wanted improved economic performance. Koreans had become so accustomed to 10 percent annual growth that even a slight slowdown was taken as recession. From the start, the public expected that the new civilian government would revitalize the economy. Even in the initial months, when it gave overwhelming support for the reforms, the public expressed discontent about the economic problems. For example, in early 1994, more than half of the respondents listed economic problems as the major failure of Kim Young Sam's government.[26]

The new government tried various measures of economic recovery, from minor fixes to major restructuring. These measures were necessary, as the once-effective Korean model of development began to show signs of fatigue. However, old practices and institutions die hard, despite the changed internal and external economic environment, because of the resistance of the vested interests (as discussed above) and habituation. The model had been so effective for so long that it was ingrained into social practices and institutions. There was a feast of rhetoric: internationalization, globalization, national competitiveness, reengineering, restructuring, and so on. But inertia prevailed. In the end, dissatisfaction with Korea's economic performance diminished public support for the regime and its reform program. If "economic reform cannot long be insulated from politics,"[27] in Korea political reform could not long be insulated from economy.

Scope, Level, and Sequence of the Reforms

As we have seen, Kim Young Sam's government set the scope of reform broadly enough to include virtually all aspects of Korean life. But the breadth of the reforms came at the cost of internal inconsistency and incoherence. For example, while the government aimed to reduce the economic concentration of the *chaebol*, at the same time it pursued strengthening national competitiveness, which involved treating the *chaebol* favorably. A similar contradiction was visible between the labor system reform and the requirements of national competitiveness. Originated as part of the quality-of-life reform, labor reform was intended to enhance labor rights. It was

26. Gallup Korea poll, January 22–February 2, 1994.
27. Joan M. Nelson, "The Politics of Economic Transformation: Is Third World Experience Relevant in Eastern Europe?" *World Politics* 45 (1993): 459.

seen by employers, however, as increasing the rigidity of the labor supply. Labor reform thus became a hotly contested issue, with the government deadlocked between the ideal of extending democracy and the exigencies of economic growth.

The initial reforms of Kim Young Sam's government were aimed largely at the political elites in the national political arena, purging and replacing elites in the state apparatuses and the political society.[28] In their typical disdain for authority and their attribution of wealth more to corruption and special favors than to industry and ability, many Koreans must have been pleased at the sight of the humiliated and expropriated public figures and applauded the reform measures.[29] Although Korean citizens had not benefited from the initial reform package, they expected those benefits to trickle down in due course. When the more tangible benefits did not come forth even after two years,[30] however, popular criticism began to rise.

28. The original reform plan aimed primarily at institutional reform. Running several thousand pages, the plan listed a total of 236 reform tasks. However, President-elect Kim Young Sam's notion of reform was largely confined to the so-called personnel reform. Kim equated reform with purges, anticorruption, and the end of money politics. See "Behind Stories of the Civilian Government (2): 'Dongsungdong Project,' the Disappeared Reform Plan" (in Korean), *Donga Ilbo*, January 3, 1998, pp. 3–4.

29. Lucian Pye is intrigued by the apparently paradoxical attitude of Koreans toward authority: they depend on an authority figure, but disdain authority. In fact, such a disrespect is a mechanism by which subordinates balance the disproportionate degree of formal deference rendered to the superordinates. See Pye, *Asian Power and Politics: The Cultural Dimensions of Authority* (Cambridge, Mass.: Harvard University Press, 1985), p. 216.

30. The term *tunnel effect* was coined by Albert Hirschman to describe the tolerance of growing inequality in the socially homogeneous developing countries. He compared the phenomenon to the drivers in a jammed tunnel feeling relieved as the cars in the other lane start to move forward. See his "The Changing Tolerance for Income Inequality in the Course of Economic Development," *Quarterly Journal of Economics* 23, no. 87 (1983): 544–66.

The Kim Young Sam government eventually shifted the focus of reform to what it called quality-of-life reforms: economic, educational, legal, welfare, and labor system reforms. However, these reforms concerned entrenched social practices that could not be modified by the president's decrees alone but had to be implemented through the bureaucracy and the politicians inherited from the ancien régime. Vested interests were now given a chance to strike back.

Virtually the only instrument that would have forced reforms on the old guard was broad mass support for the reform program. Having adopted the elite-centered, top-down approach, however, Kim Young Sam's government could not elicit such support. The citizens remained mere spectators of the reform process. By failing to seek the consent and cooperation of the citizens and by relying solely on state power, delegative reform-mongering only entrenched anti-reform forces without broadening the reform coalition.

The Problem of an Autocratic Presidency

From start to finish, reform politics in Kim Young Sam's Korea was propelled by the activist president. Although the ultimate goal was to widen and deepen democracy, the process was highly authoritarian. Why did he choose the authoritarian way to democratic reforms?

Part of the reason lay in the nature of the reforms. For example, those economic reforms that could potentially bring fundamental changes in individual wealth accumulation, business transactions, and the operation of political parties—the real-name system—were pursued without consulting with business groups and societal actors. But Kim Young Sam felt that prior public disclosure and open discussion would have effectively foreclosed or at least scaled down the reforms. The president thus chose to present the reforms as faits accomplis and force societal actors to adjust to the changed context.

As mentioned before, Kim also lacked an institutional base on which to build a strong reform coalition. Although civil society was resurrected in the course of struggles against authoritarian rule, after the transition it was too weak and fragmented to serve as the basis of a reform coalition. Political parties similarly lacked the organizational strength, programmatic coherence, and ideological discipline to sustain a reform agenda. Instead, they were led by those who had successfully captured and personified regionalist sentiments.

The heavy reliance on state powers, partly forced on Kim Young Sam by institutional conditions and partly welcomed by him as an occasion to seize the initiative and consolidate his power, provoked hostile reactions from parties, factions, and civil society. Some deplored that democracy was degenerating into civilian dictatorship. Others compared Kim's administration to what Guillermo O'Donnell terms *delegative democracy* in South America.[31] Although the lack of concrete outcomes and the sluggish economy probably contributed to the erosion of mass support for the reform program, the aforementioned criticisms were political hurdles President Kim had to overcome. When popular support for the reform program eroded, many took up the issue of the moral integrity of the reformer himself.

Admittedly, the "imperial presidency" was more apparent than real. As in many Latin American countries, the facade of the all-powerful presidency concealed the reality of a weak presidency beleaguered by relatively strong social and political actors. If the presidency had been really strong, there would have been little need to bypass the normal channels of policymaking and implementation. Reliance on decrees signified that the president could not get reforms through normal legislative procedures.

It would be wrong to conclude from this, however, that the imperial presidency was more a necessity than a choice. Instead of shoving the reforms down the throats of social groups in delegative fashion, he could have resorted to dialogue and negotiation. The presence of relatively strong organized interests (but not strong

31. "Delegative Democracy," *Journal of Democracy* 5 (January 1994): 55–69.

enough to facilitate cooperative behavior) made it difficult for President Kim to choose *pactismo* over *decretismo*. Still he could have tried to persuade, tame, or negotiate with the social groups, as President Kim Dae Jung did during the first six months of his term. Instead of seeking partners for reform in political and civil society, Kim Young Sam capitalized on his wide initial popularity as the first civilian president and a major leader of the democratic movement and sought to justify his delegative style by appealing directly to the masses.

In combination with the weakness of formal representational mechanisms, the need for popular support created strong incentives for President Kim to focus on highly visible reforms that would immediately maximize his prestige among the population. However, such a personalistic, plebiscitarian style of reform had a fatal weakness and a serious repercussion. When his moral claim became suspect, it jeopardized the reform efforts as well. And since the masses were more interested in the immediate material benefits, the reforms, which had by nature a long gestation period, had to be compromised.

Conclusion: The Limits of Embedded Reformism

If successful, Kim Young Sam's reforms would have expanded and deepened democracy in all aspects of Korean life. As this chapter has stressed, early success was mixed with subsequent failure to achieve some economic and social reforms. Although the early political reforms could be relatively easily implemented and institutionalized by the authority of the president, the later ones required a restructuring of the existing order or broad support and social consensus or both.

The authoritarian legacies not only necessitated but facilitated sweeping reforms in the initial stage. The imperial presidency, the dominance of the executive within the state apparatuses, the dwarfed legislature, the fluid political society, and the fragmented civil society, all legacies of the authoritarian years, helped President Kim carry out strong reform measures against all odds.

President Kim's delegative, autocratic style was partly driven by the institutional inheritance, but it was also consciously chosen. He appears to have believed that he had every authority to act as he saw fit since the authoritarian legacies were all around and he had the popular mandate through direct election. This leadership style worked initially, but it proved counterproductive for those reforms that required more than the presidential initiative. Instead, the way Kim executed the reforms alienated the general populace and provided his opponents with pretexts for growing criticism of "civilian dictatorship" or "reform authoritarianism." At this point, President Kim should have adjusted his political style and tactics for accomplishing reform. Instead, he clung to methods that had clearly run their course.

From the start, Kim Young Sam's reform politics was plagued by what may be called the *adopted son dilemma*.[32] He could win power by managing to be "adopted" into the ruling party through the three-party merger that created the DLP. That helped him win the presidency by increasing the inclusiveness of the ruling bloc, but it also generated a support base too heterogeneous to sustain his reform program.

The *blitzkrieg dilemma* also could have been better managed. Secrecy and surprise enhanced the effectiveness of early reforms by reducing information leakage and opponents' capacity to counterstrike, but it also impaired the legitimacy of the reform by subjecting it to the criticism of self-righteousness. For later reforms, secrecy and surprise were neither necessary nor desirable. A more deliber-

32. For a detailed discussion of the dilemmas of Kim Young Sam's reform politics, see Young Jo Lee, "The Dilemmas of Reform Politics in Kim Young Sam Government," in Choi and Lim, eds., *Korean Society and Democracy* (in Korean). He identifies ten different dilemmas.

ate and consultative approach was needed at this stage but was not forthcoming.

The *instrumentality dilemma* also plagued Kim Young Sam's reforms. Basing the legitimacy of his administration almost solely on its instrumental success in achieving reform, Kim Young Sam's government raised excessive expectations. Eventually the gap between expectation and performance generated serious discontent; the achieved reforms were taken for granted, and further performance was needed to maintain the same level of legitimacy. If President Kim had placed greater reliance on democratic procedure, he could have avoided or at least minimized this dilemma.

Kim Young Sam's reform also faced the *consistency dilemma*, the tension between comprehensiveness and coherence: to the extent that the scope of reforms was comprehensive, it was difficult to maintain consistency. Had he slowed down the pace and planned the reforms more carefully, he could have increased their consistency. However, his eagerness for historic achievements and need for instrumental legitimation kept him from such options.

Kim Young Sam's most serious problem was the *power dilemma* between democratic goals and authoritarian process. Successful reform often requires a social pact among the encompassing organization or among weak social forces. Posttransition Korea met neither condition, further weakening the social forces or strengthening the reform authority. This paradoxical situation autocratically aggrandized presidential power for the sake of democratic reforms. Such a concentration of power may have been necessary to assure implementation of reforms, but it ultimately undermined the legitimacy and sustainability of the reform process. Moreover, structural factors may constrain but do not predetermine the choice of reform method. As seen by new president Kim Dae Jung's attempts at a tripartite pact following his inauguration, Kim Young Sam could have consulted and negotiated with social forces to generate broad and sustainable support for later reforms.

Thus, the structural dilemmas that Kim Young Sam confronted were not insurmountable. They could have been overcome by publicly articulating the rationale for reforms, fine-tuning the interrelationship among the individual reform measures, expanding and refashioning the reform coalition, allowing a greater role for civil society, and embracing the legislature, the judiciary, and the local governments.

Such democratic adjustments were not forthcoming. First, President Kim's earlier and continued reliance on delegative leadership made societal actors mistrustful. Second, the controversy over the new labor law crippled his potential to enlarge the reform coalition. Then President Kim's credibility and claim to moral authority broke down as the corruption and irregularities of his close aides, including his son, were exposed in the Hanbo scandal. Finally, the onset of the 1997 presidential race made the president a lame duck.

Embedded reformism encountered limits in another direction as well. Some institutions and practices were so embedded in culture and mores that reforms were simply too difficult to achieve. This seems particularly the case with the reforms in economic areas. Here what O'Donnell calls the "paradox of success"[33] worked against reforms. The economic model adopted by the authoritarian regimes had been so successful that reforms in this area were resisted. In addition, the model included a complex of interrelated components reaching far beyond the economic realm: the regulatory role of state managers, funding of political activities, campaigning styles, political dealing and wheeling, dispensation of privileges, and so on.

A similar problem plagued the effort to reform party politics and election campaigning. President Kim Young Sam was able to win passage of the unified elections law dealing with political parties, political funds, and election management. If abided by, the new law

33. O'Donnell, "Transitions, Continuities, and Paradoxes," pp. 31–37.

would have resulted in clean politics. However, the law was so distant from actual and deeply entrenched practices that not only politicians but also citizens behaved in the age-old ways. By 1997 the law had been revised to bring it more in line with realities, but that only worsened the situation. President Kim could set the agenda, issue decrees, but could not get more complex reforms through.

Despite the apparent collapse of the reform process during the second half of President Kim Young Sam's term, it is rash to conclude that all the reform efforts were for nothing. Despite the retrogressions and failures, postreform Korean politics will never be the same. The presidential election of December 18, 1997, was the fairest and the cleanest in Korean history. Even facing defeat, the ruling party eschewed irregularities and abided by the rules, resulting in the first peaceful transfer of power in Korea's modern political history. The military maintained political neutrality throughout. Thus President Kim's efforts to clean up Korean politics had left some indelible marks. In retrospect, we can only wish that he had exhibited greater political skill and leadership to accomplish the economic and social reforms. If so, Korea might have avoided the economic crises that now torment the country.

Delayed Decentralization and Incomplete Democratic Consolidation

Decentralization as a Process to Deepen Democracy: A Neglected Research Area

Democratic transition tends to generate enormous qualitative changes not just in the political regime but also in the economic system, the social structure, and ethnic and/or territorial relations. The fact that democratic transition is essentially multidimensional and multilayered tells us that democratic transition has a tremendous revolutionary potential, shattering the old configurations of a society and remolding them into largely new ones within a certain time period. Therefore, it is not surprising that countries have encountered a series of crises, conflicts, and uncertainties after they entered into the stage of democratic consolidation.

Among the political, economic, social, and territorial transformations triggered by democratic transition, however, the least explored area in the social sciences is that of territorial transformation (with special concern for decentralization and local autonomy).[1]

---

1. Resler and Kanet note that "although a growing number of studies focus on democratization, virtually all examine the process from the national or systemic level. . . . But these studies largely neglected the role of subnational institutions and groupings." T. J. Resler and R. E. Kanet, "Democratization: The National-Subnational Linkage," *Depth* 3, no. 1 (1993): 5. See also R. A. Nickson, *Local*

This is regrettable. Democratization at the national level does not automatically bring about democratization at the local level because "authoritarian enclaves" can persist in many areas long after the national politics has been democratized.[2] Therefore, local democratization and decentralization are critical conditions for a successful consolidation of democracy since they provide citizens with ample opportunities for participation, civic education, and leadership training.[3] Democratic culture is thus nourished and democracy is entrenched as "the only game in town." Local democracy also best serves the principle of popular sovereignty. As de Tocqueville wrote in 1835, "In the township, as well as everywhere else, the people are the source of power; but nowhere do they exercise their power more immediately."[4] In this sense, local democracy is an end itself and furthermore the fountain of national-level democracy.

On the surface, the Korean case appears to fit generally well with the formulations above.[5] During the ten years after the democratic opening of 1987, decentralization and local autonomy had been vital issues, along with socioeconomic democratization. Local councils and governments have been popularly elected since 1991 and

Governments in Latin America (Boulder, Colo.: Lynne Rienner Publishers, 1995), p. 2.

2. See J. Fox, "Latin America's Emerging Local Politics," Journal of Democracy 5, no. 2 (1994): 105–16.

3. See G. Stoker, "Introduction: Normative Theories of Local Government and Democracy," in D. King and G. Stoker, eds., Rethinking Local Democracy (London: Macmillan Press Ltd, 1996).

4. Alexis de Tocqueville, Democracy in America, vol.1 (1835; reprint New York: Vintage Books, 1945), p. 64.

5. Concerning democratic transition and consolidation of Korea, most studies focused on the political aspect of democratization, while neglecting the relationship between democratization and decentralization. Thus few studies dealt with the latter issue. See, however, Ilpyong Kim and E. S. Chung, "Establishing Democratic Rule in South Korea: Local Autonomy and Democracy," Depth 3, no.1 (1993). See also Jong Soo Lee, "The Politics of Decentralization in Korea," Local Government Studies 22, no. 3 (1996).

1995, respectively, whereby authoritarian enclaves were eliminated afterward. People were given plenty of chances to participate and to practice democracy in their localities. In addition, newly elected local leaders and ordinary citizens alike enjoyed local democracy and revived the spirit of local autonomy. Considering these significant changes, decentralization and local autonomy in Korea have gone along well.

If we look at the details, however, the Korean case is a peculiar one. Above all, a strong tradition of statism and centralism still prevails in Korea. Therefore, the system of local autonomy, adopted in 1991, is seriously flawed in that major administrative and fiscal powers are not granted to local governments, although governors and mayors are directly elected by the local residents. The combination of heavy state constraints over local governments with the popular election of local leaders creates many conflicts. The leaders of local governments and councils complain about the lack of power and resources, minute regulations and supervision by the central government, and slowness of central decisions. In addition, ordinary citizens complain about the lack of institutionalized channels in which to participate in local decision making. Thus, the center-local relation in Korea produces all sorts of blames and conflicts without much progress toward decentralization and democratic deepening.

All these negative aspects lead me to the conclusion that the current system of local autonomy in Korea is basically a variant of authoritarian central control with a democratic facade. If such a system continues to exist without a fundamental restructuring, it is hard to believe that Korean democracy can be consolidated and stabilized in the near future. What is worrying is that Korean democracy may persist but not be firmly consolidated. As Schmitter pointed out: "In South America, Eastern Europe, and Asia, the specter haunting the transition is not hybridization but non-consolidation. . . . Democracy in its most generic sense persists after the demise of autocracy, but never gels into a specific, reliable, and generally accepted set of rules."[6]

Korea clearly belongs to the case of persistence but nonconsolidation. Many factors, such as the fluidity of political parties and intense political competition based on strong regionalism, are hindering democratic consolidation. But I believe that the most critical obstacles are an overcentralized state, minimal decentralization, and suppression of a full maturation of local democracy. In this sense, decentralization is delayed and hence democratic consolidation is incomplete in Korea.

From this perspective, my chapter explores three issues. First, I show the processes of decentralization and the current institutional structure of local autonomy. Second, to understand the workings of the present system and the potentials for local democracy, I examine the dynamics of local autonomy and citizen participation on the one hand and significant changes in local autonomy since 1995 on the other. Lastly, serious conflicts between the central and local governments will be analyzed and a more progressive model of decentralization will be suggested for a firm consolidation of democracy both locally and nationally.

Institutional Structure of Local Autonomy: Persistence of Centralism

Legacy of Centralism and Development of Local Autonomy in Korea

Traditionally, the Korean state has been extremely centralized, exerting a monolithic control over all localities and the general populace without any meaningful representation from below.[7] Even after

6. P. C. Schmitter, "Dangers and Dilemmas of Democracy," *Journal of Democracy* 5, no. 2 (1994): 60.

7. On this point, Gregory Henderson argues that "a miniature of the immense impedimenta of the largest and most centralized state on earth ruled Korea"

a pseudo-democracy was established in 1945, the centralist legacy has continued to prevail. Furthermore, local autonomy, if any, was an instrument of central politics.

For example, President Rhee Syngman introduced the Local Autonomy Act in 1952 for the first time in Korean history. But he constrained local councils and leaders by denying them significant powers and resources. In addition, he manipulated local autonomy and the rules governing local elections to prolong his stay in office by securing local support.[8] Between 1952 and 1956 when he maintained a relatively high level of popular support, Rhee allowed the chiefs of towns and villages to be elected either through local councils or through direct popular votes. After 1958, when he began to lose political legitimacy, however, he reversed that practice and resumed appointing them.

Local autonomy bloomed for a short period in 1960, when Rhee's personal dictatorship collapsed as a result of the student revolution. In that year, the members of local councils as well as the chiefs of local governments at all levels were popularly elected. As soon as a military regime replaced the weak democracy in 1961, however, the nascent local democracy was destroyed: local councils at all levels were dismantled, and the chiefs of all local governments again were appointed by the central government.

After a quarter century of authoritarian rule (1961–1987), local autonomy was finally reintroduced as one of the eight promises (e.g., direct presidential election, amnesty for Kim Dae Jung, etc.) in the "June 29 Declaration" of 1987, which was announced by the presidential candidate of the ruling party. Hopes of realizing that

---

(p. 23). He goes on to suggest that, after Japanese rule, war, and military coup, "Korea became as centralized as it is possible to imagine a modern culture to be" (p. 199). G. Henderson, *Korea: The Politics of the Vortex* (Cambridge, Mass.: Harvard University Press, 1968).

8. Dong-Suh Park et al., *Local Politics and Administration* (in Korean) (Seoul: Jangwon Publishing Co., 1994), pp.10–12.

promise were generated by the April 1988 National Assembly election, in which three opposition parties gained an absolute majority and the ruling party won only 87 out of 224 seats. In 1989, the Local Autonomy Act was revised to allow direct election of local councils both at the provincial and at the county level. But President Roh Tae Woo vetoed this amendment bill because he feared that his government might lose control over local politics.[9]

After the presidential veto, the three opposition parties proposed a two-stage plan in which local councils and local governments would be established in 1991 and 1995, respectively. The election for local councils was held in 1991 after the Roh government was politically buttressed by the merger of his own party and two other opposition parties in 1990.

Korea's experience with reintroducing local democracy shows how difficult it is to move from a highly centralized system of governance to a relatively decentralized one. Among other things, the national elites of the central government and the ruling party were extremely reluctant to create independent local governments and to share power with them. Because they wanted to maintain and reproduce their power without being interrupted, in a sense, they were truly centralists.

By contrast, the national elites of the opposition parties were basically ambivalent. On the one hand, for the purpose of winning elections, they wanted to weaken the firm control over localities exercised by both the central government and the ruling party. On the other hand, they wanted to maintain their own political influences over local polities and prevent strong political competitors from emerging.[10] Therefore, they introduced local autonomy gradually and with severe structural constraints. In this sense, they were as

9. Jong Soo Lee, "Politics of Decentralization in Korea," p. 64.
10. Dal-Gon Lee, "Politics of Decentralization: Changing Intergovernmental Relations in Korea," paper presented at the International Symposium, Seoul, 1995, organized by the Korean Association for Public Administration, pp. 311–12.

much centralists as were those of the ruling party and the central government. Because all the national elites of both ruling and opposition parties were centralists, local autonomy developed late in a heavily constricted form.

Centrally Constrained Local Autonomy under a Strict Ultra Vires Rule

The year 1995 was a watershed in the modern political history of Korea in two respects. First, the provincial governors and municipal mayors, who had been appointed by the central government for more than three decades, came to be popularly elected. Hence, the central government began to lose many of its almost unlimited powers to control local governments unilaterally from top down. Second, direct popular election of local leaders created a situation in which democracy could be deepened locally and consolidated nationally. As all local polities were organized democratically, the chances for any antidemocratic forces to weaken or dismantle a democratic regime now greatly diminished.

It is unfortunate, however, that so much of the centralist legacy is ingrained in the institutional structures of local autonomy. As the Local Autonomy Act (revised in 1994) stipulates in Articles 15 and 16, local governments and councils are allowed to make local ordinances only "within the scope of the national laws and presidential (administrative) orders." The same act provides the central government with numerous administrative powers and the authority to intervene in local affairs as it wishes: the power to oversee and audit, the authority to issue order for revising local decisions or ordinances, the authority to sue local governments in court, and so forth.[11]

11. The Korean governance system is hierarchically structured, involving three levels of government, all of which are constituted through popular election. The central government sets and implements basic laws and policies that have nationwide effects. Sixteen provincial governments pursue provincial-level projects and coordinate the administration of 234 county governments that manage mainly

From all these constraints, we see that the institutional structures of Korean local autonomy are founded on a strict rule of ultra vires, meaning that "local governments are not granted a general power of competence to provide services and to carry out any function not specifically prohibited by law."[12] Instead, local governments can handle only those tasks and responsibilities explicitly permitted by the national laws or delegated by the central government. In this sense, Korean local autonomy closely resembles the Jacobin tradition of France, which supposes "the one and indivisible state" in which local governments are treated as the central government's local agents, lacking any innate autonomy.

Besides tight structural constraints on rule making and administration, the central government puts an unlimited number of other restrictions on local governments. For example, it classifies all those income-elastic taxes (e.g., income tax, value-added tax) as national taxes and reserves them for itself, while allocating many of income-inelastic taxes (e.g., property tax) to local governments as local taxes. That practice results in a heavy weight of national taxes compared to local ones (78 percent versus 22 percent).[13] What is worse, only the central government has the authority to decide which and how much to tax.

---

local affairs directly related to the welfare of local residents. (The numbers of provincial and county governments are as of late 1997; see also note 20.) The problem with this system of governance is that the powers and resources are unevenly distributed among the different levels of governments.

12. D. Burns, R. Hambleton, and P. Hoggett, *The Politics of Decentralization* (London: Macmillan Press Ltd., 1994), pp. 257–58.

13. Inevitably, this practice causes serious financial difficulties for many local governments. One hundred and eighty-four local governments out of 245 (15 provincial and 230 county governments, as of late 1996) cannot meet even half of their financial needs. See Sung-Bin Im, "An Evaluation and Prospect of Local Autonomy since 1995," in *Policy Studies of 1996* (in Korean) (Seoul: Korea Research Institute for Local Administration Policy, 1997), p. 142.

In addition, the central government sets the basic rules for local organizational and personnel management. For instance, the total number of organizational divisions, requirements for specific divisions (e.g., division of planning), total number of public employees, and rules for promotion and pay raise are all regulated by the central government. Although these regulations have been lessened somewhat since 1997, the basic institutional structures remain largely intact, suffocating the autonomy and vitality of local governments.

All the above constraints and regulations create a strange administrative system that has the form of a reverse pyramid in which most important powers, functions, and resources are concentrated in the central government (see table 1). From the table, we find that the majority of administrative tasks (or functions) belongs to the central government (more than 80 percent when the delegated tasks are included), while a tiny fraction is reserved for local governments (13–18 percent).[14] Local autonomy is thus a mere appendage to the center and lacks any genuine sense of independence.

Another point to note from table 1 is that the central government continues to be reluctant to devolve administrative tasks to local governments even after governors and mayors were popularly elected in July 1995. The central government reduced the ratio of its own tasks by only 1 percent (from 75 to 74 percent), while increasing that of local tasks by 5 percent (from 13 to 18 percent). Although it is good that the central government has reduced the ratio of the delegated

14. The examples of the central (or national) tasks involve national security, diplomacy, education, macroeconomic management, and so forth that have nationwide effects and require the same national standards. Local tasks include promoting local industries, collecting wastes, taking care of local roads, and so on whose effects are limited to the specific localities. In contrast, delegated tasks include implementing administrative regulations on land use, issuing passports, collecting statistics, preventing contagious diseases, and so forth that originally belong to the obligation of the central government but are delegated to the low-tier governments for administrative efficiency.

TABLE 1   Division of Administrative Tasks between Governments

Year\Tasks	Central Tasks	Delegated Tasks	Local Tasks	Total
1993	11,744 (75%)	1,920 (12%)	2,110 (13%)	15,744 (100%)
1995	11,646 (74%)	1,246 (8%)	2,882 (18%)	15,744 (100%)

SOURCE: Ministry of Administration, *Compilation of the Central and Local Tasks* (1994 and 1996).

tasks by 4 percent, many local governments still complain that the central government did (and does) not provide them with the financial resources to implement those delegated tasks.[15] These observations reveal how strong and tenacious centralism is in Korea.

Local Politics since 1995

Regionalism and Old Patterns

Regionalism, the most critical sociopolitical cleavage in Korea, has developed alongside a highly centralized state. During the nearly three decades since 1961, when authoritarian regimes ruled with diverse clientelist devices, interregional disparity and hence antipathy worsened because those regimes distributed state resources unevenly. Regionalism, especially strong in Cholla, Kyongsang, and Chungchong, has thus become a powerful factor affecting the formation of political parties, shaping political alliances, and determining electoral outcomes.[16]

Regionalism has many negative effects on democratic consolidation. First, it precludes political competition based on policy dif-

15. See Hee-Whan Oh, "A Study on Division and Allocation of the Administrative Tasks among Governments," in *Policy Studies of 1996* (in Korean) (Seoul: Korea Research Institute for Local Administration, 1997).

16. See Kyu-Han Bae, "Electoral Processes and Inter-regional Antipathy," in the Korean Sociological Association, ed., *Regionalism and Regional Conflicts in Korea* (in Korean) (Seoul: Sungwon-Sa, 1992).

ferences and rational debates from taking root in a new democracy. Second, it deepens regional rivalry and divides national society vertically, suppressing all other important sources of cleavages. Third, and most important, it hinders the interregional cooperation necessary to overcome centralist rule, making all localities prisoners of centralism.

With regard to the last point, regionalism is dangerous not only for democratic consolidation but also for decentralization because it is used as a tool by the political leaders and parties to reproduce centralist domination. In this center-oriented regionalism, no region seeks its own political autonomy or takes pains to transform a highly centralized governance system into a more decentralized one by forming a strong interregional cooperative network.

Below the level of the regions (i.e., provincial and county levels),[17] many problems stand in the way of democratic consolidation. Above all, enough time has not yet passed for local autonomy to take a stable shape and to bring about desirable effects: only four years have passed since local autonomy was reintroduced in July 1995. Hence, a lot of confusion and uncertainty currently exist.

Several other problems can also be detected. First, the present system of local autonomy gives more power to the mayors and governors than to the local councils, whose main tasks are to pass the

17. To help readers understand the structure of Korean local governance accurately, let me give a general picture. Basically, the Korean system of local autonomy is a two-tier system. Under the central government, there is the upper tier in which seven metropolitan cities (e.g., Seoul, Pusan, Taegu) and nine provinces exist, constituting sixteen provincial governments. Below it, there is the lower tier in which 69 autonomous districts under 7 metropolitan cities and 71 ordinary cities plus 94 rural counties under 9 provinces exist, constituting 234 county governments (as of late 1997). Under the lower tier are numerous administrative units that consist of towns and villages. Seen this way, notice that *region* does not refer to any institutional unit or level of local autonomy but rather means a collection of several provinces that have spatial closeness, similarities in linguistic accent, and a strong sense of belonging.

annual budget and to monitor the activities of the local governments. Mayors and governors have the right to request a reconsider-
ation of the decisions made by the local councils when the mayors
and governors judge those decisions are against national laws and
public welfare. Their tenure is legally guaranteed (four years); local
councils cannot impeach them even when they commit serious policy mistakes. They also allocate budgets and manage their local bureaucracies. Thus, a microcosm of a strong presidency is created at
the local level.

Second, a strong mayorship or governorship can be used as a
mechanism for collusion between mayors or governors and local
magnates. Many studies report that local businessmen exert undue
influences over local governments and their heads. Many members
of the local councils are themselves from the business class and thus
form links with local heads.[18] Through this linkage, growth alliances
in many local areas seek to maximize the interests of the business
class and the wealthy elite without due consideration of the general
interest. Sometimes, as in many Latin American countries, a strong
mayor or governor uses clientelist practices to allocate local budgets
as a way to get reelected.

Third, the institutionalized channels for effective citizen participation in local government do not yet exist. For example, the referendum, initiative, and recall have not been adopted. Thus, citizens
cannot make their demands binding or make local governments
more responsible. Of course, they can influence the policies and actions of local governments through petitions, demonstrations, the
press, and so forth. But Korea lacks institutional means for en-
trenching and consolidating democracy at the local level.

18. Because so many businessmen and wealthy people are elected as the members of local councils, Kim and Chung worry about the possibility that plutocracy
may threaten local democracy in Korea; see Kim and Chung, "Establishing
Democratic Rule in South Korea," pp. 207–8.

Considering all those problems and weaknesses, we note that local autonomy needs to develop further both in institutional and in behavioral aspects. Institutionally, appropriate mechanisms are necessary to control a strong mayorship and governorship. Behaviorally, local leaders need to consider the general welfare more seriously and ordinary citizens need to be more vigilant in monitoring them. Otherwise the new local autonomy is likely to reproduce the old political problems of corruption and inefficiency and hence fail to consolidate democracy both locally and nationally.

Popularly Elected Local Governments

Despite the problems and weaknesses mentioned above, many local governments under the new local autonomy have made remarkable progress in democratic performance in several important respects.

According to a nationwide survey conducted by the Korea Research Institute for Local Administration (KRILA) in April 1996, using a sample of 645 respondents, the biggest difference, after the popular election of mayors and governors, turns out to be qualitative changes in the behaviors of both local chiefs and public employees.[19] Popularly elected mayors and governors work more diligently and are more responsive according to 50.6 percent of ordinary citizens, while only 4.0 percent give a negative evaluation (the rest answered "no difference"). A similar response was given about the behavioral changes of public employees. What has changed specifically and how? Roughly five areas of major progress can be identified.[20]

1. Local governments try hard to transform sluggish and unresponsive local bureaucracies into fast-moving and responsive ones.

19. Im, "Evaluation and Prospect of Local Autonomy since 1995," pp. 97–99.
20. On such progress, see the Korea Research Institute for Local Administration (KRILA), *Administrative Changes in the Age of Local Autonomy* (in Korean) (Seoul: KRILA, 1996, 1997).

They speed up public service delivery by reducing red tape, even providing one-stop service. Sometimes they dispatch service personnel to a client's residence or workplace to deliver public documents or to help solve administrative problems (e.g., Wonjoo City of Kangwon Province). Moreover, many local governments have introduced diverse electronic methods such as faxes, the Internet, and electronic data interchanges to maximize the efficiency of communication and service delivery. A nonstop service is now available in many areas.

2. Many local governments are trying diverse organizational innovations to make local bureaucracies more flexible and more effective. For example, some have adopted team-based organizations to overcome the rigidity of the functional-hierarchical arrangements of traditional organizations (e.g., Inchon City). Some have utilized total-quality management techniques or organized voluntary think tanks (e.g., Kangdong District of Seoul, Eumsung County of Choongbook Province). Others are trying new personnel management practices in order to recruit professional managers from the private sector and to give women more opportunities even within the strict central regulations (e.g., Kyungnam Province, Seoul City).

3. Local governments are also trying to increase their accountability. Many of them have adopted a "real-name system" of administration, which means that those who are in charge of public services print their names on the official documents (e.g., Samchuk City of Kangwon Province). This system makes all the processes and results of public services accountable as well as transparent. In addition, many local governments have introduced a local ombudsman or employ citizen monitors to oversee their faults (e.g., Nowon District of Seoul). To be more responsible, many others are awarding monetary compensation for minor administrative mistakes (e.g., Kyunggi Province).

4. Local governments have become sensitive to the demands and voices of citizens since most mayors and governors want to be reelected. Thus, they have introduced diverse channels for citizen

participation on a voluntary basis, although such participatory institutions as referendums have not yet been legalized. For example, many local governments have organized public forums and hearings (e.g., Boryung City of Choongnam). Some even allow ordinary citizens or civic organizations to request a public audit and inspection to examine the mistakes or errors committed by local governments (e.g., Yongsan District of Seoul).[21] Others provide citizens with the chance to join the local administration as honorary civil servants (e.g., Tanyang County of Choongbook Province).

5. Lastly, local governments now take a more entrepreneurial role than before in order to reduce their heavy financial dependence on the central government and also to meet increasing welfare demands. For example, some have created local public enterprises to make profits (e.g., Sangjoo City of Kyungbook Province). Some now operate public parking lots and swimming pools to gain from user fees (e.g., Kwangjoo County of Kyunggi Province). Others help private local firms by providing business funds, building industrial or science parks, and creating cooperative networks between banks, universities, and firms. Although short of funds, by organizing diverse volunteer activities, local governments also actively help the elderly, the handicapped, and broken families (e.g., Kyunggi Province), thus increasing welfare provision.

Considering all these changes, the progress made by many local governments has been remarkable. But it is too early to tell whether all the innovations will have lasting effects. It should also be noted that such changes have been made mainly by those local

21. However, it should be noted that a strong mayorship or governorship may weaken the vitality of local civil society by co-opting civic organizations. For example, civic organizations working for economic justice or environmental protection are active in many cities. But when those organizations face financial difficulties, mayors or governors often provide financial support since they feel that such organizations may threaten their authority. Thus, a close financial relationship support with political support is formed between the two. Thereby, civic organizations are co-opted.

governments that had good intentions and a strong democratic spirit. Many important institutions for effective citizen participation still wait for legalization by the National Assembly. Furthermore, many local governments run the danger of potential collusion and plutocracy. Therefore, any evaluation of the democratic performance of local governments is largely mixed at this point.

Intergovernmental Conflicts and Local Challenges

Despite the remarkable progress that many local governments have made in democratic management of their localities, Korea's system of local autonomy is inherently restrictive. Thus many intergovernmental conflicts arise out of the contradiction between local autonomy and central domination.

Intergovernmental relations have been conflict ridden since the inauguration of popularly elected local governments (see table 2). Although many other types of conflicts involve different actors, the central government lies at the source of major conflicts because it created a structurally flawed system of local autonomy in the first place.

There are usually three types of intergovernmental conflicts: conflicts around allocation of powers and authorities, conflicts around allocation of benefits, and conflicts around allocation of costs.[22] Among these three, conflicts between the central and local governments are mostly of the first type. This is understandable in that the central government holds almost all the important power and authority, as described above. Similarly, vertical relations between provincial and county governments tend to generate such

22. Young-Soo Kim, *Methods of Resolving Conflicts between Local Governments* (in Korean) (Seoul: Korea Research Institute for Local Administration, 1994), pp. 21–22.

TABLE 2 Various Types of Conflicts: July 1995–April 1996

Types of Conflicts	*Number of Cases (total = 112)*
I. Conflicts between Central and Local Governments	31
• Central government versus provincial governments	15
• Central government versus county governments	16
II. Conflicts between Local Governments	27
• Between provincial governments	4
• Provincial government versus county government	18
• Between county governments	5
III. Conflicts between Local Governments and Local Councils	19
IV. Conflicts with Local Residents	35
• Central government versus local residents	7
• Local government versus local residents	25
• Between local residents	3

SOURCE: Korea Research Institute for Local Administration, *Diverse Conflicts in the Age of Local Autonomy* (Seoul: 1996), p. iv.

conflicts because provincial governments try to retain as many powers as possible and because a clear division of powers and administrative tasks has not yet been drawn. In contrast, horizontal intergovernmental relations are in many cases known to produce benefit- or cost-related conflicts.

Faced with such conflicts, especially those involving the central government, many local governments have challenged the central government either individually or collectively. Individual challenges include the Kangwon provincial government pressing the central government to undertake the environmental assessment that is needed to redevelop poverty-stricken coal mine areas. The Taejun metropolitan government and the Gueyang district government of Inchon City quarreled with the central government regarding zoning rights. The Youngkwang county government of Chunnam province fought the central government to avoid the construction of a nuclear power plant in its area. Numerous other examples of challenges exist that were unthinkable under authoritarian rule.

The best example of collective challenges against the central government are the organized efforts of the National Mayors Conference of Korea (NMCK) that was established in September 1996 and that included mayors of district and county governments from all over the nation. Although membership in the NMCK is voluntary, it has been active and influential in pushing the central government toward decentralization and in coordinating interlocal conflicts. The NMCK especially pursues a strategy of representing the interests of the county-level governments vis-à-vis the central and provincial ones. In addition, it tries to increase its bargaining power. Considering that there has never in Korean history been any attempt to represent local interests to the central government, the NMCK is surely of epochal importance. I see the NMCK as the first organized historical bearer of local autonomy that will act as a bulwark against centralism and thus promote local autonomy.

One tactic the NMCK uses is to conduct a survey and publish the results. According to a survey of ninety-four mayors in September 1997,[23] 74 percent of the respondents negatively evaluated the central government's delegation of administrative powers and tasks since 1995; 84 percent felt that many of the national taxes should be transformed into local ones; 100 percent demanded that a special law should be established to bring about a massive decentralization; 73 percent agreed to the necessity of introducing the referendum; and 64 percent embraced the initiative as the main institution of citizen participation.

---

23. National Mayors Conference of Korea (NMCK), *Ten Tasks for the Development of Local Autonomy: A Survey Report* (in Korean) (Seoul: NMCK, 1997).

Those findings indicate that the mayors of Korea are decentralists (or localists) and at the same time democrats. Although they are not immune to corruption and favoritism, they are the guardians and advocates of local autonomy and will vigorously challenge state centralism. Thus, it is highly likely that more conflicts will arise if decentralization continues to be delayed.

Toward a Federalist Decentralization and a Strong Local Democracy

Ten years have passed since democracy replaced authoritarian rule in Korea, after which a series of elections have been held and no antidemocratic forces have attempted to dismantle democracy. However, Korean democracy is hardly consolidated, although it persists.

The nonconsolidation of Korean democracy, I argue in this chapter, is the result of strong state centralism, perverse regionalism directed toward a fierce competition for central power, and weak local autonomy. I also argue that substantial decentralization and the promotion of a strong local democracy would be stepping-stones on which democracy can move forward both locally and nationally.

At the moment, however, local autonomy is still fluid and fragile, with many political forces at the national level trying hard to manipulate it. The ruling party of President Kim Dae Jung (the National Congress for New Politics) wants to deepen partisan control over local politics to make up for its structural weakness at the national level, while the major opposition party (the Grand National Party) demands a return to the appointment of mayors (especially those of the district governments of the seven metropolitan cities) instead of direct election. Therefore, it is unclear what changes will be introduced from above.

In the near future, it seems likely that local autonomy will continue to be an instrument of central politics and at the same time an object of central domination. But such centralist control will surely bring about serious resistance from below since the mayors and other local leaders have now grown to be the historical bearers of local autonomy. Therefore, conflicts between centralist and localist forces will be inevitable.

How can this conflict-ridden and politically unproductive situation be overcome? What would be a proper model for furthering decentralization and local autonomy? I propose a normative model: that is, a federalist model to reform an overcentralized state structure.

As formulated by many scholars, federalism is a principle that organizes a political body representing the general interests (general government) and other political bodies representing partial interests (local governments) in such a way that independent status is given to each type of political body within an explicit constitutional demarcation of powers and functions.[24] If a polity is organized in such a way, the unity of the general government and the diversity of many local governments can coexist, with state powers largely dispersed and shared by many governments of different tiers. Under a federalist structure, therefore, the dangers of centralism are structurally prevented.

The reason I suggest a federalist model are as follows. First, it is the most effective way to overcome all sorts of inherent contradictions between democracy and centralism. Second, a massive devolution of powers and functions can be a good solution for managing the many negative effects of globalization that make most modern states largely "powerless states."[25] Third, only a federation can pro-

24. See P. J. Proudhon, "Isolation of the Idea of Federation," in *Uniting the Peoples and Nations: Readings in World Federalism*, comp. B. Walker (Washington, D.C.: World Federalist Association, 1863). See also G. Harman, "Intergovernmental Relations: Federal Systems," in M. Hawkesworth and M. Kogan, eds., *Encyclopedia of Government and Politics*, vol. 1 (London: Routledge, 1992).

25. M. Castells, *The Power of Identity* (Malden, Mass.: Blackwell Publishers, 1997).

vide an autonomous status to North Korea as well as South Korea when the two are finally united.[26]

Besides the above rationales for federalism, some functional arguments can also be suggested. According to Diamond and Plattner,[27] in culturally divided societies federalism can contribute to the establishment and maintenance of democracy by enabling power sharing among major ethnic groups, thus dispersing ethnic conflicts and generating intraethnic conflicts instead. If intense interregional rivalry in Korea is understood as a form of ethnic conflict, it will certainly be reduced by a federalist restructuring that curtails and disperses the powers of the central government.

In sum, I think federalist decentralization is the most fundamental and surest solution to the problems of the contradictions between democracy and centralism, a powerless state, the reunification of the two Koreas, and regionalism. That solution will be difficult to implement since the centralist forces are strong and the localist (or federalist) forces are young and weak. However, more propitious conditions for federalist reform are now emerging. Unlike previous administrations, Kim Dae Jung's government has a good understanding of federalism, and the Korean central government is

26. The unification of the two Koreas along the lines of federalism can be understood in two stages. In the first stage, the two Koreas can be unified under a united federation of Korea in which each party joins the federation as an equal partner. In the second stage, however, a united federation of Korea can and should develop into a true federation in which provincial governments, not the two central governments of the South and the North, constitute the basic units of a federation. President Kim Dae Jung mainly focuses on the first stage, whereas I emphasize both stages. See Kim Dae Jung, *Kim Dae Jung's Three-stage Approach to Reunification: A Focus on a Confederation of South and North Koreas* (in Korean) (Seoul: Atae Pyungwha Publishing, 1995). See also Kyoung-Ryung Seong, "In Search of a Decentralist Model of Korean Reunification: A Federalist Approach" (in Korean), paper presented at the Conference on Korean Reunification, Seoul, Soongsil University, 1997.

27. L. Diamond and M. F. Plattner, eds., *Nationalism, Ethnic Conflict, and Democracy* (Baltimore: Johns Hopkins University Press, 1994).

currently suffering immense economic and political crises. Drastic decentralizing reforms would be a way to cope with these crises while enhancing political legitimacy, even though many political elites and bureaucrats may resist it. In the short run, reform is likely to take the form of devolution of powers largely under a centralized unitary state. Over time, however, there could be a qualitative leap toward a federalist decentralization.

If a highly centralized state is restructured according to the spirit and principles of federalism, I believe it will greatly enhance local democracy because it disperses state power to people and localities. Federalism and local democracy could do much to consolidate and stabilize Korean democracy, whereas centralism and restrictive local democracy have made it conflict ridden and fragile.

Political Democratization
and the News Media

South Korea (hereafter, Korea) was under a dictatorship for four decades after the establishment of the First Republic in 1948. The state wielded overwhelming power over civil society, and the people suffered from the lack of political rights and civil liberties. The news media were closely controlled and supervised by the government, and the Korean press was frequently criticized as the government's "mouthpiece." As John A. Lent put it, "Suppression has been the standard in regards to the press of Korea."[1]

But times have changed. Since June 1987, when the Korean people's demand for democracy evolved into a massive uprising, Korea has undergone a sweeping transition, from traditional strongman rule to an increasingly functional democracy. The people's political rights and civil liberties, especially the freedom of expression, have rapidly increased. This change has been widely recognized by many observers, including Freedom House in New York City. Its annual reports on the state of freedom in the world indicate that Korea's political rights and civil liberties have increased dramatically since 1988, upgrading Korea from a "partly free state" to a "free state."

---

1. John A. Lent, "A Reluctant Revolution among Asian Newspapers," in Alan Wells, ed., *Mass Communications: A World View* (Palo Alto, Calif.: National Press Books, 1974), pp. 117–18.

The Korean news media have been in the midst of all this change. Governmental control over the news media has lessened, and the media have rapidly gained press freedom. The *Kwanje Ullon* (government-controlled media) under the military dictatorships are now called *Chayool Ullon* (autonomous media). After all, as one Korean-born American scholar observed, "The press in South Korea has evolved from a 'voluntary servant' to an increasingly 'equal contender' in its relationship with its government in recent years."[2]

The purpose of this chapter is to examine the process and the effects of such changes in Korea during the democratization period. The major questions raised here are threefold. One, how has the media environment altered during the democratization process in Korea? Two, how have such changes influenced the Korean news media in terms of power relations and media operations? And, three, what is the impact of the media on democratic politics in Korea?

The theoretical perspective I have adopted to answer those questions is primarily "society centered" rather than "media centered."[3] The society-centered perspective views mass media as reflecting society and as a product of social change. This view generally assumes that the various subsystems of a society depend on the general structure of the society. Therefore, as a particular subsystem of a society, the mass media depend on the society and are thus defined in a historical context. This is a theoretical position taken by the authors of *Four Theories of the Press*, who argue that "the press always takes on

2. Kyu Ho Youm, *Press Law in South Korea* (Ames: Iowa State University, 1996), p. xiii.

3. The question about the impact of the media on democratic politics is more relevant to the media-centered perspective, which sees mass media as affecting society and causing social change. The traditional media effect studies, ranging from the "magic bullet theory" of the 1930s to the more recent "powerful media model," may be the best examples of this perspective. See Leo W. Jeffres, *Mass Media: Process and Effects* (Prospect Heights, Ill.: Waveland Press, 1986), and Denis McQuail, *Mass Communication Theory: An Introduction*, 3d ed. (London: Sage, 1994).

the form and coloration of the social and political structures within which it operates."[4] They also note that the press reflects a system of social control whereby the relations of individuals and institutions are adjusted. I believe that understanding these aspects of society is basic to any systematic understanding of the press.

Using the society-centered perspective, this chapter focuses on the process and the effects of the changing media-government relationship in Korea during the past decade. To do this, I first briefly review the media-government relationship under the authoritarian regimes in Korea. Then I examine the changed media environment induced by the Declaration of June 29, 1987, and its influence on the Korean news media, including the sociopolitical place that the media currently occupy in Korean society.[5] Finally, I discuss the impact of the media on democratic politics in Korea. These explications lead me to conclude that, although the expansion of press freedom has made the Korean news media an important sociopolitical power, they need to be reformed in order to function properly in a democratic public sphere.

The News Media under Authoritarian Regimes

Following the 1961 military coup, led by General Park Chung Hee, Korea was ruled by a strong dictatorship for almost three decades.[6] During this period (1961–1987), the state had almost

4. Fred S. Siebert, Theodore Peterson, and Wilbur Schramm, *Four Theories of the Press* (Urbana: University of Illinois Press, 1956), p. 1.

5. The results of surveys conducted by the Korean Press Institute (KPI) will be frequently used for this purpose. KPI has been conducting surveys on the media audience and journalists at irregular intervals since the mid-1980s. The KPI surveys contain many interesting questions, though not all of them have been consistently asked in each survey. I will examine the change of the Korean public's and journalists' responses to those questions over time.

6. For a more extensive discussion, see Youm, *Press Law in South Korea*, chap. 4, which provides an excellent review of the history of Korean politics and press.

complete control over the civil society and the market. The news media were frequent targets of the repressive government. They enjoyed freedom only to the extent that the government allowed it, partly because most Korean rulers viewed press freedom as "grants of political favor rather than acceptance of political or civil rights."[7] During the Third and Fourth Republics, from 1961 to 1979, President Park resorted to various legal and extralegal methods to control the Korean news media, and his administration had the Korean press at its command. "Press freedom during the Park era was the epitome of the press theory of authoritarianism underlying 'development communication.'"[8]

President Park's eighteen-year authoritarian rule ended in October 1979, when he was assassinated by Kim Jae Kyu, director of the Korean Central Intelligence Agency (KCIA). After Park's assassination, the Korean news media went through a brief period of liberalization until General Chun Doo Hwan, who emerged as the undisputed strongman of Korean politics through the notorious Kwangju Massacre in May 1980, led the "new military" in an unprecedented "purification campaign" against the press in July and August 1980, forcing a sweeping structural reorganization of the Korean news media. Under the purification campaign, 172 periodicals were banned and almost 870 journalists were dismissed from their print and broadcasting jobs for various reasons, such as incompetence or antigovernment sentiments. Furthermore, in November 1980, the Korean government under President Chun forcefully closed seven daily newspapers, three private broadcasting stations, and six news agencies. The popular Tongyang Broadcasting Company (TBC) and Dong-A Broadcasting Station (DBS) were merged into the national Korean Broadcasting Corporation (KBC), and six

---

7. Raymond D. Gastil, "The Comparative Survey of Freedom," *Freedom at Issue* (January–February 1983), p. 5.

8. Youm, *Press Law in South Korea*, p. 76.

major private news agencies were merged into the Yonhap News Agency. Daily newspapers published in Seoul were prohibited from stationing correspondents in the provincial areas, and provincial dailies were not allowed to keep full-time correspondents in the capital city of Seoul.

Along with the structural reorganization of the news media, the Chun regime enacted the Basic Press Act in December 1980, which specified the rights and restrictions of the press, including access to public information and protection of news sources. Like most press laws throughout the world, however, it was more restrictive than protective of press freedom. In fact, it institutionalized the subordination of the press to political power and quickly became the symbol of the press suppression in Korea.

The Fifth Republic viewed the suppression of the press as a crucial element of political power and established systemic control of the news media through what it called "press guidelines," instructions to the press issued daily by the Department of Public Information Control (DPIC) of the Ministry of Culture and Information (MOCI).[9] Some of them were highly specific, for example, directing the press to label antigovernment protesters as "pro-Communists." In short, freedom of the press was not a reality in Korea, despite being guaranteed in the constitution.

The repression of press freedom by the government was fundamentally due to the nonexistence of a system of checks and balances in the Korean political system. In the face of this undemocratic political structure, the Korean news media struggled continuously to regain their freedom. That struggle was often likened to a "never-ending tug of war," but that analogy is not a precise picture of the

9. The press guidelines were revealed in 1986 by *Mal* (Words) magazine, which was an unregistered bimonthly published by a group of banned Korean journalists. In its special issue on September 6, 1986, it disclosed the texts of almost six hundred press guidelines issued by the MOCI between October 9, 1985, and August 8, 1986.

ever-deteriorating press situation during the Fifth Republic. The Korean government under Chun completely subdued the news media. Adjusting itself to the changed political situation rather than fighting for freedom, the Korean press defined its role as a "voluntary servant," hence being called *Kwanje Ullon*. The future of the Korean press during Chun's rule was gloomily predicted by one observer in 1986 as follows: "The hopeless situation facing the Korean press at present will remain in the future unless there is a sweeping change in the Korean sociocultural-political and legal system. Unfortunately, the chances for change are not good as long as President Chun is in power."[10]

The June 29th Declaration and the Changed Media Environment

The year 1987 marked a turning point in the history of political democratization in Korea. In June of that year the increased tension between the military regime and the opposition forces led to a massive uprising. Many observers expected catastrophic results. The regime and the opposition, however, compromised in the June 29th Declaration, which was issued by Roh Tae Woo, the presidential candidate of the ruling Democratic Justice Party (DJP) and a former military colleague of President Chun's. Although diverse views exist concerning the nature of the declaration, a generally received view presents it as "a product of a dialectic process involving resistance from below and regime concession from above."[11]

10. Kyu Ho Youm, "Press Freedom under Constraints: The Case of South Korea," *Asian Survey* 26 (August 1986): 882.

11. Sang-Yong Choi, "Democratization and Peace in Korea," in Sang-Yong Choi, ed., *Democracy in Korea: Its Ideals and Realities* (Seoul: Korean Political Science Association, 1997), p. 10.

Whatever its nature, the June 29th Declaration was a pivotal point in the history of modern Korean politics, breaking "a cycle of authoritarian rule"[12] and accelerating the democratic transition in Korea. The declaration embodied a wholesale acceptance of such popular demands as a constitutional amendment for direct presidential election. One proposal declared that the media-related regulations and practices should be reformed to promote the freedom of the press. Roh suggested that "the Basic Press Act should promptly be either extensively revised or abolished and replaced by a different law." He also emphasized that self-regulation of the news media should be guaranteed.

Since then a number of positive changes have taken place in the media-government relations of Korea. Some of these resulted in structural changes in the media industry; others were institutional, involving sociopolitical and legal systems affecting the Korean news media. The International Press Institute (IPI) reported in late 1988 that "visible and invisible restrictions imposed on the [Korean] press have been abolished in favor of a greater freedom of information and the right of the people to know has been guaranteed."[13]

For instance, the constitution, as revised in October 1987, explicitly prohibits censorship of speech and the press while guaranteeing freedom of expression. The Basic Press Act of 1980 was repealed in November 1987 and replaced by the Act Relating to Registration of Periodicals (Periodicals Act) and the Broadcast Act, legislating improvements in several respects. Additionally, the Korean government under President Roh revised several media-related laws such as the Criminal Code and the National Security Act.[14]

12. Sung-Joo Han, "South Korea: Politics in Transition," in Sang-Yong Choi, *Democracy in Korea*, pp. 21–69.

13. Peter Galliner, "World Press Freedom Review," *IPI Report*, December 1988, p. 26.

14. For a more extensive review of legislative reforms, see Youm, *Press Law in South Korea*.

The legislative reforms are a necessary but not sufficient condition for guaranteeing freedom of the press. Other institutional reforms should support the legislative reforms. We should note here that the Korean National Assembly was dominated by opposition parties during the early period of the Sixth Republic. The Korean court also made visible efforts to ensure the press's independence, thanks in part to the opposition-dominated National Assembly. As a result, the checks and balances system among the three government branches were restored to a considerable extent.

Given the more independent judiciary and the opposition-dominated National Assembly, which acted as a balance against the executive branch, the press control mechanisms of the Chun regime were either eliminated or reformed by Roh. The MOCI Bureau of Information Policy (BIP), the former DPIC (which during Chun's rule was in charge of issuing numerous daily press guidelines), was abolished, and coercive instructions were no longer issued to the press as to what should and should not be reported. The BIP's demise also led to those government agents within the media who were in charge of overseeing press activities being removed. Finally, the press card system, which permitted only those journalists with professional accreditation from the government to be employed in the news media, was repealed.

The liberalization under Roh led the Korean news media to change from a government-controlled *Kwanje Ullon* to an increasingly autonomous *Chayool Ullon* in line with the changing sociopolitical circumstances of Korea. The Korean news media were able to stretch the limits of freedom, and news coverage of previously taboo issues became routine. The degree of press freedom increased at a dramatic pace during the Roh era, a tendency that has continued after the *Munmin Chungbu* (civilian government) was established in 1993 under President Kim Young Sam.

The Korean government under Roh, however, also removed the entry barrier that gave the established media an almost monopolistic status during the entire term of the Chun administration. As a result, in another sweeping departure from the past, the Korean news media industry expanded explosively. Before the June 29th Declaration, for example, thirty-two daily newspapers, 201 weeklies, and 1,203 monthly magazines were being published in Korea. Five years later, in June 1992, these numbers had increased astonishingly: 117 dailies, 1,561 weeklies, and 2,745 monthlies—more than a 200 percent increase.[15]

The sharp increase in the number of print media was only part of the overall media expansion. With the enactment of the Broadcast Act in November 1987, the Roh administration opened up the broadcast media market. As a result, several specialized FM radio stations went on the air in 1990, and a major private TV/radio station (SBS) began to air in Seoul in 1991. In addition, under the Kim administration, five commercial TV stations went into operation in each of the five major Korean cities, excluding Seoul. By the end of 1994, ninety-seven radio stations and thirty-nine TV stations were on the air in Korea.

Perhaps the most important development during this period was the establishment of the mixed, or dual, system of public and commercial broadcasting,[16] when the monopolistic public broadcasting system of KBS and Munhwa Broadcasting Corporation (MBC), created by the coercive merger in 1980 under Chun's military regime,

15. Jin-Seok Chung, "The Significance of the June 29th Declaration in the History of Korean Press" (in Korean), *Shinmun-gua Bangsong* (Newspaper and Broadcasting) 259 (July 1992): 20–25.

16. In the "dual" broadcasting system the public service channel(s) competes with commercial or private channels. It can be categorized into three types: "public service dominant," "genuinely mixed," and "commercial dominant." See Holli A. Semetko, "The Media," in Lawrence Leduc, Richard G. Niemi, and Pippa Norris, eds., *Comparing Democracies* (Thousand Oaks, Calif.: Sage, 1996), pp. 254–79. I think that the Korean broadcasting system is close to the "genuinely mixed" dual system since the public-owned MBC is totally dependent on advertising revenue.

was finally broken up. Although KBS and MBC are publicly owned, they depend heavily on advertising revenue, which has caused the competition for market shares to increase. Competition has been even stronger since cable television (CATV) services went into operation in March 1995.

The Increased Power of the Korean News Media

Liberalization and deregulation under Roh's rule changed the media environment to a great extent. As proposed in the June 29th Declaration, Roh officially relinquished most of governmental control over the news media by removing various political, economic, and legal restrictions. Those led to increased freedom of the press as well as the breakup of the strict media cartel that had prevented new entries to the media market. President Kim's civilian government gave more impetus to those changes.

The sharp increase in press freedom since mid-1987 has been well recognized by Korean journalists and the general public. The Korean people's evaluations of the press freedom under the three Korean regimes are shown in table 1. The data indicate that both the general public and the journalists believe that the freedom of the press in Korea has significantly increased during the Roh and Kim regimes.

As a result of the dramatic change in the people's perception of press freedom, we may also expect a change in their trust of the news media. When press activities were restricted sociopolitically as well as legally under the military regimes, the Korean people's trust in the news media was relatively low since they perceived the press as a mouthpiece for the authoritarian government. This was especially the case for the broadcast media that had been under the government's strong control.

As the Korean press changed from the *Kwanje Ullon* to an increasingly autonomous *Chayool Ullon*, however, the people's trust

TABLE 1   Press Freedom under Three Korean Regimes according to Journalists and the General Public (in percent)

Regime	1993[a]	1995[b]	1993[c]
Chun Doo Hwan	25%	30%	30%
Roh Tae Woo	51	46	45
Kim Young Sam	70	60	69
Number of respondents	727	1,024	1,196

[a]Korean Press Institute, "The Journalist's Responsibility and Ethics: The Third Survey," Research Report 93-3, 1993, p. 50. Measured by a scale ranging from zero ("totally unfree") to one hundred ("totally free").

[b]Korean Press Institute, "The Journalist's Responsibility and Ethics: The Fourth Survey," Research Report 95-2, 1995, p. 66. Measured by a ten-point scale and transformed into a hundred-point scale.

[c]Korean Press Institute, "Audience Opinion Survey: The Sixth Survey on Media Influence and Media Trust," Research Report 93-5, 1993, p. 158. Measured by a hundred-point scale.

in the news media has gradually increased (see table 2, which indicates that the Korean people's trust in newspapers has significantly increased in the 1990s). This tendency is even greater for television. In most democratic societies, television is generally perceived as a more trustworthy medium than newspapers because of the differences in their historical development. In Korea until the 1980s, however, television had been far behind newspapers in terms of media trustworthiness. This situation changed in the 1990s, and, indeed, television enjoys more trust from the public, the majority of which—about 70 percent of the population—prefer it as the most trustworthy medium.

The Korean news media of today enjoy unprecedented press freedom and the people's trust. What implications does this have in the changed sociopolitical circumstances of Korea? Since Carl Hovland's pioneering works on source credibility in the early 1950s,[17] a

17. See, for example, Carl I. Hovland and Walter Weiss, "The Influence of Source Credibility on Communication Effectiveness," *Public Opinion Quarterly* 15, no. 4 (1951): 635–50.

TABLE 2 Korean People's Trust in News Media: 1986–1994

Media Trust	1986	1990	1992	1993	1994
Newspaper					
Question 1[a]	3.31	3.56	3.58	—	—
Question 2[b]	2.92	3.39	3.40	3.56	3.97*
Television	3.06*	3.24	3.38	3.52	4.08*

NOTES: Entries are the mean results of a five-point scale ranging from one ("don't trust at all") to five ("trust very much"); those with asterisks were measured by a four-point scale and adjusted to a five-point scale. The data are based on the Audience Opinion Surveys on Media Influence and Media Trust conducted by the Korean Press Institute (KPI). The KPI survey, however, did not measure media trust in 1988 or TV trust in 1986. The 1986 TV data are from Myung Chey, Kwon Tai-Hwan, and Hong Doo-Seung, eds., *Social Research [Sahoe Chosa]: 1979–1988* (Seoul: Institute of Social Sciences, Seoul National University, 1989), p. 689. The sample size for each survey was 1,200, but the actual number of respondents fluctuates from 1,127 to 1,199 depending on respondents' lack of answers, 'don't know' answers, or both.

[a]"How much do you trust the newspaper that you subscribe to?"

[b]"How much do you trust Korean newspapers in general?"

number of studies have shown that the more trustworthy the source, the greater the effects of the mediated messages. When the people's trust in the news media is relatively low, as was the case in Korea under the military dictatorship, the media have little influence on public opinion. If an issue is politically sensitive, people tend not to believe the information provided by the media because they suspect that it might have been distorted by governmental pressure. Instead, they would tend to depend on interpersonal communication channels such as rumors. This was certainly the case under Chun's rule.

In the age of *Chayool Ullon*, however, the people believe what the media present, and public opinion is thus formed on the basis of information provided by the media. The media reflect it through daily reporting, which, in turn, influences the people's perceptions of what public opinion is. By this seemingly circular process, the media have a large role in defining the public agenda and forming public opinion. The media's power in public agenda setting and opinion formation would be even greater if the once military-dominated society suddenly entered a democratic phase, as there is no single dominant sociopolitical group.

Korea was in this same situation after the breakdown of the military forces in the late 1980s. The military began to lose its power rapidly under Roh's rule and was completely purged from the Korean political landscape under President Kim's *Munmin Chungbu*. The military's decline left a power vacuum in Korea's sociopolitical world. The question was, Who would fill the vacuum? The Korean people believe that it has been filled up mostly by the press.

The perceptions of Korean journalists and the general public about the power of various social groups in Korea are shown in table 3. Journalists are seen as one of the most influential groups in Korea by both the general public and the journalists themselves. About 20 percent of journalists and 13 percent of the general public believe that journalists are *the* most influential group today in Korea. More important, journalists are perceived as the group whose influence has increased most (and decreased least) under the civilian government. This is in striking contrast to the military, which was seen as one of the least influential groups.

The unprecedented power of the Korean press has often been criticized. A Korean journalism professor warned that "the Korean press has become a Frankenstein that creates a political power and exerts uncontrolled power arbitrarily."[18] In fact, the Korean news media are presumed to be a greater influence than the media of most democratic countries. Comparative estimates by journalists of the actual and ideal influence of the news media on public opinion in the United States, the United Kingdom, Germany, and Korea are presented in table 4. The journalists of each country were asked to estimate, on a scale of zero to ten, how strong they thought the influence

18. Hyo-Sung Lee, "The Problems of Korean Media Industry" (in Korean), paper delivered at the Seminar on the Journalist's Professional Ethics and the Direction of Korean Media Industry, Yousung, Korea, September 10, 1993, p. 11.

TABLE 3   Perceived Power of Social Groups in Korea (in percent)

	MOST INFLUENTIAL			INCREASED	DECREASED
	1993[a]	1993[b]	1996[b]	1993[a]	1993[a]
Politicians	38.7%	55.7%	56.5%	19.2%	9.4%
Journalists	21.8	12.3	13.6	32.7	2.5
Officials	19.5	14.3	13.3	11.5	17.6
Businessmen	12.6	6.6	5.3	8.8	10.7
Lawyers	3.7	2.0	6.4	17.0	5.6
Military	1.6	5.5	1.6	0.3	46.3
Religious	1.2	2.4	2.1	3.1	2.8
Professors	0.8	0.3	0.6	7.6	5.1
Total	99.9[c]	99.1[d]	99.4[d]	100.2[c]	100.0

NOTES: Entries are the percentages of respondents who answered to these questions: "Below is a list of the important social groups that affect our society. Which do you think is the most influential group today in Korea? Which do you think has increased/lost its influence most under Civilian Government?"

[a] Sample: journalists (n = 727). Korean Press Institute, "The Journalist's Responsibility and Ethics: The Third Survey," Research Report 93-3, 1993, p. 97.

[b] Sample: general public (n = 1,200). Korean Press Institute, "Audience Opinion Survey: The Sixth Survey on Media Influence and Media Trust," Research Report 93-5, 1993, p. 170, and "Audience Opinion Survey: The Eighth Survey on Media Influence and Media Trust," Research Report 96-2, 1996, p. 167.

[c] Percentages do not add up to 100 percent because of rounding.

[d] Percentages do not add up to 100 percent because "don't know" responses are excluded.

of the media was on the formation of public opinion. They were then asked how much influence the press should have on public opinion. Both questions attempted to get at how much political clout the journalists *thought* they had versus how much they *should* have.

As indicated in table 4, Korean journalists' estimates about the media's ideal and actual influence are higher than those of the U.S., British, and German journalists. That is, Korean journalists think that the press should have great influence and that the Korean press is very influential, much more than it should be.

Note, however, that the majority of the Korean people under-estimate the role of the Korean news media in the democratization

TABLE 4 Comparative Estimates by Journalists of
Actual and Ideal Influence of News Media on Public
Opinion

	U.S.A.[a]	U.K.[a]	Germany[a]	Korea[b]
Ideal	5.96	5.90	6.01	7.58
Actual	7.39	7.30	5.93	8.60
N	991	405	450	727

NOTES: Entries are the mean results of a ten-point scale in which zero was
"no influence" and ten was "a very great influence."

[a] From David H. Weaver and G. Cleveland Wilhoit, *The American Journalist: A Portrait of U.S. News People and Their Work*, 2d ed. (Blooming-
ton: Indiana University Press, 1991), p. 142.

[b] Korean Press Institute, "A Comparative Study of Korean and American
Journalists," (in Korean), Research Report, 93-4, 1993, p. 35.

process. According to a survey conducted by the KPI in 1993, about
74 percent of the Korean people believed that the Korean news media had not played a leading role in the democratization of Korean
society but instead took advantage of it.[19] This underestimation is
shared among Korean journalists; more than 80 percent agreed with
the people's view.[20]

In fact, it was not easy for the government-controlled *Kwanje
Ullon* to play a significant role in the democratization process.
Nonetheless, the Korean news media took more advantage of the
fruits of democratization than any other social sector. Thanks to the
democratic reforms that started in mid-1987, the Korean press
became an autonomous *Chayool Ullon* and had a chance to

19. Korean Press Institute, "Audience Opinion Survey: The Sixth Survey on
Media Influence and Media Trust" (in Korean), Research Report 93-5, 1993,
p. 180.

20. Korean Press Institute, "The Journalist's Responsibility and Ethics: The
Third Survey" (in Korean), Research Report 93-3, 1993, p. 88, and "The Journalist's Responsibility and Ethics: The Fourth Survey" (in Korean), Research Report
95-2, 1995, p. 123.

maximize its influence, given the power vacuum created by the military's decline.

The Impact of the Media on Democratic Politics in Korea

Although it cannot be denied that the expansion of press freedom is a result of the democratization process, it is also true that the autonomous media played an important role in bringing about democratic change in Korea. For instance, the transfer of power between the ruling and opposition parties, which occurred as a result of the presidential election in 1997, could not have been possible without free news media.

One important change brought about by the freedom of the press is the expanded political discourse, with previously tabooed antiestablishment views being accepted within the establishment. This trend was accelerated not only by the previously established media but also by the progressive media that had just entered the establishment. For example, in May 1988, the newspaper *Hankyoreh Shinmun*, with thousands of antiauthoritarian citizens as stockholders, was launched. That newspaper became the voice of blue-collar workers and university students and played a large part in expanding political discourse within the establishment.

One effect of the news media's expanding political discourse is easing the extreme social conflict and tension between the establishment and the antiestablishment. Politics under the past authoritarian military regime can best be described as "politics of the street": a confrontation between the government's physical force, such as the police, and the antiestablishment's mass mobilizations. During the democratization process, however, such politics of the street gradually became the politics of discourse, giving Korean democracy a chance to arise not from a revolutionary overthrow of the regime but through a moderate and gradual process of reformation. In fact, the radical antiestablishment forces that had sought revo-

lutionary change through mass mobilization quickly lost their influence, as witness the decline of the student movement.

In contrast, the politics of discourse helped ignite a moderate citizen movement. One of the most dynamic forces in Korean society
since the 1987 democratization movement has been the emergence
of various civil groups dealing with issues such as the environment,
health, traffic, women's rights, consumer complaints, the media, and
so on. Their basic strategy is to create a receptive public sentiment
through the politics of discourse. Under the authoritarian regime,
which restricted the freedom of the press, civil society had to rely on
the politics of the street; with the advent of democracy and the politics of discourse, the foundation for civil movements was laid.

The politics of discourse also implies media politics: the emphasis of media within the political process. Although widely criticized, today's democratic politics are everywhere changing into
media politics, and Korea is no exception. As a result of democratization, the freedom of the press has increased greatly; this in turn has
strengthened the influence of the media, making the government
and politicians sensitive to the climate of opinion.[21] The reformation
policies begun during Kim Young Sam's government—for example,
the disclosure system for civil servants' personal wealth and the real-
name system in financial transactions—could not have succeeded
without the support of the media. Another example is one of the Kim
government's greatest achievements: military reformation. With the
media's unanimous support, the Kim government did away with
what had been for thirty years Korea's greatest obstruction to democracy, thus ushering in the "civilian government." In today's

21. Nowadays in Korea it is not uncommon to see various important government policies changed or scrapped as a result of media coverage. For instance,
President Kim Young Sam, who was sensitive to media reaction, had six prime ministers during his five-year term and replaced almost all the other ministers several
times each. According to the press, such actions damaged the Kim administration's
continuity, resulting in the current economic crisis.

economic crisis, the tripartite agreement between government, management, and union was successful not only because of President-elect Kim Dae Jung's political prowess but also because public opinion was reflected in the mass media. Without the pressure of public opinion, such a deal between the conservative *chaebol* and the radical workers would have been extremely difficult.

Evidence that Korean politics are changing into media politics can best be seen in elections. Historically, Korean elections have relied on massive public rallies and private corps and hence necessitated astronomical amounts of election funds. Such an expensive election system is one of the main causes of corruption and clientelism, also known as the "Korean diseases."[22] This style of election campaigning is also impractical because of the restricted number of voters that can be contacted through the party system and the candidate's private corps. That the positive use of media during the election could end such impractical, high-expense campaigning became a popular sentiment. As a result, since the presidential election of 1988, mass media, television in particular, have become an essential part of campaigning. During the 1997 presidential election, the first TV debates between presidential candidates were aired, ultimately defining Korean elections as media elections.

However, it is difficult to forsee how such an election system — in which the candidates' individuality and personal image are given priority over the differentiation between parties on the basis of ideology and policy — will affect Korean democracy. In general, today's politics tend to depend excessively on the reality construction of the

22. The indictment of two former presidents, Chun Doo Hwan and Roh Tae Woo, over the slush fund scandal plus President Kim Young Sam's political crisis owing to the Hanbo scandal all had some connection with illegal election funds.

mass media. The effect that the mass media will have on the future of democracy remains to be seen.

Conclusion: News Media for Democratic Consolidation

The democratic transition that Korea has undergone over the past decade is characterized as the development of liberal pluralism: removing legal and institutional oppression, decentralizing socio-political power, introducing a real market economy, tolerating diverse values and ideas, and so on. The Korean news media have undergone this change and are flourishing. As some observers put it, they are "freer than ever to criticize the government, address formerly taboo issues, and expand with virtually no restraint."[23] Indeed, they are living through a golden age mainly because of the democratic reforms that started in mid-1987.

In this golden era, however, the Korean news media are facing another challenge: pressure from the market. As discussed earlier, liberalization and deregulation under the Sixth Republic led to an explosive expansion of the news media industry, resulting in heavy competition for market shares. In particular, the print media have been competing for a relatively limited market and, as a result, are suffering from chronic deficits.

Given the market-driven situation, the Korean news media are experiencing what France Vreg called "the dilemma of the pluralist media in a capitalist society"[24]: a decline in quality and in content

23. John V. Heuvel and Everette E. Dennis, *The Unfolding Lotus: East Asia's Changing Media* (New York: Freedom Forum Media Studies Center, Columbia University, 1993), p. 10.

24. France Vreg, "Dilemmas of Communication Pluralism in Social Systems," in Slavko Splichal, John Hochheimer, and Karol Jakubowicz, eds., *Democratization and the Media* (Ljubljana, Yugoslavia: CCC, University of Ljubljana, 1990), pp. 10–32.

due to severe market competition. Indeed, the Korean media have been frequently criticized for sensationalism and commercialism. The "turn off TV" campaign, conducted by various organizations in 1993, is an example of such social opposition.

As a result of the intensive market competition, Korean journalists are increasingly influenced by media owners and executives. That is, the role of political power, which controlled the *Kwanje Ullon* during the military dictatorship period, is being rapidly replaced by capital in this age of *Chayool Ullon*. In surveys conducted by the Journalists Association of Korea (JAK) in 1991,[25] about 40 percent of Korean journalists answered that media owners, executives, and advertising sponsors are "the most influential groups or forces affecting press activities." The percentage of respondents who gave the same answer increased to 50.1 percent in 1993. Interestingly, the percentage of respondents who answered "the government" as the most influential was only 11.0 percent in 1991; that figure dropped to about 8.4 percent in 1993.

These findings suggest that it may be necessary to promote "journalistic freedom," as distinguished from "press freedom,"[26] for Korea's democratic consolidation. In Korea, freedom of the press has been traditionally related to freedom *from* governmental restraints. As one Korean-born American scholar argued, however, "this passive notion should now be changed to the positive freedom *for* democratizing Korea."[27] To realize this new goal, then, journalists'

---

25. Journalists Association of Korea, "The 1991 Survey for the Korean Journalist's Opinions" (in Korean), *Journalism* (winter 1991): 298–322, and "The 1993 Survey for the Korean Journalist's Opinions" (in Korean), *Journalism* (summer 1993): 348–78.

26. John C. Merrill, *The Dialectic in Journalism: Toward a Responsible Use of Press Freedom* (Baton Rouge: Louisiana State University Press, 1989). He says that "journalistic freedom concerns a relationship between the journalists working for a news media and the executives and editors of that news media, while press freedom concerns a relationship between the press and the government" (pp. 34–35).

27. Youm, *Press Law in South Korea*, p. 70.

professional activities must be free from constraints imposed by capital as well as those imposed by government.

Journalistic freedom may best be promoted by the so-called internal democratization of the news media themselves, which involves ensuring journalist's editorial rights and activating press unions. Support from civil society is also crucial in protecting this freedom. For a full-blown democracy to establish itself, civil society needs a free and socially responsible press that functions in a democratic public sphere. In return, civil society should support the journalists' internal democratization and guard against any possible restraints imposed on the press by capital as well by government.

In the interests of the democratic consolidation of Korea, however, it is also important for the Korean news media to eliminate some years-old corrupt practices of their own, including *chonji* journalism and the *kijadan*. *Chonji* is a monetary gift in an envelope from news sources. Although most Korean journalists agree that *chonji* is ethically unacceptable, many habitually receive it.[28]

The *kijadan* are exclusive press clubs that exist in government ministries, city halls, police offices, political party headquarters, and so on. They are made up of groups of journalists assigned to the same "beat"; nonclub members are often denied access to those same news sources. The *kijadan*, then, protect their members' professional interests and function as a channel through which news sources provide information and sometimes *chonji*.

Unless these old practices are reformed, it will be difficult to consolidate democracy in Korea. The Korean journalists must realize that those practices abuse the freedom of the press. An American journalist wrote in an article titled "How Koreans Squander Press Freedom" that "The press is rudely learning that the exercise of

28. Jae-Chon Yu, "Social Change and the Journalist's Professional Ethics" (in Korean), in Jae-Chon Yu, ed., *Hankuk Sahoe Beundong-gua Ullon (The media and social change in Korea)* (Seoul: Sohwa, 1985), pp. 51–92.

freedom is complex."[29] Arguing that editors and reporters are making decisions they never had to make before, they must realize the power of their words for Korea's democratic consolidation. In the end, only by strengthening the journalists' professional ethics through *chajung* (self-purification) will Korea be able to advance a step closer toward a democracy.

29. David E. Halvorsen, "How Koreans Squander Press Freedom," *Asian Wall Street Journal*, September 22, 1992, p. 10.

Reforming the *Chaebols*

The *chaebols*—Korea's huge family-owned and family-managed business conglomerates—grew enormously in economic and political power under the careful guidance and protection of successive military regimes.[1] Since the inauguration of the democratic Sixth Republic in 1988, the *chaebols* have become one of the main targets of democratic reform.[2] As the first civilian president of the Sixth Republic, Kim Young Sam attempted to carry out sweeping *chaebol* reforms to achieve democracy in the marketplace, not just in the political arena. With few personal ties to the *chaebols*, his successor,

1. A growing body of literature on the *chaebol* includes Seoung Noh Choi, *The Analysis of the 30 Korean Big Business Groups for 1996* (Seoul: Korean Economic Research Institute, 1996); Dong Seok Cho, *The South Korean Chaebol* (Seoul: Maeil Kyungje Shinmunsa, 1997); Eun Mee Kim, *Big Business, Strong State: Collusion and Conflict in South Korean Development, 1960–90* (Albany: State University of New York Press, 1997); Kyu Uck Lee and Jae Hyung Lee, *Business Group in Korea: Characteristics and Government Policy* (Seoul: Korea Industrial Economics and Trade, 1996); and Management Efficiency Research Institute, *Analysis of Financial Statements—Thirty Major Business Groups in Korea* (Seoul: Management Efficiency Research Institute, 1997)

2. The Fair Trade Commission of the Ministry of Finance and Economy identifies each year (since 1993) the thirty largest business conglomerates and subjects them to government regulations on cross-investments with total assets of over 6 billion Korean won.

Kim Dae Jung, has also been seeking to restructure the age-old system of crony capitalism based on the *chaebols* in order to simultaneously promote democracy and the free market. This chapter details and critically assesses the *chaebol* reform policies of the Kim Young Sam government and then compares them with the *chaebol* reform policies that have subsequently been pushed more successfully by the Kim Dae Jung government and the International Monetary Fund (IMF).

Reform Policies of the Kim Young Sam Government (1993–98)

An important policy objective of the Kim Young Sam presidency was to reform the *chaebols* as a means to achieving democratic values in the marketplace.[3] Democratic management *internal* to the *chaebols* refers to the following two issues: separation of ownership from the top management, without leaving any sacred group of family-cum-managers untouched, and transparent management, such that the family-cum-managers are prevented from making decisions with little regard to the principles of the market. Democratic values in the marketplace, which are *external* to the *chaebols*, focus on the *chaebols'* unfair advantages in the market vis-à-vis small- and medium-sized enterprises (SMEs) and foreign corporations. By making the internal structure and the external relations of the *chaebols* democratic, the marketplace would become fairer for all players, according to the Kim Young Sam government.

The first set of reform policies to enhance democratic values in the internal management of the *chaebols* focused on transparency to curb the unfair advantage the *chaebols'* founding family members en-

---

3. Mu Park, "New Economic Policy of the Kim's Government," *Shindonga* 11 (1992).

joyed in managing their own business and to ultimately separate management from ownership. The undemocratic management practices of the *chaebols*, which allowed the founding families to not only own but effectively manage the conglomerates, became an important target of reform. Unfortunately, most of the policies in this category—pursued through the New Five-Year Economic Development Plan (July 1993) and the Revisions of the Fair Trade Act (1992 and 1994)—failed to separate the founding families from management.

The second set of reform policies sought to remove the unfair economic and political advantages the *chaebols* enjoy vis-à-vis South Korea's SMEs and foreign corporations. Here again the instruments were the New Five-Year Economic Development Plan and the Revisions of the Fair Trade Act, along with the two "real-name" reforms, requiring the use of the actual names of the parties in financial transactions (August 1993) and in real estate registration (July 1995). Specific policies included reducing government protection and subsidies for the *chaebols* and removing/revising policies that allowed the *chaebols* to enjoy unfair advantages as compared with other domestic and foreign firms. An example of such unfair advantages is the cross-investment and collateral allowed among *chaebol* member firms, which enabled the *chaebols* to have easy access to bank loans. The goal of the Economic Planning Board's (EPB)[4] policies—The New Five-Year Economic Development Plan, and the Fair Trade Act—was to abolish the undue advantages of the *chaebol* member firms and thus level the playing field for all enterprises, including small- and medium-sized, independent ones. Again, these policies largely failed. In fact, some of the measures intended to improve fair trade directly contradicted the principle of competition; thus the *chaebol* reform policies as a whole produced mixed results.

---

4. The Economic Planning Board merged with the Ministry of Finance on December 23, 1994, and became the Ministry of Finance and Economy.

The third set of *chaebol* policies evolved around increasing their global competitiveness. This goal included measures that sometimes contradicted the above-mentioned reforms. For example, "economies of scale" were emphasized for key sectors, which allowed some corporations to become megacorporations with government support and subsidies. This policy went directly against *chaebol* reform policies, which were aimed at reducing the *chaebols'* unfair advantage in the domestic market based on their large size and affiliated member companies.

Among the leading policies introduced to increase global competitiveness were the Segyehwa (Globalization Drive, beginning in 1994), the 1995 deregulation policy, and the Ten Percent Competitiveness Campaign (1996). Of these three, only the deregulation policy was successful. Even in this case, however, critics argued that it was carried out without a concomitant policy to curb unfair business activities. In other words, deregulation only made it easier for the *chaebols* to continue to accumulate and concentrate capital in the hands of a few and to allow their businesses to further diversify into unrelated sectors.

The Kim Young Sam government's specific policy measures to reform the *chaebols*, their objectives, and their results are summarized and detailed in table 1 (see appendix 1 for their chronology). As shown in the table, most of the policies geared toward achieving a democratic marketplace failed; in contrast, the policies that succeeded (those related to global competitiveness) meant that the largest *chaebols* were once again major beneficiaries of government action. In particular, the *chaebols* were favored in terms of overseas direct investment and by the increased concentration of ownership facilitated by deregulation. Furthermore, since a democratic internal structure was not achieved in the *chaebols*, the founding families continued to exert great influence, including making decisions for overseas investments and diversifying the businesses.

TABLE 1 Kim Young Sam Government's *Chaebol* Policies: Goals and Implementation

Broad Objectives	Policy Goals	Policies (Year) and Specific Policy Measures	Result: Implementation (Yes/No/Partial)
Democracy in Market	Democracy in internal management	The New Five-Year Economic Development Plan (1993) • Division of ownership • Separation of ownership from management	No No
		• Decrease in the share of nonvoting stocks from 50 percent to 25 percent of total	No
	Democracy in external relations (fair trade to political-economic ties)	Third revision of Fair Trade Act (1992) • Restrict debt-payment guarantees among *chaebol* member firms to prevent reckless diversification into unrelated sectors	No
		The New Five-Year Economic Development Plan (1993) • Specialization of business activities into two to five main areas	No
		• Limit *chaebol* investments in financial institutions and media	Partial
		• Limit mutual loan guarantees among *chaebol* member firms	No
		Real-name financial transaction system (1993) • Ban the use of false/borrowed names in all financial transactions	Yes

TABLE 1–*Continued*

Broad Objectives	*Policy Goals*	*Policies (Year) and Specific Policy Measures*	*Result: Implementation (Yes/No/Partial)*
		Fourth revision of Fair Trade Act (1994)	
		• Decentralization of ownership via limiting the *chaebols'* investment in other firms from 40 percent to 25 percent	No
		Revision of Fair Trade Act (1994)	
		• Decentralization of ownership • Restriction of total investment from 40 percent to 25 percent	No
		Real-name real estate registration system (1995)	
		• Ban the use of false/borrowed names in all real estate transactions	Yes
Global Competitiveness	Competitiveness	Segyewha (globalization drive) (1994–)	
		• International market orientation by enlarging production capacity and opening export offices overseas	Yes
		• Deepening linkages and interconnections of economic activities on a worldwide basis	Yes

Global enterprises	Deregulation (1995)	• Remove barriers to free competition, pursuit of organizational reform	Yes
	Ten Percent Competitiveness Campaign (1996)	• Implement plans to increase efficiency and productivity	Yes
	Ease restrictions on overseas direct investment (ODI) (1994–96)	• Relax regulations against ODI	Yes
		• Abolish negative list for sectors and regions for ODI	Yes

Outcomes of President Kim Young Sam's Reform Policies

Reports published in 1994 and 1995 indicate that, less than two years after the inauguration of President Kim Young Sam, the *chaebol* policies appeared to have failed.[5] Although several minor measures, including limiting *chaebol* investments in financial and media institutions, were put into practice, most of the significant measures to limit the influence of the *chaebol* were not implemented successfully. In fact, several of the currently bankrupted *chaebols* expanded recklessly during this period into unrelated business sectors, hastening their demise. The IMF and others have argued that the failed *chaebol* policies of the Kim government allowed the *chaebols* to continue the disastrous management practices that paved the way for the financial crisis of 1997.

To understand the *chaebols'* response to some of the Kim Young Sam government's reform policies, let us focus on the public posture of the Federation of Korean Industries (FKI), an interest group established in 1961 that represents the opinions of the large enterprises, in particular the *chaebols*.[6] The real-name financial transaction system was hailed in both the domestic and the foreign media as a key to transparency in all economic transactions in South Korea. In particular, the policy improved transparency in *chaebol* management and limited political financing and political kickbacks by the *chaebols*. The system also made it difficult to establish "slush funds" that were used as political kickbacks and bribes to govern-

5. Baek Man Lee, "President Kim Young Sam's *Chaebol* Operation, Only Time Is a Matter," *Shindonga* 6 (1993).

6. The FKI was founded in 1961 as the Korea Businessmen's Association with thirteen members. Its first chairman was the late Lee Byung-Chul of the Samsung *chaebol*. It changed its name to FKI in 1968. As of 1995, 475 companies were members. The leadership of the FKI has been under the leading *chaebol* of Korea. The current acting chairman is Kim Woo-Choong of the Daewoo Group, with fifteen vice-chairmen representing South Korea's largest and most influential *chaebols* including Hyundai, LG, SK, Hyosung, and Hanjin.

ment officials and politicians. The *chaebols* welcomed this policy, feeling that it freed them to focus on innovative management and quality improvements.[7] Thus on October 12, 1993, the FKI established the Committee for Strengthening National Competitiveness, which stated that businesses would seek growth and development, not through collusive ties between businesses and politicians but through enhanced productivity and competitiveness.[8]

After the financial crisis erupted in November 1997, however, the FKI asked the government to abolish the real-name financial transaction system,[9] arguing that it contributed to the financial crisis by reducing the private sector's savings and encouraging the overconsumption that led to the trade deficit. This argument could not be supported, however, because private-sector savings had been gradually decreasing since their peak of 32 percent in 1987, not just after the real-name system became effective.[10] In fact, the total savings rate of the private and government sectors increased in 1995, and the level of consumption was in line with the up-and-down pattern of overall economic growth. Thus, funds hidden away in private safes were the real problem, not the lack of money flowing into the industrial sector.[11] Confronted with the public's outcry, however, the FKI swiftly withdrew its proposal.[12]

The Fair Trade Act was also a matter of great dispute between the government and the private sector. In response to the Revision of Fair Trade Act in 1996 by the Fair Trade Commission (FTC), the FKI issued a strong declaration of opposition. The *chaebols* argued that the commission was moving against the trend toward deregulation and the opening of markets by strengthening rules aimed at

7. *Segye Ilbo*, February 13, 1994.
8. Ibid.
9. *Chosun Ilbo* (digital English edition), November 13, 1997.
10. Ibid.
11. *Hangyorae*, November 27, 1997.
12. Ibid.

"stifling" business activities.[13] They contended that the commission's asking the top thirty *chaebols* to eliminate cross-payment guarantees by the year 2001 was unconstitutional because it infringed on the freedom to engage in private contracts by banks and borrowers. The FKI also took issue with the commission's plan to retain the right to nullify corporate mergers it deemed anticompetitive. The FKI said that it was an arbitrary practice, going against the government's move toward making rules more transparent. The FTC countered that the *chaebols* opposed the revision in an effort to protect their vested interests.[14]

In response to the Kim Young Sam government's globalization and deregulation policies, the *chaebols* and the FKI were skeptical. Their assessment was that, despite numerous reform packages, pronouncements, and slogans, the Kim government had failed to achieve real progress in deregulation. From the standpoint of business, the bulk of the government's measures were mere window dressing, dealing mainly with the simplification of procedures and formalities rather than genuine reform.[15]

The *chaebols'* reaction to the deregulation policies of the Kim Young Sam government was articulated in an interview with the chair of FKI, Choi Jong-Hyun (CEO of SK group), in January 1995.[16] Choi argued that past deregulation policies had been ineffective and futile, though he did concede that the Kim Young Sam government had shown some initiative by streamlining government offices first, in line with improving efficiency in the private sector. Choi strongly urged the government to lower interest rates, which he said hampered the conglomerates' global competitiveness. The FKI favored deregulation of the financial and foreign exchange sys-

13. *Korea Times*, August 15, 1996.
14. Ibid.
15. *Korea Business Review*, January 1997.
16. *Shindonga*, January 1995, pp. 236–45.

tems and abolition of all regulations on *chaebols* (such as those regarding economic concentration, shares of bank ownership, and fair trade) that could inhibit their global competitiveness. Further, the FKI opposed any attempt by the government to impose on the highly diversified *chaebols* a specialized and coherent business structure (a policy that had been pressed unsuccessfully by the government numerous times over the past three decades).

In January 1997, the Deregulation Promotion Office of the FKI conducted a survey of the top thirty business groups, individual manufacturing companies, financial institutions, private research centers, and academia. The FKI identified one hundred key issues for deregulation, which were classified into five basic categories consisting of finance, overseas investment and trade, manpower, promotion of competition and trade, and land (see table 2).

The proposed measures envisioned eliminating all government controls and regulations so that a free market could be realized. If such a market were created, businesses would be rewarded for creativity and innovation, not for their connection to politicians and government officials. However, the recommendations said nothing of the changes or improvements the businesses would be willing to make in response. In fact, the suggestions proposed that the largest ten *chaebols* be free from any governmental restrictions, which were initially imposed to curb their unfair advantages in the marketplace. Together these suggestions would have not merely allowed but promoted the expansion of the largest *chaebols*.

Overall, then, the effort to discipline and in a sense democratize the *chaebols* failed during the five years of the Kim Young Sam presidency (1993–98). As noted above, the government's efforts to reduce the unfair advantages of the *chaebols* were not implemented successfully. Policies aimed at separating the founding families from management and enhancing transparency in management practices failed. Measures to enhance global competitiveness, which removed restrictions and regulations, in contrast, allowed the largest *chaebols*

TABLE 2   The Federation of Korean Industries' Key Issues for Deregulation

Finance	• Abolish ceiling on loans to top ten business groups • Abolish the requirement for advance approval for the acquisition of real property by the top ten business groups • Ease restrictions related to onerous capital increases and abolish the ceiling on additional capital infusions for subsidiaries of the top ten business groups • Relax controls on the issuance of bonds overseas • Ease controls on foreign loans for plant facilities • Abolish controls on the start-up of financial businesses • Revise requirements for banks to make available loans to small and medium enterprises on a proportional basis
Overseas investment and trade	• Abolish requirements for equity funding for overseas investment • Expand opportunities for nonfinancial businesses to engage in financial activities in other countries • Ease formalities for reporting or approval of overseas investment • Abolish the limit currently imposed on the receipt of advance export payment • Increase commodities and commodity groups that can be imported on a deferred payment basis and extend the period of payment.
Manpower	• Revise the Labor Standard Law to allow employers to lay off surplus employees based on their own discretion • Revise the Labor Standard Law to allow employers to change work hours as they deem necessary • Simplify the procedures for employing foreign workers • Ease controls on the number of work hours for female workers

TABLE 2—*Continued*

Promotion of competition and trade	• Revise the criteria under which large businesses are classified
	• Revise the criteria under which monopoly businesses are classified
	• Ease controls on the founding of holding companies and prohibition of mutual investment between subsidiaries of the same business groups
	• Lower the ceiling on required capital infusions
	• Ease controls on payment guarantees for subsidiaries of the same business groups
	• Ease controls on the ownership of businesses
	• Ease the requirements on business specialization
Land	• Abolish the approval for land transactions and ease the requirements for reporting land transactions
	• Ease controls on land owned by business enterprises for purposes other than their general business
	• Revise the requirements for the appraisal of environmental feasibility
	• Integrate the amount of development costs and capital gains tax
	• Ease controls on the start-up of high-technology industries

SOURCE: *Korea Business Review,* January 1997, 192.

to expand their businesses into often unrelated sectors and thus to overextend themselves. In particular, the removal of regulations on overseas investments disproportionately favored the largest *chaebols,* which (in comparison to the smaller *chaebols* and independent enterprises) had significantly greater access to the huge amounts of credit and technology necessary for such investments. In fact, the five largest *chaebols* continued their expansion by means of enormous overseas investments, which added to their already staggering burdens of debt.

Chaebol Reform under Kim Dae Jung

The IMF's standby agreement, signed on December 5, 1997, with the South Korean government, includes important corporate restructuring plans in addition to extensive restructuring of the financial sector.[17] The IMF has demanded reform in two main areas of corporate governance and structure: greater transparency in management and the creation of a level playing field for all private enterprises. The first area includes "the adoption of improved accounting standards, independent external audits, provision of consolidated financial statements, and enhanced disclosure requirements." The latter involves banning mutual loan guarantees among *chaebol* member firms, which often leads to increased debt financing of the *chaebol* firms. Most important, the latter provision requires that the South Korean government not intervene in bankruptcy cases (in the past, often based on political factors, *chaebol* firms had been protected from bankruptcy). The IMF criticized this type of market intervention, saying it had contributed in a major way to the financial crisis. The South Korean government was also blamed for several forced mergers between sound and unsound companies, which eventually led to insolvency of the merged company. In addition to the above two measures targeted at corporate restructuring, the IMF requested the opening of the domestic bond market to foreign investment, which would help draw the *chaebols* away from their extreme dependence on bank loans.

In 1998, the largest *chaebols* (e.g., Samsung, Hyundai, and LG) announced major restructuring plans, which included massive layoffs of managers and employees and a sharp reduction of operations. Nationally, unemployment, which had hovered at around 2 percent in 1996, averaged 7 percent in 1998 and was expected to soar further in 1999, when 170,000 workers at the top five *chaebols* were expected to lose their

---

17. International Monetary Fund (IMF), "IMF Approves SDR 15.5 Billion Stand-by Credit for Korea," *IMF Press Release* no. 97/55, 1997.

jobs.[18] The IMF's restructuring requests, however, went far beyond mere belt tightening. They sought to break the tight grip over management held by the founding families of the *chaebols*, even when they owned less than 10 percent of the entire stock. The termination of bank lending based on political favoritism also promised to foster the growth of SMEs.

Following his election to the presidency in December 1997, and even before formally assuming office in February 1998, Kim Dae Jung moved quickly to press for fundamental structural reform of the economy, in response to the country's worst economic crisis in half a century. On January 13, 1998, President-elect Kim got the chairmen of four of the largest *chaebols*—Hyundai, Samsung, LG, and SK[19]—to agree to (1) provide consolidated corporate balance sheets for each *chaebol* by 1999, as a means to improve transparency in management; (2) eliminate cross-investments and payment guarantees among *chaebol* member firms; (3) reduce the high debt/equity ratio of corporations; (4) specialize into a small number of key sectors; and (5) strengthen the responsibility of the CEOs and upper management. The president-elect also urged the *chaebol* leaders to invest their personal funds in the *chaebols* to improve their financial structure. These policies promised to make the *chaebols* smaller in scale but more competitive by focusing them around a narrower and more viable range of business activities.[20] In addition to the five above-mentioned reforms, the Kim Dae Jung government sought corporate restructuring, which would be driven by the financial institutions. This included establishing fair loss-sharing practices and adopting measures to facilitate the restructuring process[21] (see figure 1).

18. *New York Times*, January 24, 1999, p. 3.
19. Daewoo is one of the largest four *chaebols*. However, its chairman, Kim Woo Choong, did not attend the January 13, 1998, meeting. The president-elect excused Mr. Kim from the meeting so that he could continue his overseas business transactions. See *Chosun Ilbo* (digital), January 13, 1998.
20. Ibid.
21. *Corporate Restructuring: Performance and Future Plan*, Financial Supervisory Commission, January 1999.

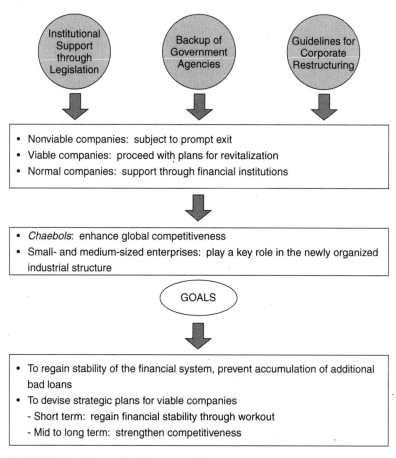

FIGURE 1   Vision for Corporate Restructuring

Although implementing these programs would be difficult, the depth of the economic crisis, the extreme financial dependence and distress of the *chaebols,* and the intensity of international pressure and scrutiny gave the *chaebols* little choice but to comply with the broad contours of the reform agenda.

A major element of the Kim Dae Jung (and the IMF) reform policy has been to reduce the extreme diversification of the *chaebols,* compelling them to concentrate on a narrower range of businesses.

Thus, in accordance with the principle of specializing into key sectors, each of the top five *chaebols* has envisaged business restructuring plans (see table 3).

In one of its most ambitious initiatives, the Kim government forced the top *chaebols* to swap businesses in multibillion-dollar deals designed to consolidate their activities. Thus in what became known as the "big deals," the Samsung group reluctantly agreed to turn over its fledgling car manufacturing affiliate to the Daewoo group, which is much stronger in that area, and the Daewoo group agreed to transfer its hard-pressed electronics unit to Samsung, which has its greatest strength in that sector. The LG group also agreed to transfer its computer chip division to the Hyundai group. (A chronology of the "big deals" among the largest five *chaebols* is presented in appendix 2.) Beyond this, the Kim Dae Jung government has also ordered the *chaebols* to reduce their huge corporate debts and stop debt guarantees of their affiliates.

Institutions and organizations for *chaebol* restructuring were established by the Kim Dae Jung government, of which the Tripartite Commission[22] was a major achievement. The president used his image as an ally of the working class to bring in labor leaders to this forum. Without the active inclusion of labor in the processes of

22. The second Tripartite Commission was officially launched on June 3, 1998, when President Kim Dae Jung appointed the members of the commission. Its origins date back to the "Great Compromise" of February 6, 1998. This proposal was drawn to establish the commission as a permanent body to allow economic players to exchange views and consult and cooperate among the members in order to overcome the economic crisis and consolidate public support. An official related to the commission was quoted as comparing the first Tripartite Commission with the second commission as follows: "The first Tripartite Commission fomented partnership among the tripartite members by reaching a great compromise in this time of a national crisis. The second Tripartite Commission, on the other hand, is an institutionalized arena, where all the economic players, based upon mutual trust, will hold open discussions concerning immediate tasks and devise proper measures to implement the tasks. As a consequence, it will greatly contribute to the construction of a permanent tripartite partnership."

TABLE 3 Business Restructuring Plans of the Top Five *Chaebols* (December 17, 1998)

Chaebol	Hyundai	Samsung	LG	Daewoo	SK
Key industrial sectors	Automobile, construction, chemical, electronics, financial/ services	Electronics, financial services, trade/service	Chemical/ energy, electronics/ telecommuni- cations, service, financial services	Automobile, heavy industry, trade/ construction, financial services	Chemical/ energy, electronics/ telecommuni- cations, construction/ distribution, financial services
Reduction of affiliates	63 → 30	65 → 40	53 → 30	41 → 10	42 → 20
Debt/equity ratio (targeted for end of 1999)	533% → 194%	370% → 197%	414% → 168%	505% → 199%	466% → 200%
Inviting foreign capital investment	8.484 billion U.S. dollars by 2002	5 billion U.S. dollars by end of 1998	7 billion U.S. dollars by 2000	6.5 billion U.S. dollars by end of 1999	2 billion U.S. dollars by end of 1999

SOURCES: *Agreement for the Restructuring of the Top Five Chaebol*, Financial Supervisory Commission, December 7, 1998; *Hankuk Kyongjae Shinmun*, September 27, 1998.

designing and implementing *chaebol* restructuring programs, the *chaebol* reform policies would have failed, for the immediate losers in the *chaebol* restructuring are the workers, who stand to lose their jobs due to mergers and "big deals." Although the Tripartite Commission has experienced a great deal of difficulty, its existence reflects the Kim Dae Jung government's ability to bring in the major parties to the *chaebol* talks.

As of January 1999, full implementation of the five programs of reform was under way as follows:

- To enhance transparency of management, the External Auditors Committee was established to foresee the implementation of transparency standards, and penalties for fraudulent audit reports have been strengthened (revision of Law concerning the External Auditing of Joint-Stock Companies, February 1998).

- New corporate cross-guarantees were prohibited for the thirty largest *chaebols* as of April 1998 (revision of Fair Trade Act, February 1998), and financial institutions are prohibited from demanding cross-guarantees from affiliates when extending loans (revision of Credit Management Regulation, April 1998).

- High debt/equity ratios were improved through agreements between the *chaebols* and creditor banks (Capital Structure Improvement Plan: CSIP) for debt/equity ratio reduction and divestiture. In addition, interest payments on borrowings higher than five times the equity capital will be excluded from income tax deduction starting in 2000 (revision of Corporate Income Tax Law, February 1998).

- Plans to streamline business sectors were announced by the top five *chaebols* and included in the CSIPs.

- The responsibilities of the CEOs and upper management were enhanced through revision of laws on minority shareholders rights and institutional investors (revision of Securities and Exchange Act, February and May 1998; revision of Securities Investment Trust Business Act, September 1998).

To speed up the restructuring process, the Kim Dae Jung government established a Corporate Viability Assessment Committee in May 1998 and reviewed the viability of 313 companies. As a result, fifty-five were classified as nonviable in June 1998 and placed under careful scrutiny. Their status as of January 1999 is summarized in table 4.

By the beginning of 1999, these sweeping reform and restructuring measures seemed likely to have a lasting effect on the *chaebols* and indeed the entire economy and society. Although promising to make the Korean economy much more dynamic, flexible, open, transparent, and globally competitive in the medium to long run, they brought widespread bankruptcies and layoffs in the short term, as the economy shrank by 6 percent in 1998. Some forecasts envision modest (2 percent) economic growth for 1999, but it will be some time (if ever) before Korea returns to the heady days of 7 to 10 percent annual growth rates.

Concluding Remarks

From the above analyses, we can see that President Kim Young Sam's efforts to reform the *chaebols* were a failure and that that failure contributed to the devastating financial crisis that swept South Korea in late 1997. Ineptness and corruption on the part of Kim's government, and the contradiction between different *chaebol* policies, were all at least partly to blame for the failure, which in turn obstructed the democratization of the marketplace and of society as a whole.

In the depth of the economic crisis that erupted in November 1997, it fell to Kim Dae Jung, a lifelong political outsider, to tackle

TABLE 4 Status of Fifty-Five Nonviable Companies (January 1999)

Status	THE TOP 5 CHAEBOLS		CHAEBOLS RANKED 6–30		OTHERS		Total
	Group	Company	Group	Company	Group	Company	
Liquidated	Hyundai	Sunil Shipping, Hyundai Equipment	Dong-Ah	Dong-Ah Engineering	Donguk	Dongkuk Elec.	25 (45%)
	Samsung	Samsung Watch, Hanil Wire, Daedo Phar., Yichun Electric	Hanwha	Otron, Hanwha Travel	Woobang	Taesung Const.	
			Hyosung	Tongkwang Plastic, Hyosung One Number, Hyosung Media	—	Yangyoung Paper, Daihan Textile	
	Daewoo	Korea Ind. System	Kohap	Kohap Fine Chemical			
	SK	Kyongjin Shipping	Shinho	Shinho Trading, Shinho Electronic, Young Jin Tech., Korea Tungsten			
			Keopyung	Keopyung Ind. Development, Keopyung Const.			

TABLE 4—*Continued*

Status	THE TOP 5 CHAEBOLS		CHAEBOLS RANKED 6–30		OTHERS		Total
	Group	Company	Group	Company	Group	Company	
Consolidated	Hyundai	Hyundai Livart, Hyundai Aluminum	Kohap	Kohap Textile	Kabool	Shin Han Industry	13 (24%)
	LG	LG Electro-components, Wonjeon Energy, LG ENC	Haitai	Haitai Stores	Hankook Synth.	E-hwa	
	SK	SK Warehousing	New Core	Newtown Project, Sidae Chuksan, Sidae Distribution			
Sold	Daewoo	Orion Elect. Component, Dong Woo Consulting, Daechang Enterprise	Kohap	Kohap I & T, Kohap FCN	—	Woojung Hospital	10 (18%)
	LG	LG Owens	Haitai	Haitai Confectionery	Hanil	Namju Development	
	SK	My TV Co.					
Court receivership					Hanil Tongil	Hanil Synthetic Ilhwa	2 (4%)
Under review	Daewoo	Korea Automotive Fuel	Ssangyong	Burma Petroleum	Hanil	Shinnam Development, Chinhae Chemical	5 (9%)
			Haitai	Haitai Electronics			
Total		20		23		12	55

SOURCE: FSC (1999).

the urgent and historic challenge of restructuring the country's badly battered *chaebols*, the flagship of its national economic success over the previous decades. Ironically, many of the reform measures pursued by Kim Dae Jung were similar to those of his predecessor, but several new factors enabled Kim Dae Jung to succeed where Kim Young Sam had failed. The first was the gravity of the economic crisis itself. With the economy reeling from its worst crisis in half a century and hardship spreading rapidly, the *chaebol* owners no longer could claim state favors, indulgence, or protection, for had they, they risked being labeled unpatriotic and having even harsher reform measures imposed on them. The second factor (related to the first) was the intense international pressure for reform, particularly from the IMF. Without far-reaching restructuring of the financial institutions and the *chaebols*, the IMF standby agreement would be in serious jeopardy and the South Korean economy would lack both the emergency credit from the IMF and the rating of creditworthiness from private capital markets necessary to overcome the financial crisis. The *chaebols'* compliance was thus considered critical for the survival of the entire South Korean economy. Third, the Kim Dae Jung government is relatively insulated from the class interests of the *chaebols*. Unlike previous governments, which had close, collusive ties to *chaebol* leaders based on kinship, schooling, and other elite social networks, the Kim Dae Jung government enjoys less intricate and formal ties. This provides the Kim presidency with the freedom to implement painful reform policies that *chaebol* owners have resisted in the past. The fourth factor was the creation of the Tripartite Commission and its forging an uneasy alliance among the three parties to implement *chaebol* restructuring programs. By appealing to all parties to sacrifice for the good of the nation, the Tripartite Commission was able to make the *chaebol* restructuring more successful in the Kim Dae Jung government, compared with its predecessor, which lacked such an institution.

Finally, the last factor is President Kim Dae Jung's reputation inside and outside South Korea as a heroic advocate of democracy. He is seen as someone who risked his life to challenge authoritarian regimes and thus fostered an image of a "clean government." This provided him with widespread popular support at the start of his term. Although Kim Young Sam's image as a democratic reformer also conferred great popularity early in his term, Kim Dae Jung's image was even stronger and more internationally acclaimed. Kim Dae Jung, after all, had been a political outsider all his life, while Kim Young Sam came to power as the candidate of the ruling party. All of this gives rise to guarded optimism that Kim Dae Jung's *chaebol* reform policies will indeed effect a permanent restructuring of the nature of South Korean business and of state-business relations.

It is possible, however, that some of these assets could be squandered. As unemployment rises, labor protests will increase and so too could nationalist reaction against the alleged foreign imposition of painful reforms. The Kim Dae Jung government's lack of class ties and personal experience with *chaebol* owners may also present difficulties. This weakness of informal bonds could make it difficult to utilize nonpolicy measures to exert influence when the *chaebols* resist the reform measures. Initially, some observers also worried that the lack of management skills would make it difficult for the Kim government to provide tangible guidelines for reform, although this concern abated somewhat as vigorous reforms were pursued.

Undoubtedly, the *chaebol* restructuring programs of the Kim Dae Jung government to date have not all been equally successful or sound. First, restructuring in the largest five *chaebols* appears to be much slower than that of the small *chaebol*. Second, all five of the largest *chaebols* declared financial institutions as one of their key sectors, which does not match the goal of reducing *chaebol* competition in certain sectors. Third, corporate restructuring as a whole is seen as lagging behind that of the financial sector and is seen as a main factor in Korea's low international rating for investment. Finally, the government put an undue burden on the banks to restructure the *chaebols,* making the banks responsible for restructuring their own institutions as well as their creditees—the *chaebols.* This protects the government from criticism if the *chaebol* restructuring fails.

For all his liabilities and weaknesses as a political outsider from Cholla, a region that was long discriminated against politically and socially, Kim Dae Jung has been vigorously dismantling the age-old structure of crony capitalism and restructuring the major conglomerates that have controlled more than three-quarters of South Korea's gross domestic product. The fact that Kim Dae Jung brings with him the outsider's fighting spirit and his close connections with labor and other social groups bodes well for him. Some worry, however, that his micromanagement style and the underdog mentality that he acquired during his long years as a political outcast may make it difficult for the reform process to go swiftly and smoothly. With the success of the reform effort rides not only the future of the country's economy but of democracy itself.

APPENDIX 1

Chronology of Key Events and Policies Related to the *Chaebols:* The Kim Young Sam Government (1993–98)

February 25, 1997	Inauguration of President Kim Young Sam
March 1997	Introduction of a hundred-day plan for the new economy
July 1, 1993	Implementation of the New Five-Year Economic Development Plan (1993–97)
August 12, 1993	Enforcement of the real-name financial transaction system
October 1993	Improvement of foreign exchange system
November 1993	Implementation of the second-stage financial liberalization plan
October 21, 1994	Collapse of the Sung-Soo Bridge
November 17, 1994	Announcement of the Segyehwa Initiative
December 3, 1994	Government organizational restructuring and establishment of Ministry of Finance and Economy (MOFE)
December 1994	Implementation of the third-stage liberalization of interest rates
June 27, 1995	Local elections
June 29, 1995	Collapse of the Sam-Poong Department Store
July 1, 1995	Enforcement of the real-name and real estate registration system
November 16, 1995	Arrest of former president Roh Tae Woo
December 3, 1995	Arrest of former president Chun Doo Hwan
October 1996	Campaign to raise competitiveness by 10 percent
November 1996	Approval of Korea's membership to the Organization for Economic Cooperation and Development
December 26, 1996	Forceful pass of the labor law and National Security Act law in the National Assembly
January 23, 1997	Bankruptcy of the Hanbo Steel Company

May 17, 1997	Arrest of President Kim Young Sam's son Kim Hyun Chul
July 15, 1997	Bailout of the Kia Group
November 21, 1997	Request of emergency loan to the IMF
December 18, 1997	The fifteenth presidential election
December 20, 1997	Pardon of the two presidents, Chun and Roh

APPENDIX 2

Chronology of the "Big Deals" of the Largest Five *Chaebols* (1998)

January 13, 1998   In a meeting with the top four *chaebol* leaders, President-elect Kim Dae Jung urged them "to enhance global competitiveness through focusing management capabilities on a narrower and more viable range of business activities."[23]

January 23, 1998   In an interview with Asahi News, President-elect Kim conveyed that "the *chaebol* groups need to resolve most of their subsidiaries, leaving only 3–5 key business areas."

January 30, 1998   Park Tae-Joon, then head of the United Liberal Democrats Party, stated that "Big Deal is one of the five principles in the *chaebol* reform."

April 20, 1998   President Kim Dae Jung meets with six key economic institution leaders and points out that "the conglomerates should sell healthy and promising companies"; FKI chair-elect Kim Woo-Choong replied that "the restructuring efforts will be visible in the second half of 1998."

23. "Big Deal Chronology of Top Five Chaebol," *Chosun Ilbo*, September 4, 1998.

June 10, 1998	Chief Presidential Secretary Kim Joong-Kwon mentions that "the *chaebols* will announce Big Deals Agreements in the immediate future."
	FKI rebuts, announcing "there has been no discussions on Big Deals."
June 16, 1998	In a cabinet meeting, President Kim mentions that "the Big Deals are blocked by resistance of one conglomerate (Hyundai)." He urges that the top five *chaebols* should set a good example for the rest of the conglomerates.
June 17, 1998	President Kim requests of the six key economic institutions' leaders that "the Big Deals should be agreed through FKI."
June 19, 1998	In a special meeting of FKI, member CEOs announce "active implementation of Big Deals, joint-ventures, and mergers and acquisitions, under principles of free market economy and corporate autonomy."
July 26, 1998	"An autonomous and preliminary Big Deal Agreement among the top five *chaebols*" is announced at the first meeting of political-economic policymakers.
August 3, 1998	President Kim conveys that "the restructuring of core businesses of the *chaebol* are making little progress."
August 4, 1998	The minister of industry and energy, Park Tae-Young, reports to the Blue House on the "Blueprint for Restructuring in Ten Industrial Sectors of Redundant Investments."
August 7, 1998	Agreement on restructuring by industrial sectors, including big deals by the end of August, is drawn at the second meeting of political-economic policymakers.
August 10, 1998	The first meeting of the restructuring task force of the FKI.
August 13, 1998	Agreement on the big deals among the top five *chaebols* is made at the second task force meeting of FKI.
September 3, 1998	Announcement of the final big deal agreements in seven business sectors by the top five *chaebols*.
October 7, 1998	Announcement of the first business restructuring plan in seven business sectors by the top five *chaebols*.

**Mark Andrew Abdollahian, Jacek Kugler,
and Hilton L. Root**   **8**

Economic Crisis and
the Future of Oligarchy

Korea's annual growth rate of 6.6 percent from 1960 to 1992 made
it the best-performing emerging market in the world. Such sustained
performance required institutional and policy adaptability to respond to changing global economic trend.

However, many of the policies that helped jump-start the economy in the past are irrelevant in today's global economic marketplace.
The financial crisis of and since 1997 is the most serious challenge to
Korea's future prosperity since the Korean War. Surmounting the obstacles to future growth will depend on the country's resolve to undertake long-term structural reform. This is a difficult task for any country,
as success inevitably creates strong vested interests, deeply ingrained
habits, and a tendency to seek salvation in the solutions of the past.
Will Korea resist this temptation and forge ahead with a new development strategy, opening the society and economy to entrepreneurial
risk taking and making the ordinary Korean an owner of capital?

This study was funded by the Milken Institute. We are grateful to Jongryn Mo, professor at the Graduate School of International Studies at Yonsei University in Korea, for
hosting the Milken Institute in Korea and for his essential role in helping the Milken
Institute team collect data. We would also like to thank Peter M. Beck, director of research and academic affairs, Korea Economic Institute of America, for providing the
data for figures 2 and 3 and table 1.

By diligently implementing macroeconomic austerity, Korea has inspired hope that it will be the first East Asian country to recover from the financial crisis of late 1997. One year after austerity was introduced, the currency rebounded, the stock market doubled in value, and reserves were replenished. However, the strengthening of balance sheets will be temporary if the structural reforms needed to keep the problems from recurring encounter stiff resistance. Can emerging Asia's star performer overcome the hurdles to comprehensive institutional reform? Returning to the path of rapid sustained growth will require Koreans to put aside differences and coordinate their divergent interests. As in the rest of Asia, politics remains the primary obstacle to economic reform in Korea.

Crisis and Opportunity

Crisis brings change when key groups realize that their survival is at risk. The institutional reforms that turned England, France, and Japan into economic powerhouses all came out of crisis. In each case, the state's fiscal capacity had shrunk to the point where elites had to cooperate to restore basic governmental capacity so that they could compete over the future allocation of resources.[1]

Korea's first generation of institutional reforms was similarly born. After General Park Chung Hee seized power in 1961, the threat of national disintegration induced the construction of new institutions. To overcome opposition from deeply entrenched interests, President Park built needed public support on the premise that the benefits of growth would be shared by all.[2] To make his promise of shared growth credible, Park worked to control endemic bureau-

1. Hilton Root, *The Fountain of Privilege: Political Foundation of Markets in Old Regime France and England* (Berkeley: University of California Press, 1994).

2. Hilton Root and J. Edgardo Campos, *The Key to the East Asian Miracle: Making Shared Growth Credible* (Washington, D.C.: Brookings Institution, 1996).

cratic corruption and to provide broad-based access to basic health and education. By upholding standards of civil service integrity and not grabbing the profits of the private sector, Park demonstrated that his government could be a reliable partner in the development process.[3] Confidence in the regime's survival grew, which in turn prompted the private sector to invest in the long term.

The economic policies and practices that helped South Korea escape threats to its survival in the 1960s created interests that stand in the way of change today. Those policies and practices also created chronic internal weaknesses that cannot withstand global economic integration. For example, privileged access to government-subsidized credit is a vestige of a government/business interface that initially helped the government coordinate national resources to pursue long-term growth priorities. A highly supervised and centralized credit system that worked by fostering export contests was never fully transformed into a system of market-based financial discipline. Long before the financial system collapsed in December 1997, this underlying structural weakness had been the subject of a government study (released in 1993) showing that financial markets suffered from significant political interference on behalf of the *chaebols* and lacked the capacity for adequate prudential supervision.[4]

Corporate governance was deeply flawed; with little accountability to minority shareholders or workers, conglomerates could migrate dangerously from their core competencies. Labor rigidity inhibited entrants into new product markets. However, Korea's outstanding growth figures led to procrastination.

Since the collapse of the Korean currency, the won, in November 1997, new voices promising dramatic reform have been heard from the center of government. Elected president in December

3. Hilton Root, *Small Countries, Big Lessons: Governance and the Rise of East Asia* (London: Oxford University, 1996).

4. *Shifting towards the New Economy: Korea's Five-Year Economic Plan, 1993–1997* (Seoul: Korea Institute for International Economic Policy, July 1993).

1997, Kim Dae-Jung outlined a new vision for Korea's future in which small and medium-sized enterprises (SMEs) would become the engines of growth and new employment, as in the United States. On a speaking tour in the United States, Kim promised to end "government-controlled economic growth that made it possible for the nation's economy to be controlled by the collusive link between politicians and businessmen and government influence over finance."[5] Foreign direct investment and enhanced opportunities for SMEs would become the two pillars of a new, more competitive economy. Pledging to end monopoly power, President Kim advocated diversification of ownership and knowledge in order to encourage the introduction of new trades and industry. At the 1998 Asia Pacific Economic Cooperation (APEC) meetings in Kuala Lumpur, Kim emerged as Asia's champion of international economic integration through trade openness and financial liberalization.

Nevertheless, fully one year after the initial agreement with the IMF, Korea's five largest conglomerates are stronger than ever within the Korean economy, dominating credit allocation and leaving little for their weaker partners. Domestic competition has decreased rather than increased. Indeed, opportunity has become further concentrated rather than diffused. Where thirty *chaebols* once reigned, now just five dominate, thus increasing the leverage of each one over the government. SMEs have been hit hardest in the economic shakedown; many have had to lay off staff and liquidate enterprises. How did the *chaebols* grow stronger under the nose of their historically strongest critic?

Structural Weakness of Political Institutions

Korea lacks the institutions for complex democratic politics and the vote trading necessary to promote and implement a policy dia-

5. President Kim Dae-Jung, speech, April 23, 1998.

logue about basic reforms. The legislature does not provide an arena for disputing parties to negotiate on important policy issues.[6] The absence of appropriate interest-group intermediation has held back economic recovery by preventing consensus on the necessity for restoring economic well-being by recapitalizing South Korean banks. President Kim will need taxpayer support for such a measure, but he has been reluctant to borrow the capital needed from citizens; he would have to explain where the money was going and how it would be spent. Similarly, he has shied away from requesting new taxes, for fear of damaging his standing with the public. On this issue, he is supported by the *chaebols*.

Kim is reported to have said that "Asian-style democracy in which governments are built around a powerful leader who dictates economic policy is the fundamental cause of Asia's current financial crisis."[7] Consistent with this observation, Korea still does not possess an administrative apparatus to adequately defend the political rights of its citizens. Many of the existing institutions were derived from the period of martial law. As we see in chapter 3 of this volume, the National Assembly is subordinate to the executive branch in policymaking. The courts and chief prosecutor have limited independence from the executive branch. Hence, laws can be enforced only if the president wants them enforced.[8]

Without a strong legislature to provide a stable mechanism of interest intermediation, international donor pressure may be needed to settle a deal between state, labor, and business in Korea. In

6. Jongryn Mo, "The Political Origins of the Asian Economic Crisis: Democracy, Gridlock, and Failed Economic Reforms in South Korea," Yonsei University and Hoover Institution, August 24, 1998.

7. *Bloomberg*, January 9, 1998.

8. For example, a law exists that allows firms to dismiss redundant labor with government authorization. However, when Hyundai attempted to apply the law, the government refused to authorize the dismissal and forced Hyundai to rehire its workers.

particular, the IMF and the World Bank might jointly play such a mediating role.

The IMF Program

Korea needed the IMF in late 1997 to avoid imminent default on its payments. Efforts to maintain the currency at precrisis levels vis-à-vis the dollar had depleted its reserves. Depreciation of the currency (from 850 to as much as 2,000 to the dollar) would have made it difficult to pay down international debt denominated in dollars. In its analysis, the IMF articulated the importance of long-term structural reform to prevent a recurrence of the crisis. Nevertheless, this message was overshadowed by the macroadjustments that led the IMF to release $21 billion. Insistence on the primacy of long-term issues was unusual for the IMF, but it reflected a consensus that if Korea does not abandon "authoritarian developmentalism," the inefficient deployment of resources will continue to make the economy vulnerable to crisis.

Ironically, the most controversial part of the reform program, macroeconomic austerity, has been implemented, while the less controversial microstructural reforms have lagged. Many prominent economists have publicly criticized the IMF's commitment to austerity. In fact, two major multilateral institutions, the World Bank and the IMF, have been feuding over the merits of austerity.

Although there is much disagreement on macroadjustments, little disagreement exists over the structural reforms that the Korean economy needs. Almost everyone agrees that the conglomerates must focus on core specialties, that they must be subject to financial market discipline, that cheap credit for government favorites must end, and that a market for corporate control must be developed in order to hold management accountable to shareholders.

Similarly, there is agreement that labor costs have escalated beyond productivity gains since 1987. Labor-market flexibility should approach the standards of Korea's competitors, especially if foreigners are to find ownership of Korean assets attractive. Yet, more than one year after the collapse of the currency, the banking system has not been recapitalized, numerous bankrupt businesses remain, excess capacity has yet to be rationalized, and the labor market is still less flexible than those of Korea's industrial competitors.

Why, then, has the usually controversial macroeconomic austerity package been so easily carried out? Macroeconomic reform programs, often overseen by a single ministry, require little political consensus to implement. Structural change, by contrast, requires political consensus, which has been difficult to construct. Although most Koreans agree on the necessity of reform to restore general well-being, the groups that have the most power to influence reform have no motivation to initiate changes that may challenge their positions in the long run. The top five *chaebols* and organized labor have felt little of the pain and, in fact, have seen their power enhanced. Thus, these politically significant players are averse to change because it threatens their preferred political positions.

Although President Kim claims broad support for reform, support fragments when each issue is separated. Koreans view the *chaebols*, labor, and financial markets as part of an implicit social bargain in which *chaebols* receive public financial support in exchange for a commitment to labor stability. No one part of Korea's social contract can be separated from the other without rupturing the overall bargain. Since the key issues are interdependent, solving any one issue requires progress on the other: labor reform is needed for *chaebol* reform, financial sector reform is needed to reform the *chaebols*, *chaebol* reform creates flexible labor markets, and so forth. This triangle constitutes a package of agreed social responsibilities. As a result, a coordinated political deal is needed to restore consensus and overcome the stalemate. This deal must address all three pillars of Korea's corporatist past: industrial concentration, labor security, and a centralized financial system.

Reforming the Financial System

Korea's financial system is an ineffective intermediary between savers and investors. Too few actors have incentives to collect information to make financial markets function effectively; thus, existing financial institutions do not effectively match capital with profitable investment opportunities.

The financial sector has not evolved in tandem with an increasingly sophisticated private sector; it has become dysfunctional and vestigial. In the 1960s, a centralized financial sector funded a mercantilist offensive by allowing government to direct credit to companies that exported successfully. An export yardstick provided a market-based criterion for credit allocation. In the 1980s, the government withdrew its direct control. It continued to indirectly approve credit allocation, but it could no longer track how much was borrowed. Nevertheless, the government was responsible for implicitly funding the banking system, leaving considerable margin for abuse. The banks could borrow overseas, and, although the debt was implicitly backed by the government, government supervision was weak. At the same time, lenders believed the government was committed to maintaining its currency and had the means to do so. Long-standing exchange-rate pegs encouraged financial institutions to borrow abroad, convert the borrowed funds into domestic currency, and then lend domestically. International investors did not think they had to worry since their investments were brokered by local banks that were presumed to have government backing. Meanwhile, Korean intermediaries had little motive to develop the necessary skills in credit analysis, as they believed their loans were backed by the government.

The banks never acquired an adequate supervisory framework for another reason: the government insured the financing requirements of the conglomerates and implicitly underwrote their risks. Since the banks did not choose projects or make decisions about which firms should expand, they did little monitoring. They provided finance essentially at the direction of state planners. But neither the planners nor the banks had an incentive to independently assess the plans they were financing and, as a result, did not acquire the skills necessary for effective loan assessment.

Without appropriate accounting, would-be bank regulators could not regulate the banks, which in turn could not regulate the borrowers. The government was unaware of how much borrowing occurred offshore and did not have realistic estimates of debt-equity ratios. It seems they were not able even to count the number of subsidiaries belonging to each *chaebol* group. The absence of fundamental information did not seem to matter. Credit was allocated on the basis of personal relationships or collateral. The largest borrowers got the rosiest assessments, since it was understood that they could always borrow more to pay off existing debts. So long as the economy grew, the potential of the *chaebols* was considered unlimited. This general lack of oversight and transparency served the interests of the large industrial interest groups that dominated Korean society. By providing policy loans, the government had in effect exempted firms from bearing the risk of investment.

The massive quantity of nonperforming loans was actually a by-product of government policy that allowed a small group of financially unfit companies to defy the laws of profit maximization. The reforms necessary to exit this impasse now threaten the interests of this powerful group. In effect, both the banks and the government have been captured by the very industrial concerns that they created.

The first reform challenge is to clean up nonperforming loans. In 1998, the government established a vehicle for acquiring nonperforming loans from the Korea Asset Management Corporation (KAMCO). For reformers, this is only an initial step; for conservatives it is sufficient to restore the country's financial well-being. Real reform requires a transfer of the skills and information necessary for running the financial system from the government to market-based institutions, forcing domestic banks to take full responsibility for the loans they authorize.

Progress in the financial sector is a prerequisite for restructuring the enterprise sector. The erosion of profit margins, low return on equity, and low return on capital all reflect a lack of financial discipline. Banks must be able to allocate credit on the basis of an objective assessment of a borrower's cash flow prospects. Korea is chided for failing to establish accounting standards, which are considered a precondition for effective bank regulation. Active credit analysis, however, will thrive when loans are resold, which means that alternatives to banks must be developed. Greater independence for the central bank's inspection of the financial sector will ensure that these standards, once introduced, are maintained.

The Politics of Financial Reform

Although there is political consensus within Korea for general financial sector reform, there is no agreement on the extent of desired reforms. The policy steps necessary for financial system reform and the divisions among the preferences of key actors are shown in figure 1. The final step in the reform process would align Korean banks with Western institutions, whereas the first step represents Korean banking policies at the onset of the current economic crisis. Koreans recognize the need to solve the nonperforming loan problem and recapitalize their banks. In this regard, solving the current loan problems is only the first step; decentralizing financial decisions through institutional reform is essential. Discussions on financial reform are polarized. Each coalition is committed to a different step in the process. The IMF and World Bank (backed by many Korean technocrats) advocate deep reforms; the *chaebols* see the problem simply as a liquidity issue; and President Kim advocates the inter-

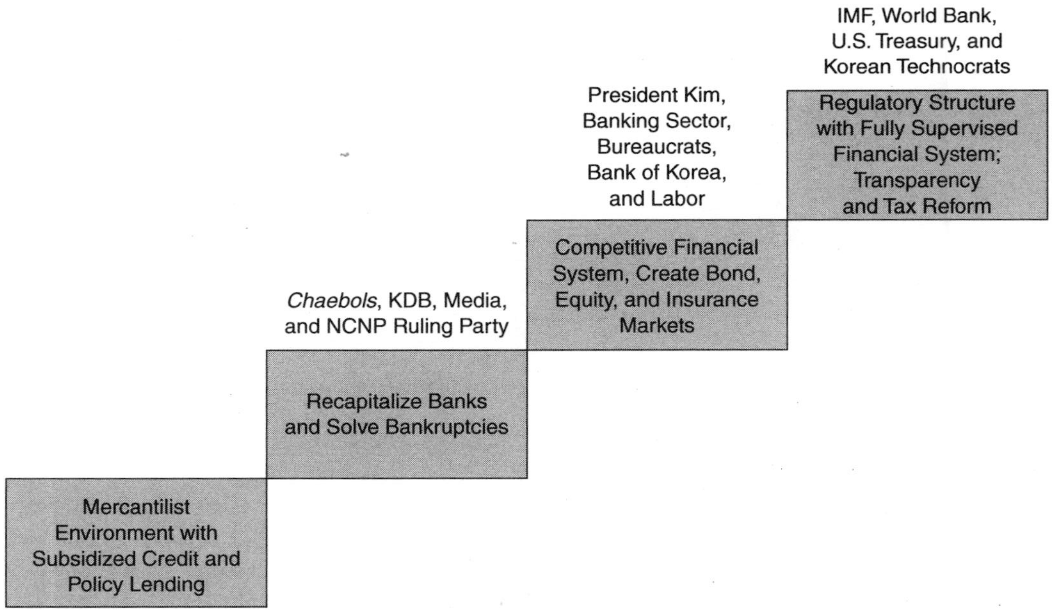

FIGURE 1 Korean Financial System Reform: Policy Steps in the Reform Process

mediate step of moderate institutional reforms. The parties have not been willing to compromise.

Believing that the path to prosperity includes financial reforms, President Kim currently is willing to take steps toward a competitive financial system, including the promotion of open bond, equity, and insurance markets and a Western-style investment banking structure. The majority of Koreans support moderate financial reform as well. Presidential allies include the Korean academic community, the Financial Supervisory Committee, the Ministry of Finance and Economics, the banking sector, the media, the National Congress for New Politics (NCNP) ruling party, the United Liberal Democrats (ULD) coalition party, and the Grand National Party (GNP) opposition party.

Despite a broad-based consensus for needed change, the *chaebols* are poised to persuade their traditional allies to thwart presidential calls for reform and to oppose IMF and World Bank demands for dramatic change, thus maintaining a deadlock on banking reform. The longer reform fails, the more dissent will grow. Delaying reform entrenches positions on all sides, decreasing societal support for any reform.

Breaking Up the Credit Oligarchy:
The Key to Financial Market Reform

Extensive financial market development is necessary to correct the underemployment of capital. Although most Koreans support the institutional reforms to create a competitive financial system, the *chaebols* and conservative political parties in Korea advocate only recapitalizing banks and are hostile to foreign ownership of troubled financial institutions.

Korea is constantly chastised for not attaining universal standards of accounting. The IMF position on banking reform placed heavy emphasis on overcoming the chronic problem of poor accounting by mandating international accounting standards through legislation and governmental audits. The assumption that active monitoring is a product of legislation is a frequent misconception of the international donor approach. Experience outside Korea suggests that active credit analysis is a by-product of an active market for loans.

When a few banks dominate the loan market, as in Korea, they have little incentive to invest in developing the skills of active credit analysis. Banks became specialized in catering to the particular needs of the companies they financed because the government mandated that they focus on particularly narrow segments of the economy. An oligarchic credit system thrives on protecting special information about the markets, structures, and performance of its clients. Making that information easily available allows rivals to use the information to expand their own businesses. In addition, greater public disclosure risks exposing information about possible nonperforming assets.

Not surprisingly, the major banks in Korea have used their control over information to control the loan market. An active assessment of loan performance may threaten their ability to continue controlling the loan supply. Recapitalizing the banking sector as it existed would allow continued domination of the credit market by the large financial institutions—the very organizations that have no incentive to actively monitor their loans.

Requiring regulatory disclosure through legislation supported by technical assistance will never be as effective as liberalization. Only if direct political interference and the danger of confiscation are eliminated will companies seeking credit want to disclose convincingly. Then the skills of credit analysis will migrate to their higher-value users—the companies that buy and sell loans—and they will therefore have an interest in active assessments of loan performance.

Thus, active credit assessment will come with an active market for loans. Transparency, improved corporate accountability, and governance all facilitate proper risk pricing via the transmission of market signals and emerge along with rating agencies and credit analysis when institutional investors and issuers freely seek each other. Regulatory review, creditors' rights, and covenant structures are all products of economic competition that come into being as the government steps out of the direct management of credit allocation. Breaking up the monopoly of a few large lenders will do more to develop credit analysis than trying to regulate it into existence. Bringing foreign banks into the Korean market will be an important step in this direction.

Reforming the *Chaebols*

The weakness of financial-market supervision promoted unhealthy industrial development. After the government stepped in to prevent large firms from going under, they became "too large to fail," further consolidating their grip on credit. This paved the way for their almost unlimited expansion into unrelated businesses. First, the government conferred preferential status to industries by relieving them from competitive pressures. Then it allowed the firms to expand into areas in which they had no competitive advantage through the practice of cross-guarantees within *chaebols*. Internal cross-financing made it possible for *chaebols* to grow in seeming defiance of market forces. Although expansion started with government support of preferred sectors, firms soon moved into unrelated sectors, using finance derived from the core specialty; electronic manufacturers, for example, eventually came to own hotels and golf courses and a host of other subsidiaries (see figure 2). To an extraordinary degree Korea's *chaebols* have diversified into unrelated businesses, when compared with their industrialized counterparts (see figure 3). The large number of subsidiaries in unrelated businesses and their staggering debt-to-equity ratios, fostered by the deeply flawed financial system, are reported in table 1.

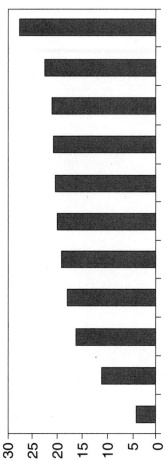

FIGURE 2 Average Number of Subsidiaries for the Top Thirty *Chaebols*, by Year.

SOURCE: Yoo Seong-min, "Evolution of Government-Business Interface in Korea: Progress to Date and Reform Agenda Ahead," working paper, Korean Development Institute, November 1997.

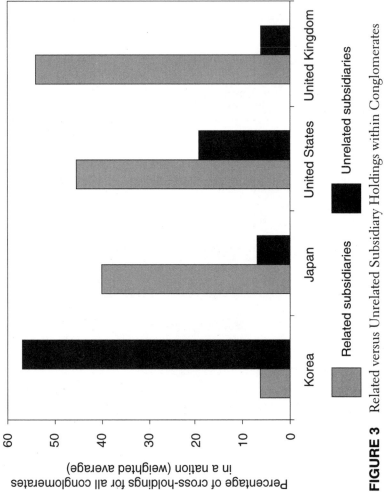

FIGURE 3 Related versus Unrelated Subsidiary Holdings within Conglomerates

Transfer pricing within a conglomerate enables one subsidiary to subsidize another, thereby allowing unprofitable subsidiaries to operate. It also prevents SMEs from operating in areas where *chaebols* are not efficient. Many conglomerates were dragged down by their affiliates. For example, Kia Motors, despite having world-class production facilities, was dragged down by its failing sibling companies: Specialty Steel, Asia Motors, and Kaisan.

The balance between large and small businesses became disproportionately weighted toward the large firms to the point where they could dump their problems into the laps of smaller enterprises. *Chaebols* were known to force the acceptance of promissory notes with unfavorable terms on smaller firms and to pressure those firms to cut prices on products they sold to the large *chaebols*. Eventually, many were driven out of their specialized niches. Thus President Kim has asserted that "if *chaebols* restructure, it will create competitiveness for companies and more jobs for workers."[9]

It is widely recognized that the reform of the *chaebols* must restrict the practice of cross-guaranteeing loans and cross-shareholding in order to trim back their lines of business to core specialties. Other key reforms include protection for the rights of small shareholders; meaningful, independent roles for boards of directors and auditors; an active market for mergers and acquisitions to discipline management; and an active role for financial institutions as investors. In the long run, the government must shed its habit of allocating resources by decree and instead set up fair competition laws to break the collusion of business and politics. Once a culture develops where individual Koreans own shares and demand a return on their capital, business accounting practices will fall into line with international accounting standards.

9. *Bloomberg*, April 29, 1998.

TABLE 1 Top Twenty Korean *Chaebols*: Size and Breadth

	Company	DEBT/EQUITY RATIO (IN PERCENT)		1998 Assets (in billion won)	In-Group Shareholding (in percent)	NUMBER OF SUBSIDIARIES	
		1996 (end)	1997 (end)			1996 (end)	1997 (end)
1	Hyundai	376%	579%	73,520	56.2%	57	62
2	Samsung	206	371	64,536	46.7	80	61
3	Daewoo	337	472	52,994	38.3	30	37
4	LG	313	506	52,773	40.1	49	52
5	Sunkyong	320	468	29,267	44.7	46	45
6	Hanjin	619	908	19,457	41.4	24	25
7	Ssangyong	297	400	15,645	42.0	25	22
8	Hanwha	619	1,215	12,469	33.0	31	31
9	Kumho	465	944	10,361	40.1	26	32
10	Dong-Ah	320	360	9,054	54.2	19	22
11	Lotte	179	216	8,862	22.8	30	28
12	Halla	2,930	n/a	8,562	49.5	18	18
13	Daelim	344	514	7,001	34.2	21	21
14	Doosan	625	590	6,586	49.7	25	23
15	Hansol	290	400	6,268	37.3	23	19
16	Hyosung	315	465	5,249	44.9	18	21
17	Kohap	472	472	5,193	39.4	13	13
18	Kolon	350	434	4,894	45.1	24	25
19	Dongkuk	323	324	4,865	51.0	17	17
20	Dongbu	338	338	4,626	47.8	34	34

Top 30	387	519	404,180	43.0	27.3	26.8
3,179 Korean manufacturing companies	317	396				
Japan	193					
Taiwan	86					
United States (1996)	154					

SOURCE: Peter M. Beck, "Revitalizing Korea's Chaebol," *Asian Survey* 38 (1988): 810–1035.

The Politics of Enterprise Reform

Chaebol reform addresses the very foundation of Korea's corporatist society. President Kim clearly has stated that the future of Korea is tied to the development of SMEs and has attempted to reduce *chaebol* overcapacity through legislation. The policy steps toward enterprise reform are depicted in figure 4.

The final step toward real reform would require *chaebol* owners to accept diversified ownership structures with management-sharing concessions, voting rights, and corporate transparency. This is a far cry from the current, almost unimpeded control over business and resources that *chaebol* owners enjoy. Koreans disagree strongly on the economic and political feasibility of *chaebol* reform. Labor, technocrats, and the ruling NCNP demand a diversified management and ownership structure with voting rights. President Kim, supported by the Fair Trade Commission (FTC), IMF, and World Bank, advocates that ownership reform be limited to ending internal cross-guarantees with some management sharing and diversified ownership. However, the ULD and GNP do not support such reforms and instead advocate less-extensive changes that focus only on diversifying ownership and consolidating assets. Under pressure from labor, Kim has advocated far more extensive reforms than his traditional political constituency is willing to accept. However, many Koreans fear that tampering with the *chaebols* through ownership reform risks killing the geese that lay the golden eggs.

The "big 5" *chaebols*—Hyundai, Samsung, Daewoo, LG, and SK—prefer to legalize holding companies but would be willing to consolidate around core competencies while maintaining management control. The president, the Ministry of Finance and Economics, and the president's Blue House bureaucrats want the big 5 *chaebols* to make further concessions. In response, the *chaebols* might accept the third step—diversified ownership reforms without management sharing—as token concessions to be made over time.

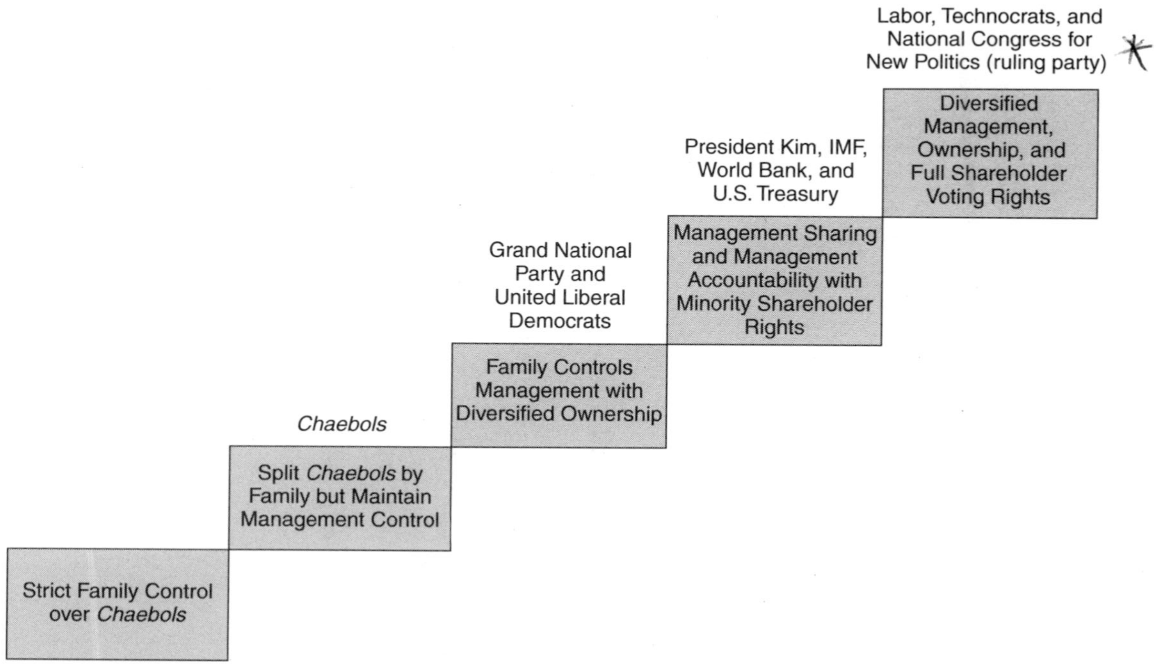

Strict Family Control
over *Chaebols*

Split *Chaebols* by
Family but Maintain
Management Control

Chaebols

Family Controls
Management with
Diversified Ownership

Grand National
Party and
United Liberal
Democrats

Management Sharing
and Management
Accountability with
Minority Shareholder
Rights

President Kim, IMF,
World Bank, and
U.S. Treasury

Diversified
Management,
Ownership, and
Full Shareholder
Voting Rights

Labor, Technocrats, and
National Congress for
New Politics (ruling party)

FIGURE 4   Korean Enterprise Reform: Policy Steps in the Reform Process

However, such changes fall far short of the demands for significant reforms by President Kim, the IMF, and the World Bank. Currently, political support for fundamental *chaebol* reform is weak and will likely decrease if the *chaebols* accept only minimal reforms. By paying more attention to *chaebol* reform, the FTC, along with the GNP and ULD, could prompt the *chaebols* into accepting this deal at an earlier time. The outlines of a possible policy compromise that would result if the *chaebols* moved up one step in the reform process while labor, Korean technocrats, and the NCNP moved down one step are seen in figure 5.

The Economic Implications of Enterprise Reform

The *chaebols* can no longer defy the financial laws of gravity; systemic corporate restructuring is necessary. Effective equity markets will not form until *chaebols* can be broken up into units whereby economic performance can be more directly observed. In their present formulation, *chaebol* components cannot be assessed according to the criteria set for a normal economic rate of return and shareholder value. Developing efficient equity and bond markets would require diversification of *chaebol* ownership and the establishment of minority shareholder rights.

Initially, the big 5 *chaebols*, responsible for 32 percent of corporate sales in 1997, had the opportunity to restructure themselves. They first agreed to halve the number of their subsidiaries, then use the proceeds to pay off existing debts. Next, the government demanded that the *chaebols* end their cross-subsidiary loan guarantees and prepare consolidated financial statements. The government also emphasized that it would penalize intragroup trading. When it was clear the *chaebols* were not responding to the government's insistence that all payment guarantees across different affiliates in different industries end by 1998, the Blue House stiffened its resolve.

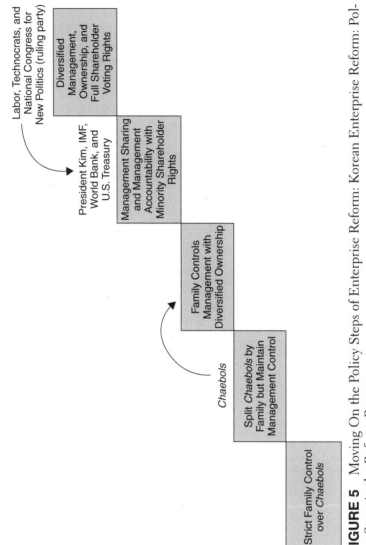

FIGURE 5 Moving On the Policy Steps of Enterprise Reform: Korean Enterprise Reform: Policy Steps in the Reform Process

Thirty-five years ago, General Park rounded up the *chaebol* leaders and threw them in jail until they complied with national development goals. This time, President Kim could do no more than insist that financial institutions limit their bond holdings to any one *chaebol* at a maximum of 15 percent of their portfolio. This did not move *chaebol* reform far forward on the scale of ownership transparency and management accountability, the key issues. Moreover, the *chaebols* can evade the regulations, for example, by establishing ghost companies overseas.

Koreans view the government-*chaebol* agreement on voluntary restructuring, called the "big deal," as a significant step toward industrial consolidation. It is premised on the belief that consolidation around core competencies will eliminate the danger to otherwise healthy companies of being brought down by their nonperforming assets. But what is accomplished when Daewoo, already debt ridden, acquires Sangyong Motors, or when overleveraged Hyundai acquires the debts of Kia Motors? The larger companies created are no more efficient than the ones they replaced; loss-making companies are not shut down, and excess capacity persists.

In its first year, the restructuring plan focused on the development of a time frame and on the specific affiliates to be spun off. However, this simply allows the conglomerates to dump on the public assets that are unsalvageable and keep the jewels for themselves. Under the new reform, the *chaebols* are consolidating value for themselves at the public's expense. Moreover, the big deal does not replace the need for effective market discipline that comes when capital markets reward effective corporate strategies with investor capital. The big deal is trying to replace the market with government. This might have made sense when the private sector was weak and lacked experience, but it makes no sense now, in an era when the private sector is more knowledgeable than the government.

Labor Reform

Labor-market rigidity has in turn been a key factor weakening the competitiveness of Korean industry. Companies cannot adjust to business cycles and are forced to accept high costs of maintaining labor during recessions, making economic cycles more extreme than they need to be. As a result, Korean assets have been unattractive to foreign investors. Foreign merger and acquisition specialists report that bankrupt companies may need to lay off as many as one-third of their employees before multinational companies will consider investing. Although the government enacted new laws in early 1997 to increase labor-market flexibility, it refused to allow Hyundai to use them to lay off eight thousand workers. A contentious strike ensued, forcing President Kim to intervene. Foreign confidence in labor reform sank when only several hundred workers were let go.

Korea has one of the most rigid labor markets in the world. Directed and financed by cheap government credit, the *chaebols* subsidized social stability during economic downturns by keeping their employees and thousands of subsuppliers working. In return, the government furnished the conglomerates with a compliant labor force. This job security arrangement, coupled with an economy that historically has had low levels of unemployment, prevented the development of a flexible labor market.

How might the government mobilize support for improved labor-market flexibility? One incentive would be a national safety net that includes those not presently covered and that extends benefits for those who are cut off after a short period. Clear and credible rules governing layoffs are crucial to bolstering foreign direct investment, particularly among bankrupt companies.

Properly structured equity arrangements provide management with direct incentives to run companies more efficiently. Regulations allowing Korean companies to use equity ownership, particularly employee stock ownership plans (ESOPs) and stock options, offer management alternatives to cash to motivate employees. Moreover, investors prefer companies with high management-ownership ratios. Increased equity incentives would also help unlock Korea's highly developed human capital.

The Politics of Labor Reform

In 1998, the Korean government took the first policy step toward labor reform by allowing temporary layoffs of permanent employees among firms that have obtained government approval. Since Korea has no national unemployment insurance system, labor opposes unrestricted layoffs, relying on the president's commitment to overseeing them. Layoff reform faces stiff impediments. As business and labor interests clash, most Korean political and social groups recognize the difficulty in initiating substantive labor reform. Moderate labor groups (such as the Federation of Korean Trade Unions, or FKTU), government bureaucrats, the Ministry of Labor, and most political parties recognize the need for some mechanism to expand layoffs without provoking a political backlash. However, temporary or permanent layoffs are acceptable to the majority of Koreans only if the government maintains control over which employees and sectors are affected. Radical labor groups (such as the Korean Confederation of Trade Unions, or KCTU) continue to push for the old system of implicit lifetime employment, and President Kim continues to advocate government control over layoffs in order to retain domestic political support.

The IMF, the World Bank, and the *chaebols* all advocate real labor market reform, making strange bedfellows indeed. They would like to see an unrestricted and flexible labor market similar to Western standards. However, recognizing the domestic political pressures for maintaining current controls and fearing public protests targeted at the entire package of IMF/World Bank reforms, the IMF and the World Bank have refrained from pushing for significant labor reform. They fear that protests targeted at reforms suggested by them could exacerbate the situation. By contrast, the *chaebols'* stake in labor reform is much greater, and hence they will continue to pursue a much more flexible labor market. The range of preferences for labor market reform in Korea is depicted in figure 6.

Most Koreans believe that a flexible labor market could expose the nation to social upheaval. Consequently, when strikes and protests do occur, the government's inclination is to make political concessions to soften radical labor demands and appease moderates. While there is no returning to the "lifetime employment" of the past, labor reform seems likely to remain limited to temporary layoffs under government supervision.

Toward a Grand Reform Bargain

Although labor seems unwilling to make significant concessions toward a system of labor-market flexibility comparable to Korea's international competitors, a grand bargain may be possible, for the predominant, moderate wing of organized labor is willing to trade employment security for real participation in the management and decision-making of the *chaebols*. Consequently, *chaebol* reform is closely connected to labor reform, and, as the preceding analysis has shown, real *chaebol* reform also requires financial reform. Hence, Korea may only overcome the deep structural roots of its economic crisis with a comprehensive approach to reform that seeks the following key outcomes:

- A more flexible contract-labor market that labor will support
- A competitive financial system that a majority of Koreans will support
- Diversified *chaebol* ownership with management sharing and minority shareholder rights

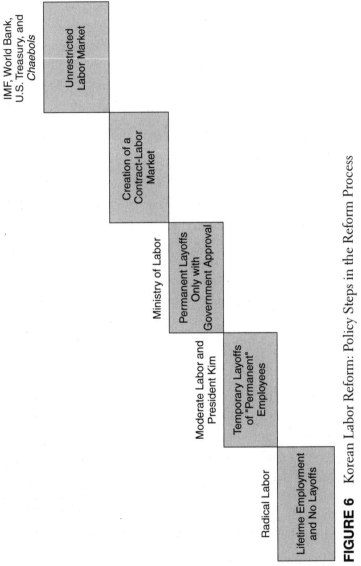

FIGURE 6   Korean Labor Reform: Policy Steps in the Reform Process

Such a comprehensive reform bargain would not only open and revitalize Korea's economy but could be politically feasible. By supporting President Kim's proposals, the IMF and the World Bank could bolster the reform process. A strengthened president could then push the major parties to collectively bargain on *chaebol*, bank, and labor reforms. Each party would gain on the issues that are important to each while conceding others in a package deal allowing for a higher level of liberalization than has been attained so far. A key to striking such a deal is to identify what is politically acceptable in Korea.

A window of opportunity for comprehensive reform exists. Although labor supports the IMF and the World Bank on *chaebol* ownership reform, labor opposes their calls for a flexible labor market. The *chaebols* agree with the IMF/World Bank position of creating a flexible labor force in Korea and oppose their position of diversifying ownership and management sharing. Meanwhile, President Kim is seeking a political consensus for levels of reform not far from IMF/World Bank objectives. Aligning these interests on banking and labor reform could generate an effective bargain while effecting more substantive *chaebol* reform. A deal between the *chaebols* and the president (possibly brokered by the international financial community) could break the present stalemate by linking labor and banking reforms. To gain the economic advantages of a more flexible labor market, the *chaebols* might make concessions on financial reform. Likewise, Kim could offer labor flexibility in return for financial-sector reform. This agreement could result in the promotion of open bond, equity, and insurance markets, coupled with the emergence of a contract-labor market that allows some permanent layoffs. (See figure 7.)

Such a brokered deal would require the president, IMF, World Bank, and *chaebols* to build domestic support to avoid opposition from labor. Once a deal between the president and *chaebols* was struck, labor might well allow progressive reform toward the creation

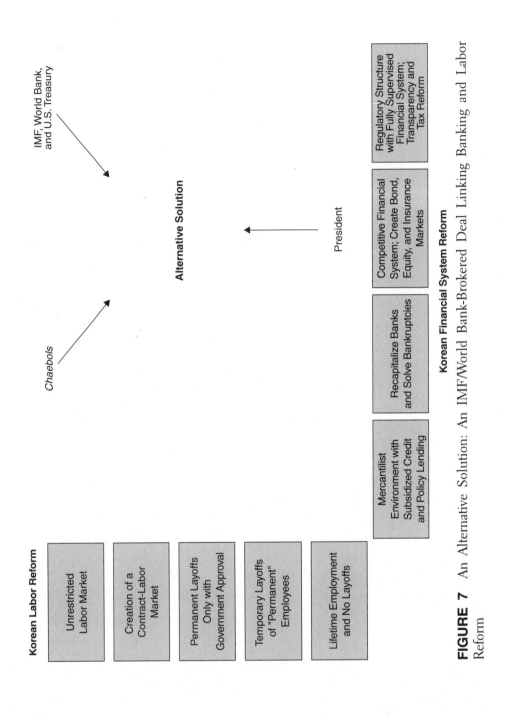

Korean Labor Reform

| Unrestricted Labor Market |

| Creation of a Contract-Labor Market |

| Permanent Layoffs Only with Government Approval |

| Temporary Layoffs of "Permanent" Employees |

| Lifetime Employment and No Layoffs |

Chaebols

IMF, World Bank, and U.S. Treasury

Alternative Solution

President

Korean Financial System Reform

| Mercantilist Environment with Subsidized Credit and Policy Lending |

| Recapitalize Banks and Solve Bankruptcies |

| Competitive Financial System; Create Bond, Equity, and Insurance Markets |

| Regulatory Structure with Fully Supervised Financial System; Transparency and Tax Reform |

FIGURE 7 An Alternative Solution: An IMF/World Bank-Brokered Deal Linking Banking and Labor Reform

of a contract-labor market, rather than risk losing further societal support as the public realizes how entrenched labor interests impede Korea's economic future. Moreover, in contrast to the pattern of past secret agreements, this new style of engagement would entail openness and the building of a broad social agreement.

Successful banking and labor reform would have a second important payoff: it would give President Kim Dae-Jung the necessary political capital to achieve his *chaebol* reform initiative, allowing management sharing, meaningful minority rights, and management accountability. By allowing some labor participation in the management process, a broad-based societal consensus could be created. Such a comprehensive, brokered package of liberalization measures would not give Korea the level of openness and flexibility of a Western economy, but it would produce a new and durable foundation for economic competitiveness and dynamism for political cohesiveness.

Conclusion

The IMF assumed that, once out of the danger zone, Koreans would focus on what went wrong and the president would have time to build support for reforms. After the agreements were signed, President Kim confidently asserted that "we have become keenly aware of the consequences of not adjusting to exchanges in the world and of losing competitiveness."[10] In fact, the opposite occurred: support for Kim's reforms waned. The five largest *chaebols* defiantly went to the international credit market to secure more loans for more acquisitions. They had to be coerced to comply with what was initially intended to be voluntary restructuring. The liberalization program set forth in the IMF accord is on a much grander scale than any

10. *Bloomberg*, December 3, 1997.

political group in Korea would find acceptable. If he attempted to introduce such radical reforms, President Kim would risk destabilizing his political base, which even for a proponent is a highly unrealistic expectation. Essential to crafting a stable reform bargain is to build on what is feasible by discovering where support for reform rests. Here the IMF proposals were lacking.

The hopes of the IMF and the World Bank to reform Korea's basic economic institutions were based on the notion that the interests of the government parallel those of the governed. Motivated to revitalize his economy, Kim, it was presumed, would do what informed opinion deemed the best overall bet for the country's future. This approach to economic policy reform assumed the task was a matter of identifying the best possible program and then coordinating national resources to achieve that result (i.e., place the right experts in the right positions and the rest would be easy). However, experts in Korea had been trying to get the government's attention about the weakness of financial institutions for some time. Even before the crisis the right people were in the right places but to no avail. The politicians were not listening—and not because they did not understand.

Much can be learned about the role of crisis in generating support for lasting reforms from Korea's experience. IMF officials did not prepare themselves with appropriate knowledge about what was politically feasible before going into negotiations and then relied too much on declarations of goodwill expressed by the president and his technocratic advisers. They did not recognize that the positions they advocated lay outside of what was acceptable to any single group other than internationally trained economists and therefore took a position potentially harmful to the president. They also failed to see the interconnectedness of the issues with which they were dealing, ignoring the importance of labor reform for gaining support for financial-market liberalization.

Crisis can bring change when the interests of key players are at stake. In Korea's case, once the country had been rescued from immediate disaster, the groups that the president depended on to stay in office had little to gain and much to lose from radical change. Although these influential groups represent a minority of Koreans, Korean civil society is still relatively undeveloped. Political parties are weak and are organized around regions and personalities rather than issues. Hence political authority is highly dependent on a few well-organized interest groups. These groups were in many cases stronger after the crisis than before.

If a single universal message stands out from Korea's experience of the currency meltdown, it is that, before the bailout, the overall condition of the economy was everybody's concern. After the bailout, each group could again concentrate on its own affairs, ignoring the plight of the nation.

Recovery without comprehensive reform is unlikely to be politically secure or socially durable. Although partial reform has opened the country to greater foreign ownership, it also makes the country ripe for future discord and social conflict. Labor has not gained management reform; the industrial empires still have a politically driven credit system to exploit. The few winners now own more of what is profitable and are discarding loss-making activities on the public. If the costs of restructuring are not borne evenly, a populist backlash remains a distinct possibility, making today's foreign investment a target for tomorrow's unrest.

The Evolution of Popular Support for Democracy during Kim Young Sam's Government

> "In many ways it [Korea] is a democratic society, and it yearns for international recognition as an open and advanced country. Yet the democratic filaments are intertwined with autocratic ones to make a social fabric that is sometimes baffling to outsiders."
>
> *Nicholas Kristof, 1996*

For survival and growth, all democracies depend on their citizens' continuing and widespread support. Popular support is not only crucial for their legitimacy but also vital to their effective performance.[1] As government *by* the people, democratic rule cannot be justified

The surveys reported in this paper were supported by grants from the National Science Foundation, the Korean Legislative Development Institute, the Asia Foundation, and the Aspen Institute.

1. William Mishler and Richard Rose, "Five Years after the Fall: The Trajectory and Dynamics of Support for Democracy in Post-Communist Europe," paper presented at the John F. Kennedy School of Government Workshop on Confidence in Democratic Institutions, Washington, D.C., August 25–27, 1997. See also David Easton, "A Reassessment of the Concept of Political Support," *British Journal of Political Science* 5 (October 1975): 435–57. Dieter Fuchs, Giovanna Guidorossi, and Palle Svensson, "Support for the Democratic System," in Hans-Dieter Klingemann and Dieter Fuchs, eds., *Citizens and the State* (New York: Oxford University Press, 1995), pp. 323–53.

unless a large majority accept it. As government *for* the people, it cannot promote citizen welfare on a continuing basis without a reservoir of support that is sufficient to weather periods of policy failures and public dissatisfaction.[2] As Diamond and Gibson, Duch, and Tedin point out,[3] the beliefs, values, and attitudes of ordinary citizens structure, as well as limit, the pace and possibilities of democratic change.

Popular support is especially important to democratizing countries. Without exception, those countries lack the reserves of popular support and confidence in democratic politics that their predecessors had accumulated over long periods of time. In newly democratizing countries, moreover, the cultural norms of the previous authoritarian or totalitarian regimes cohabit with the institutions and procedures of democratic rule.[4] Therefore, for new democracies like the one in Korea to consolidate, an increasing number of citizens must not only accept the ideals and practices of democratic politics but also dissociate themselves from the authoritarian past. As theorists of political culture argue, the political customs, habits, and manners of the mass public are important es-

2. Russell Dalton, "Citizens and Democracy: Political Support in Advanced Industrial Democracies," paper presented at the John F. Kennedy School of Government Workshop on Confidence in Democratic Institutions, Washington, D.C., August 25–27, 1997.

3. Larry Diamond, "Toward Democratic Consolidation," *Journal of Democracy* 5 (July1994): 4–17. James L. Gibson, Raymond M. Duch, and Kent L. Tedin, "Democratic Values and the Transformation of the Soviet Union," *Journal of Politics* 54 (May 1992): 329–71.

4. Peter McDonough, Samuel Barnes, and Antonio Lopez Pina, "The Nature of Political Support and Legitimacy in Spain," *Comparative Political Studies* 27 (October 1994): 349–80. Guillermo O'Donnell, "Illusions about Consolidation," *Journal of Democracy* 7 (April 1996): 34–51. Doh Chull Shin and Huoyan Shyu, "Political Ambivalence in South Korea and Taiwan," *Journal of Democracy* 8 (July 1997): 109–24.

pecially for the process of democratic consolidation.[5] As the subjective foundation of democratic regimes, those dispositions and sentiments not only shape the contours and dynamics of the consolidation process but also influence its ultimate fate.

This chapter attempts to assess the problems of and prospects for the consolidation of Korean democracy by examining perceptions of and support for democratic politics among its electorate. How do ordinary Koreans understand democracy? Do Koreans view democracy more in the sense of political ideals than of political practices? How broad and deep is their support for democracy? Is their democratic support a mile wide but only inches deep? Is their democratic support on the rise or in decline? Is it impervious to short-term economic and other policy failures? This chapter addresses these questions with four parallel surveys of the Korean electorate conducted in 1993, 1994, 1996, and 1997, during Kim Young Sam's government.

After a brief review of earlier research on the idea of attitudinal support for democracy, the chapter introduces a conceptual framework featuring democratic support as a multilevel and multidirectional phenomenon. A discussion follows of how the various levels of democratic support were measured and how the surveys of the Korean mass public were conducted. Based on the analyses of these surveys, the chapter then examines the depth, character, trends, and durability of Koreans' support for democracy. Finally, the chapter discusses the implications of its major findings for the future of democratic consolidation in Korea.

5. Diamond, "Toward Democratic Consolidation," pp. 4–17. Juan J. Linz, and Alfred Stepan, *Problems of Democratic Transition and Consolidation: Southern Europe, Southern America, and Post-Communist Countries* (Baltimore: Johns Hopkins University Press, 1996).

Conceptualization

Much of the earlier survey research on mass orientations toward democracy is based on David Easton's[6] conception of political support. According to Easton, political support "refers to the way in which a person evaluatively orients himself to a [political] object through . . . his attitudes." This notion differentiates political support among the various categories of its objects—political community, political regime, and incumbents, the occupants of political authority roles. It also differentiates the nature of political support in terms of the extent to which its objects are specific or general. Political support may be of a diffuse or specific nature; it depends on whether the objects involved represent a set of abstract values and principles or whether they refer to the specific actions and performance of government institutions or officials. In Easton's conceptual framework, political support is a multilevel phenomenon of a diverse nature.

As a component of political support, democratic support is also viewed as a multilevel phenomenon, which ranges from diffuse feelings of generalized affect for democratic political values to instrumental judgments of specific political behaviors. As a multilevel phenomenon, democratic support is differentiated first into two broad categories: normative and empirical. The empirical category is further differentiated into three subcategories, which focus, respectively, on political institutions, processes, and performance. From this categorization and subcategorization of democratic political life, four distinct levels of support for democracy are distinguished. These four levels may be characterized as normative, institutional, procedural, and behavioral in nature.

The normative level deals with democracy in principle, while the other three levels are concerned with the different aspects of

6. Easton, "Reassessment of Political Support," p. 436.

democracy in practice. Democracy as a normative phenomenon involves only political ideals and values. Therefore, democratic support at this first level refers merely to a loose attachment to the positive symbols, which democracy represents in principle. Democracy as an empirical phenomenon, in contrast, involves the fundamental institutions and processes comprising a political regime and the actual workings of the regime itself and the performance of the occupants of structural roles (authorities). Support for democracy in practice refers to favorable evaluations of the structure and behavior of the existing regime.

Within the normative level, which focuses on ideals and values of democratic political life, the idea of democracy is differentiated from that of democratization, which is a movement toward it. Within the structure of democracy known widely as constitutional order or regime in Easton's framework, a further differentiation is made between institutions and the processes of their actual operation. Within the behavioral level, a similar differentiation can be made between the performance of the democratic regime and that of its leadership, which is often called the government.

In short, democratic support is conceptualized as a multilevel phenomenon featuring (1) attachment to the ideal of democratic politics and the ultimate goal of democratic change, (2) the endorsement of the institutions of democratic governance, (3) preference for democratic processes, and (4) approval of the way in which institutions function and incumbents apply policies to problems. This multilevel model builds on the Eastonian framework of political support; however, several refinements of the original framework are attempted so that it can be made more suitable for the study of countries in democratization.

Within each of four broad levels of democratic support, specific components are differentiated to discern significant variations in the amounts as well as the quality of such support. In fledgling regimes where "democracy is a goal, a dream, and something that is worth defending until it has been proven not worth defending,"[7] support for democracy in principle cannot be viewed as the residue of democracy in practice, as is known in old established democracies like the United States.[8] Naturally there can be a wide gap between what citizens of new democracies understand democracy to be ideally and what they experience as political reality.

There can also be a wide gulf between their embrace of democracy as representative institutions and their actual commitment to the authentic processes of representative democracy. As O'Donnell[9] notes, representative democratic institutions can coexist with the undemocratic habits of the authoritarian past; this is especially true in the world of new democracies. Between the processes of representative and delegative democracy, the citizenry of new democracies may remain in favor of the latter for a long period. It is therefore important to determine whether support for democracy is qualitatively different (i.e., of a representative or delegative nature). The reconceptualization of Easton's framework allows for drawing such qualitative distinctions in support for democracy.

The reconceptualized model, as outlined above, holds that democratic support is a multilevel and multidimensional phenomenon. As a multilevel phenomenon, it embodies all the necessary levels—values, institutions, processes, and performance—of democratic political life. As a multidimensional entity, it takes into consideration the qualitatively different aspects of democratic life at each level. In short, the proposed model is capable of offering a more comprehensive and balanced account of democratic support

7. Marta Lagos, "Latin America's Smiling Mask," *Journal of Democracy* 8 (July 1997): 125–38.

8. John R. Hibbing and Elizabeth Theiss-Morse, *Congress as Public Enemy: Public Attitudes toward American Political Institutions* (New York: Cambridge University Press, 1995).

9. Guillermo O'Donnell, "Delegative Democracy," *Journal of Democracy* 5 (January 1994): 55–69. O'Donnell, "Illusions about Consolidation," pp. 34–51.

than that achieved in earlier research. Much earlier research has been concerned exclusively with either democratic ideals or practices. Whether either idealist or realist in its substantive focus, the same research has often overlooked qualitative differences in democratic support within and between its levels.[10]

As stated above, the reconceptualized model is predicated on the assumption that democracy is a normative and empirical phenomenon, and support for it is thus divisible and variable across its objects. This assumption is reasonable in view of recent survey findings. Many citizens of new democracies often support the various ideals of democracy but withhold support for their democratic regimes when they find them falling short of those ideals.[11] An increasing number of citizens in old democracies, in contrast, have lost confidence in the performance of representative institutions but remain supportive of the system of representative democratic governance itself.[12]

In addition, the revised model takes into account that support for democratic rule does not necessarily mean the rejection of authoritarianism among citizens of new democracies. Having lived most of their lives within authoritarian politics and cultures, citizens tend to embrace both authoritarian and democratic solutions at the same time.[13] With little knowledge about democratic theory and limited

10. Dalton, "Citizens and Democracy." Gabor Toka, "Political Support in East-Central Europe," in Hans-Dieter Klingemann and Dieter Fuchs, eds., *Citizens and the State* (New York: Oxford University Press, 1995), pp. 354–82.

11. Fuchs, Guidorossi, and Svensson, "Support for Democratic System," pp. 323–53. Lagos, "Latin America," pp. 125–33. See also Shin and Shyu, "Political Ambivalence," pp. 109–24.

12. Hans-Dieter Klingemann, "Mapping Political Support in the 1990s: Global Analysis" (paper presented at the John F. Kennedy School of Government Workshop on Confidence in Democratic Institutions, Washington, D.C., August 25–27, 1997. Joseph Nye, ed., *Why People Don't Trust Government* (Cambridge: Harvard University Press, 1997).

13. Nicholas Kristof, "At Crossroads of Democracy, South Korea Hesitates," *New York Times*, July 10, 1996, A3. David I. Steinberg, "Consolidating Democracy in South Korea," paper presented at the international conference "Consolidating Democracy in Korea," Seoul, June 19–20, 1996.

experience in democratic politics, they choose democratic solutions for some problems while rejecting those for other problems. Without any apparent sense of contradiction, even for the same problems, those democratic novices may alternate from time to time between the democratic and nondemocratic approaches "not as hypothetical alternatives but as lived experiences."[14] The endorsement of democratic institutions and procedures and the rejection of authoritarian alternatives should be considered together to advance an accurate understanding of support for new democracies.

Assembling the Survey Data

The basic data for the present study are assembled from four parallel surveys conducted in Korea during the Kim Young Sam government (1993–97). The Institute of Social Science at Seoul National University conducted the first of these surveys in November 1993 (n = 1,198). Korea-Gallup conducted the next three surveys in November 1994 (n = 1,500), in January 1996 (n = 1,000), and in May 1997 (n = 1,117).[15]

From these surveys, four pairs of questions have been selected to measure democratic support at the four levels identified above (see appendix A for the wording of the questions). The first pair consists of one four-point verbal item tapping general belief in democracy and a ten-point numerical scale measuring the extent of personal desire for democratic change. The second pair consists of four-point verbal scales measuring the general endorsement of vot-

14. McDonough, Barnes, and Pina, "Political Support in Spain," p. 350.
15. For survey methodology, see Doh Chull Shin and Richard Rose, *Koreans Evaluate Democracy: A New Korea Barometer Survey,* Studies in Public Policy no. 292 (Glasgow: Centre for the Study of Public Policy, University of Strathclyde, 1997).

ing and elections. The third pair consists of one verbal scale assessing the desirability of democratic processes and another ten-point numerical scale tapping their suitability. The fourth pair includes two ten-point numerical scales tapping, respectively, satisfaction with the functioning of the democratic regime called the Sixth Republic and that of the Kim Young Sam government. In addition to these four pairs, two more pairs are selected to measure the extent to which Koreans are psychologically disengaged from authoritarian institutions and processes.

Breadth and Depth

How broad is the support of the Korean people for democracy at each of the four levels? To explore this question, the two items selected for each level of democratic support are first rescaled into a three-point scale ranging from 0 (no support) to 2 (strong support) by collapsing all negative categories into one single category. Then the numbers of rescaled items registering support (some or strong) are counted to construct a simple index estimating the breadth of democratic support at each level. As shown in table 1, the values of this index range from a low of 0 when none of the two rescaled items register support to a high of 2 (full) when both items register support.

TABLE 1 Comparing Democratic Support across Four Levels

	AMOUNTS (%)		
Support Levels	*None*	*Some*	*A Lot*
Democracy in principle	2.0	11.8	86.2
Democratic institutions	10.8	31.3	57.8
Democratic processes	10.7	36.3	53.0
Democratic performance	61.1	29.7	9.2

SOURCE: 1997 Korea Barometer Survey.

Scrutiny of the data in table 1 reveals a great deal of difference in the amount of support among the four levels. It also reveals a steady downward tendency from the top to the bottom level: the more abstract or general the level of support is, the larger it becomes. Specifically, a large majority (86 percent) believe in the values of democracy and democratization, 58 percent endorse democratic institutions, 53 percent embrace democratic processes, and a small minority (9 percent) approve of the way both the democratic regime and the Kim Young Sam government perform. Between the two extremes is a difference of 77 percentage points, which indicates a great deal of variation in the way the Korean people understand democracy. To a large majority, it does not mean much more than an abstract ideal or a distant goal.

Another important feature of table 1 is that more than three-quarters of those surveyed are merely attached to the ideal of democratic politics without being satisfied with its practice. In other words, the democratic political system that Koreans admire as an ideal differs a great deal from the political system under which they currently live. Among the Korean population as a whole, democracy tends to symbolize an unfulfilled dream, or unrealized goal, even after a decade of experimenting with it.

Further analysis of the data reported in table 1 reveals how deeply democracy has captured the minds of the Korean people. While nearly nine out of ten (86 percent) Koreans are fully attached to democracy in principle, less than a third (32 percent) are committed to all the necessary institutions and processes (second and third levels) required of a democratic regime. When only strong supporters of those institutions as well as processes are taken into account, less than 2 percent (1.7 percent) become unqualified supporters of a truly representative democratic regime as a political ideal and enterprise. Equally surprising is that virtually none (0.3 percent) express unqualified satisfaction with every aspect of democratic politics.

How broad is the Korean people's overall support for democracy in principle as well as in practice? How many Koreans are totally alienated from democracy? How many are strongly supportive of it at all levels? To answer these questions, let us look at the percentages expressing at least some degree of democratic support from none to all four levels and the percentages expressing strong support from one to the four levels (see figure 1).

As expected, nearly everyone in Korea expresses some support at one or more levels. Only 3 people in the entire sample of 1,117 respondents expressed no support at any level. By sharp contrast, more than four out of five (85 percent) Koreans expressed some support at more than two levels. Virtually no Korean is totally alienated from democracy, and an overwhelming majority support democracy to some degree. This finding confirms the hypothesis that democratic support is widespread throughout every segment of the Korean population.

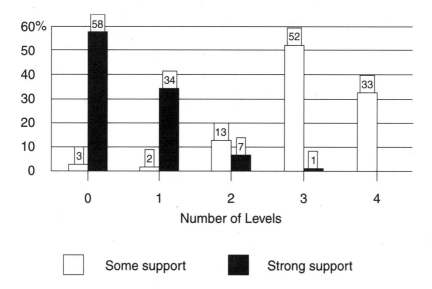

FIGURE 1 Overall Amounts of Democratic Support (in percent)
SOURCE: 1997 Korea Barometer Survey.

How deep is their overall democratic support? This question is addressed by counting the number of levels at which a majority express strong support. Of the four levels surveyed, nearly three-fifths (58 percent) do not express strong support at any level, and a third (34 percent) strongly support democracy at only one level. Less than 1 percent (0.7 percent) strongly support democracy at more than two levels, and no Korean in the survey strongly supports it at all four levels. In short, a vast majority of the Korean people remain shallow in their support of democracy. These findings make it reasonable to conclude that Korean support for democracy is a mile wide but only a few inches deep.

Character

For democratic attitudes to serve as a potent force promoting the pace and possibilities of democratic change, they must be more than internally structured among themselves. Externally, they have to be dissociated from an authoritarian belief system. Holders of democratic and authoritarian attitudes are so cross-pressured that they are likely to remain ambivalent about any necessary reforms for democratic consolidation—such as the expansion of limited democracy and the removal of authoritarian residues.

How many Koreans still support authoritarian institutions? How many prefer authoritarian processes to democratic ones? The 1997 survey asked two pairs of questions to help discern people's orientations toward authoritarian institutions and processes. Proauthoritarian responses to each pair are counted to estimate the overall amount of support for authoritarian institutions and processes. The percentages expressing authoritarian support on a three-point scale ranging from a low of 0 (none) to a high of 2 (full) are reported in table 2.

When asked whether the army or a strongman should rule the country, 15 and 19 percent gave affirmative responses. An examination of those responses reveals that a large majority (72 percent) en-

TABLE 2 Support for Authoritarian Rule

Support Levels	AMOUNT (%)		
	None	Some	A Lot
Institutions	71.7	22.5	5.8
Processes	14.4	45.2	40.4

SOURCE: 1997 Korea Barometer Survey.

dorse neither of these two authoritarian institutions. About a fifth (22 percent) endorse one of those institutions, and one-sixteenth (6 percent) endorse them both. Obviously not every Korean is willing to reject the political institutions of the authoritarian past. Yet a large majority have successfully disengaged themselves from the powerful instruments of the military authoritarian regimes.

Nonetheless, an even larger majority have failed to disengage themselves from the political processes of the authoritarian past. Nearly two-thirds (66 percent) subscribe to the most prominent authoritarian process by agreeing with the statement that "the dictatorial rule like that of a strong leader like Park Chung Hee would be much better than a democracy to handle the serious problems facing the country these days." Moreover, about three-fifths (61 percent) favor the legislative practices of the authoritarian past by agreeing with the statement that "if a government is often restrained by an assembly, it will be unable to achieve great things." When these two authoritarian responses are considered together, a vast majority (85 percent) are found still in thrall to one or the other process of the authoritarian past.

The paradox of Korean support for democracy becomes clearer when support for democratic institutions is juxtaposed with support for authoritarian processes. The endorsement of democratic institutions is more often than not accompanied by a choice of authoritarian solutions. Even among those who affirm the democratic institutions of both voting and elections, only a small minority (16 percent) reject both authoritarian institutions and processes.

Consequently, a large majority of the Korean people still live in a state of political ambivalence—desiring to live freely under democratic institutions while simultaneously refusing to sublimate authoritarian means to democratic freedom.

The paradoxical nature of Korean support for democracy is highlighted further by the two types of democrats and authoritarians recognized by the Korean people (see table 2). Representative democrats endorse democratic institutions and reject authoritarian methods. Delegative democrats fully endorse democratic institutions but, unlike representative democrats, refuse to reject authoritarian methods fully. Unlike democrats, authoritarians refuse to endorse some or all democratic institutions. Yet hard authoritarians refuse to endorse all those institutions while accepting authoritarian solutions fully. Soft authoritarians, in contrast, do not fully reject democratic institutions or fully accept authoritarian methods. Of these four types, the two of delegative democrats and soft authoritarians are the most politically ambivalent.

As expected from the data reported in table 1, institutional democrats constitute a majority (58 percent) of the Korean population. Among the democrats, who support the electoral institutions of representative democracy, delegative democrats outnumber representative democrats by a margin of five to one. In Korea today, there are five "fair weather" or "expedient" democrats for every representative democrat. Representative democrats, moreover, account for less than one-tenth (9 percent) of the entire electorate. Among the authoritarian minority, soft authoritarians outnumber hard authoritarians by a large margin of seven to one. Hard authoritarians account for 5 percent.

When delegative democrats and soft authoritarians are considered together, we can see that a large majority (86 percent) of the Korean population are politically ambivalent, holding democratic and authoritarian attitudes at the same time. The politically ambivalent are more than nine times as numerous as genuine democrats (9 percent), who fully endorse democratic institutions while

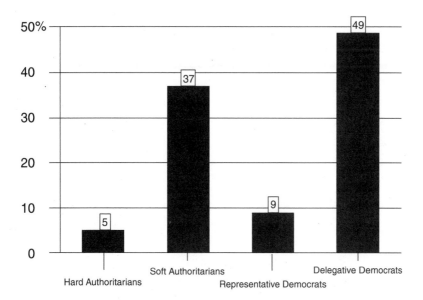

FIGURE 2 Types of Regime Supporters (in percent)
SOURCE: 1997 Korea Barometer Survey.

rejecting authoritarian solutions to the same degree. They are also seventeen times more numerous than genuine authoritarians (5 percent), who opt for fully authoritarian solutions without endorsing any democratic institutions. From a numeric point of view, the politically ambivalent, not the true believers in authoritarianism, pose the most serious threat to the advance of Korean democratization.

Trends

The consolidation of new democracies requires more than broad and deep support. As Mishler and Rose[16] aptly point out,

16. William Mishler and Richard Rose, "Trajectories of Fear and Hope: Support for Democracy in Post-Communist Europe," *Comparative Political Studies* 28 (January 1996): 553–81.

"stable or increasing support facilitates the survival of democratic regimes, whereas declining support puts regimes at increasing risk." Such stable support makes it possible to complete the democratic reforms already adopted and launch more needed reforms for the expansion of limited democracy in those countries confronting a large number of pressing problems.

Has democratic support been susceptible to change during the Kim Young Sam period? For the direction and trajectory of democratic support at its three different levels, see figure 3. At the most abstract level, involving the values of democracy, support has been stable with few upward or downward shifts in the percentage expressing desire for democratic change. The shifts in the relative size of those embracing democracy in principle have been smaller than three percentage points during the five-year period. As they did in 1993, more than nine out of ten Koreans remain attached to the positive symbols of democracy.

This pattern of stable support at the normative or symbolic level contrasts sharply with what has been observed in two other levels featuring democratic processes and performance. In those other two levels, the magnitude of percentage shifts has been large (greater than 10 percentage points) and their direction has been mostly downward rather than upward. These changes testify to a high level of temporal instability and a notable decline in support at the democracy-in-practice level. This confirms the hypothesis that Korean support for democracy as a viable political system is fragile.

In 1994, when the Kim Young Sam government was two years old, three-quarters (76 percent) of the Korean people believed that democracy would be suitable for the situation of their country at that time. By the time he left office, about three-fifths (63 percent) believed that democracy was a suitable political system for the realities of their country. Thus during this three-year period alone, we see a decline of 13 percentage points in those adhering to democratic processes. Much sharper declines occurred in positive views on the

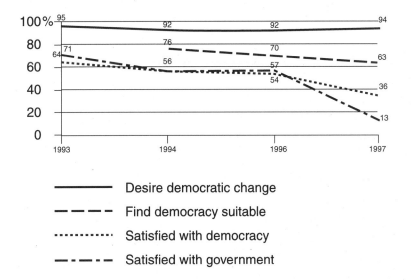

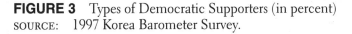

FIGURE 3 Types of Democratic Supporters (in percent)
SOURCE: 1997 Korea Barometer Survey.

workings of the democratic regime and the performance of the Kim
Young Sam government. Those expressing satisfaction with "the way
democracy is working in Korea" went from 64 percent in 1993 and
55 percent in 1996 to 36 percent in 1997. Those expressing satisfaction with "the way the Kim Young Sam government handles problems facing our society" dropped more sharply, from 71 percent in
1993 to 56 percent in 1994 to 57 percent in 1996 to 13 percent in
1997. Only small minorities approved of the regime and government, both of which had once been applauded by large majorities.

Undoubtedly, the direction and magnitude of all these changes
suggest a systematic erosion of support at the level of democracy in
action. Although the aggregate percentages reported in figure 3 cannot tell us who has moved away from their earlier commitment to
democracy as a collective enterprise, significantly fewer support
democratic practice today than five years ago. Nonetheless, supporters
of democracy as a political goal or dream remain an overwhelming

majority—as they did five years ago. As the Eastonian model holds, Koreans are capable of distinguishing between the different types of support (i.e., diffuse and specific). Their specific support for democracy responds to the way their expectations and demands are actually met. Their diffuse support, in contrast, is of a generalized and enduring nature and remains impervious to short-term forces.

Durability

If new democracies are to survive and thrive, their citizens must "make clear distinctions between government performance and the legitimacy of democratic institutions."[17] When citizens are able to blame the governments and policies that democratic elections have produced instead of the democratic institutions themselves, the new democratic regimes can continue to exist and function as legitimate entities. When citizens begin to attribute policy failures to the institutions themselves, democratic regimes no longer remain a preferable alternative to nondemocratic ones. When support for democracy in principle declines immediately in response to the poor performance of the national economy or other policy failures of the democratically elected government, moreover, democratic support becomes ephemeral rather than durable; there is not enough support to withstand economic and political crises.[18] In short, the democratic citizen must be sophisticated enough to distinguish between the legitimacy of the regime and the performance of incumbent politicians.

17. Raymond M. Duch, "Economic Chaos and the Fragility of Democratic Transition in Former Communist Regimes," *Journal of Politics* 57 (February 1995): 121–58.
18. Dalton, "Advanced Industrial Democracies." Gibson, "Mile Wide," pp. 396–420.

According to this model of democratic citizenship, democratic support is durable to the extent that citizen dissatisfaction is directed at the performance of incumbent officials rather than the workings of a democratic regime. Do Koreans tend to direct their dissatisfaction toward the popularly elected government or the newly installed democratic regime itself? I address this question by comparing the proportions choosing only one of those two targets to blame (see table 3). Whereas only 3 percent blame the democratic regime, 27 percent blame the elected leaders. Even among those perceiving declines in the national economy, regime bashers are still outnumbered by government bashers by the same margin. Yet the prevalent pattern is to blame both the Kim Young Sam government and the newly installed democratic regime. Nearly two-thirds (64 percent) of the respondents refused to distinguish between the two entities of a different nature, which supports the hypothesis that Korean support for democracy remains generally rudimentary or tentative.

Since the first year of the Kim Young Sam government, the proportion of regime bashers has declined steadily and significantly, by more than four-fifths, to 3 percent from its high of 17 percent in 1993. Conversely, the proportion of government bashers has increased steadily and sharply, to 27 percent from its low of 9 percent in 1993. Even among those Koreans complaining about the performance of the national economy, the proportion of government

TABLE 3 Apportioning Dissatisfaction

TARGETS		ENTIRE SAMPLE (*in percent*)			ECONOMICALLY DISCONTENTED (*in percent*)		
Government	*Regime*	*1993*	*1996*	*1997*	*1993*	*1996*	*1997*
Yes	Yes	18.6	26.8	60.9	23.3	35.9	63.5
Yes	No	8.9	15.0	26.6	8.8	17.6	26.5
No	Yes	16.8	15.0	3.2	16.8	14.8	3.0
No	No	55.7	43.2	9.3	51.0	31.7	7.0

SOURCE: 1997 Korean Barometer Survey.

252 DOH CHULL SHIN

bashers has expanded while that of regime bashers has shrunk. From these findings, it is clear that the durability of Korean support for democracy improved during the Kim Young Sam government.

How resilient have Korean attachments to democratic values been in the face of the sagging national economy and a series of other major policy failures during the latter years of the Kim Young Sam government? By comparing and tracing the percentage of idealist or normative democrats among three subsamples of the Korean population—(1) the economically dissatisfied, (2) the governmentally dissatisfied, (3) the economically as well as governmentally dissatisfied—we see that an overwhelming majority of the Korean people remain steadfastly attached to their desire to live in a democracy (see table 4a). Even among those who are troubled by both economic failures and governmental blunders, more than nine out of ten Koreans surveyed prefer to live in a democracy, as they did three years ago. This is another piece of unambiguous evidence confirming the durability of support for democracy in principle.

Unlike such support in principle, support for democracy in action, as measured by perceptions of its suitability for the Korean situation, is not resilient, especially to governmental performance. The Korean people are more reluctant to continue their support for the democratic regime when they judge that their government is malfunctioning (see table 4b for the percentage differentials). To a substantial minority (about 20 percent), support for democracy as a viable political regime appears contingent on the performance of its popularly elected government. During the 1994–97 period, however, there has been little change in the percentage refusing to support democratic practice among those who are dissatisfied fully (i.e., economically and governmentally). A substantial majority (61 percent) of those fully dissatisfied continue to support it, as they did three years ago. When taken together, these findings suggest that Korean commitment to the practice of democratic politics is not highly vulnerable to the vagaries of economic and political forces.

TABLE 4 Resilience of Democratic Support

a. Democracy in Principle (desire for democratic change)
(in percent)

Domains of Performance	1994 Sat.	Dis.	Dif.	1996 Sat.	Dis.	Dif.	1997 Sat.	Dis.	Dif.
Economy	96.8	94.7	+2.1	95.6	90.9	+4.7*	97.0	94.0	+3.0
Government	98.1	93.4	+4.8*	96.3	91.7	+4.6*	97.1	94.3	+2.8
Both	98.3	92.6	+5.7*	97.6	90.0	+7.6*	98.0	93.7	+4.3

b. Democracy in Practice (democratic suitability)
(in percent)

Domains of Performance	1994 Sat.	Dis.	Dif.	1996 Sat.	Dis.	Dif.	1997 Sat.	Dis.	Dif.
Economy	82.0	71.2	+11.2*	75.4*	68.4	+7.0*	66.1	63.5*	+2.6
Government	88.7	65.0	+23.7*	82.5*	61.3	+21.2*	81.2	61.7*	+19.5*
Both	90.3	62.8	+27.5*	82.8*	56.9	+25.9*	78.9	61.5*	+17.4*

NOTES: Sat.: satisfied; Dis.: dissatisfied; Dif.: difference.

Entries are percentages of the economically and/ or governmentally satisfied or dissatisfied who expressed support for democracy.

*Statistically significant at the .05 level.

SOURCE: 1997 Korea Barometer Survey.

Conclusion

The principal purpose of this inquiry has been to examine the support of the Korean people for democracy from a variety of perspectives and to assess the prospects for the consolidation of their incipient democratic rule. Starting from the premise that the pace and path of democratic consolidation depends on how the masses express their support for democracy, the previous sections examined the breadth, depth, durability, and stability of democratic support in Korea.

The results of the four parallel surveys presented here reveal that the overall support of the Korean people for democracy has not broadened, deepened, or stabilized appreciably since Kim Young

Sam became the first civilian president of the democratic Sixth Republic. Instead, those findings suggest that democratic support in Korea tends to remain superficial, fragmented, and mixed with authoritarian habits; however, support for democracy in principle is broadly distributed and increasingly resilient to the rapidly changing realities of economics and politics. Even after one decade of the democratic experiment, Koreans' support for democracy in practice is neither a mile wide nor more than a few inches deep. However, their attachments to democracy in principle are wide and fairly deep.

Even after a decade of the democratic experiment, most Koreans are neither strongly committed to the fundamentals of democratic rule nor fully disengaged from the authoritarian habits of formulating and implementing policies. Perhaps they are simply democrats by convenience. Only a small minority are authentic democrats strongly committed to expanding the current practice of limited democracy and removing the residue of authoritarian rule. Therefore, this minority must lead the drive for the consolidation of Korean democracy. Given the slow and uncertain process of cultural democratization in the past decade, it seems highly optimistic that Koreans will form a truly democratic nation in a single generation. It would be more accurate to think that they are in a long march that requires several generations.

APPENDIX A

Survey Questions

A. **Democratic Values**

Q32. Let us consider the idea of democracy, not its practice. In principle, how much are you for or against the idea of democracy—very much for, somewhat for, against somewhat, or against very much?

Q38C. Here is a scale ranging from a low of 1 to a high of 10. On this scale, 1 means complete dictatorship and 10 means complete democracy. The closer to 1 the score is, the more dictatorial our country is; the closer to 10 the score is, the more democratic our country is. To what extent would you personally desire our country to be democratized?

B. **Democratic Institutions**

Q14. How much influence do you think the votes of people like yourself have on the way this country is governed—a lot, some, a little, or none?

Q15. Do you agree or disagree with the following statement: The best way of choosing our government is an election that gives every voter a choice of candidate and parties—definitely agree, somewhat agree, somewhat disagree, or definitely disagree?

C. **Democratic Processes**

Q33. With which of the following do you agree most?
1. Democracy is always preferable to any other kind of government.
2. Under certain situations, a dictatorship is preferable.
3. For people like me it doesn't matter if we have a democratic or nondemocratic government

Q39a. Here is a scale measuring the extent to which people think democracy is suitable for our country. On this scale, 1 means complete unsuitability while 10 means complete suitability. During the present Kim Young Sam government, to what extent is democracy suitable for our country?

D. Democratic Performance

Q25a. On the whole, how satisfied or dissatisfied are you with the way the Kim Young Sam government handles the problems facing our society? Please choose a number on this scale ranging from a low of 1 (complete dissatisfaction) to a high of 10 (complete satisfaction).

Q25b. On the same scale, where would you place the way democracy works in our country?

E. Authoritarian Institutions

Q17. Our present system of government is not the only one this country has had, and some people say we would be better off if the country was governed differently. How much do you agree or disagree with the following:

Q17a. The army should govern the country—agree strongly, agree somewhat, disagree somewhat, or disagree strongly?

Q17b. Better to get rid of Parliament and elections and have a strong leader decide everything—agree strongly, somewhat agree, somewhat disagree, or strongly disagree?

F. Authoritarian Processes

Q36. How much do you agree or disagree with the statement that the dictatorial rule like that of a strong leader like Park Chung Hee would be much better than a democracy to handle the serious problems facing the country these days—strongly agree, somewhat agree, somewhat disagree, or strongly disagree?

Q28b. How much do you agree or disagree with the statement that if a government is often restrained by an assembly, it will be unable to achieve great things—agree strongly, agree somewhat, disagree somewhat, or disagree strongly?

Mass Perceptions
of Democracy

Any effort to analyze progress toward democratic consolidation —
whether in Korea or elsewhere — must examine popular beliefs and
attitudes. One key aspect of this cultural dimension of consolidation
involves the extent to which the mass public supports the democratic system over any feasible alternative (legitimacy), or, in the
formulation of Linz and Stepan, an attitudinal and behavioral commitment to democracy as "the only game in town."[1] Here we find
both positive and negative signs for democratic consolidation in Korea. The cross-national survey data of Rose and Shin show that Koreans, like the manifestly democratic Czechs, have a strong aversion
to the plausible undemocratic regime alternatives: rule by the army,
rule by a dictator, or a return to communist rule (in the Czech Republic). This evidence, they maintain, lends support to Winston
Churchill's famous dictum that any kind of democracy is preferable
to any kind of undemocratic regime.[2] At the same time, a "hollow-
ing out," or leveling off, of democratic aspiration is also observed in

1. Juan J. Linz and Alfred Stepan, *Problems of Democratic Transition and Consolidation* (Baltimore: Johns Hopkins University Press, 1996).
2. Richard Rose and Doh C. Shin, "Discerning Qualities of Democracy in
Korea and Post-Communist Countries," a paper delivered at the "Conference
on Democratization and Globalization in Korea: Assessments and Prospects,"
Seoul, Korea, August 18–19, 1997; Doh Chull Shin and Richard Rose, *Korean*

the Korean case. Shin and Shyu found no growth in the desire of Koreans for greater democracy after the significant rise in democratic preference observed in the surveys of 1991 and 1993. In 1991, the mean preferred level of democracy was 6.3 on a ten-point scale, rising to 8.4 in 1993 but stabilizing at 8.6 in 1994 and 1996.[3]

Perhaps closely linked to the normative question of what kind of political system people want is the issue of how they *perceive* the political system they actually have and how they compare its qualities with previous ones and with the type of regime they expect in the future. Measuring these types of perceptions also enables us to assess an important issue in the study of democratic consolidation: How do people evaluate their political system's progress in democratization? To the extent that the mass public broadly perceives—across all major social and political groups—that the formally democratic system is in fact democratic, and substantially more so than the previous authoritarian regime, would seem to augur well for democratic consolidation. To the extent that the public at large, however, or major sections of it, doubts the very democraticness of its political system, its legitimacy would also figure to be more fragile. Recent cross-national studies suggest that the political quality of a new democracy—its perceived degree of democraticness—constitutes an independent and even preeminent basis of mass public support for the political system.[4]

This chapter employs public opinion survey data to examine how Koreans assess their new democracy as they experienced it under the government of President Kim Young Sam (1993–98), who

Evaluative Democracy: A New Korea Barometer Survey, Studies in Public Policy 292 (Glasgow: Centre for the Study of Public Policy, University of Strathclyde, 1997).

3. Doh Chull Shin and Huoyan Shyu, "Political Ambivalence in South Korea and Taiwan," *Journal of Democracy* 8, no. 3 (July 1997): 109–24.

4. Richard Rose, William Mishler, and Christian Haerpfer, *Democracy and Its Alternatives* (Oxford: Polity Press; Baltimore: Johns Hopkins University Press, 1998); Larry Diamond, *Developing Democracy: Toward Consolidation* (Baltimore: Johns Hopkins University Press, 1999).

was the first civilian president popularly elected since the military coup of 1961. The Kim Young Sam government is usually regarded as the beginning of the consolidation stage for Korean democracy, whereas the Roh Tae Woo government is regarded as its transitional stage. To put the evaluations of democracy under Kim Young Sam in a dynamic political context that may permit some inferences to be drawn about progress toward democratic consolidation, we will also examine how people perceived the level of democracy under the military authoritarian regime of Chun Doo Hwan and what level of democracy they expect for the future.

The analysis that follows is based on data from three national surveys conducted by the Sejong Institute in 1995, 1996, and 1997. Samples were drawn randomly from the adult populations nationwide (with the exception of Cheju Island). The sample size for 1995 is 1,800 and that for 1996 and 1997 is 1,500.

Assessments of Democratization

How do Koreans evaluate the level of democracy under different governments and their country's overall progress in democratization? In our three nationwide surveys, respondents were asked to "grade" the level of democracy during each of the last three governments (Chun Doo Hwan, Roh Tae Woo, and Kim Young Sam) and the expected level of democracy in five to ten years, using a ten-point numerical scale where the score of one represents "complete dictatorship" and ten "complete democracy." People evaluated the Kim Young Sam government as the contemporary one while simultaneously assessing the level of democracy of the previous two governments.

As we can see in table 1, the perceived levels of democracy of the two governments of Chun and Roh were rated, on average, well below six, indicating that both governments were viewed as less than

TABLE 1 Mean Score of Democratization Ratings on Ten-Point Scale

Years	1995 Survey (n = 1,800)	1996 Survey (n = 1,500)	1997 Survey (n = 1,500)
Chun Doo Hwan government (1981–87)	3.3	3.1	3.6
Roh Tae Woo government (1988–92)	4.5	3.9	4.7
Kim Young Sam government (1993–97)	6.1	6.0	5.9
Next five to ten years	7.7	7.9	7.7

democratic. Although the Roh government was rated as more democratic, its average score was consistently well below five. Only with the Kim Young Sam government do Koreans believe that they achieved democracy. Yet even the Kim government was not widely perceived as providing a high or "complete" level of democracy, as its average score in each of the three surveys was only about six on the ten-point scale. Only 61 percent of respondents in the 1997 survey gave a rating of six or higher for the Kim Young Sam government, which means that four in ten respondents perceived the Kim government as undemocratic or only very ambiguously democratic. Across all three surveys, however, Koreans appear optimistic about the future development of democracy in their country, expecting a level of democracy in five to ten years of 7.7 (1995), 7.9 (1996), and 7.7 (1997). In each case, these scores are one and a half to two points higher than the mean perceived level of democracy at the time.

Across the three surveys, one can also observe some decline in people's perceptions of democratic progress. The average democracy rating of the Chun government fell during the period 1995–96 but increased in 1997. From 1996 to 1997 there was also a rise in the retrospective democracy rating of the Roh Tae Woo government, while the democracy rating of the contemporary Kim Young Sam government slightly declined. Moreover, while the expected level of future democracy rose 0.2 in 1996 from 1995, it fell back in 1997 to the 1995 level. In short, Koreans' assessment of their current democracy and future democratic prospects regressed slightly and their view of the past authoritarian government became more positive. As a result, the gap between the democracy ratings of the Kim Young Sam government and its authoritarian and quasi-democratic predecessors narrowed between 1995 and 1997. Economic failures, popular disenchantment with corruption scandals, and President Kim's reform policies might be responsible for this setback. The impact of economic decline on the people's democratic perceptions will be examined later.

Since the above observations are based on the average democracy rating of each government, an additional indicator is needed to see how serious the 1997 setback was in perceived democratization of the current and future democracy. Clearly, Koreans in 1997 perceived progress in democratization from the past to the present and expect democratic improvement to continue in the future. A great majority of Koreans viewed the Kim Young Sam government as more democratic than the past authoritarian Chun government; 83 percent of Koreans gave a higher democracy rating to the Kim government than the Chun government, while 8 percent rated the Chun government as more democratic. Moreover, an overwhelming majority of Koreans (85 percent) expected that their future governments would be more democratic than the current one (see table 2). Despite the modest erosion in 1997, this broad popular perception of significant progress in democratization, as well as the expectation for continued future progress, augur well for democratic consolidation in Korea.

TABLE 2   Past Changes and Expectations for Future Democratization in 1997 (in percent)

Direction of Change in Level of Democracy	Between Past and Present (n = 1,498)	Between Present and Future (n = 1,495)
Deterioration (−)	7.54	3.81
No change (0)	9.55	10.84
Improvement (+)	82.91	85.35

Perceptions of Democratization

What factors account for the differences in Koreans' perceptions of democracy under the previous two governments, the contemporary Kim Young Sam government, and an expected future government? First, demographic backgrounds such as age, educational attainments, income level, and residential area were tested. Among demographic variables, income level and residential area show statistically meaningful differences in the 1997 survey. Interestingly, income level has a curvilinear relationship with the democratization evaluation of the Kim era. The lowest income group (less than 1.5 million won a month) assigns the lowest democratization score; Kim's democratization score increases as household income level rises. A higher-income group (with more than 3.5 million won a month), however, gave Kim Young Sam's government a lower democratization score than the intermediate-income groups. This downturn in the assessment of Kim's democraticness among upper-class Koreans may be a result of his government's economic reforms, such as the "real-name" financial accounting system, which impinged on their financial interests. As regionalism is an important factor in explaining Korean political alignments and opinions, a person's regional background affected his/her experiences of democratization more than any other demographic variable. This factor is examined separately below.

Second, ideological orientations (progressive versus conservative, or anti- versus progovernment) are often considered as explanatory variables for different political attitudes in Korea. They do not, however, explain the differences in perceptions of democracy and democratization. Yet party affiliation does have an important effect. Since the opposition Democratic Party split—into the main opposition National Congress for New Politics (NCNP) and the minor opposition United Liberal Democratic Party (ULD)—after the 1995 survey was carried out, the data sets for 1996 and 1997 were checked to determine continuity of party affiliation. Not surprisingly, supporters of the ruling New Korea Party (NKP), which was renamed in 1997 as a successor to the Democratic Liberal Party (DLP), gave the Kim Young Sam government a much higher democracy rating (6.8 average for both years) than did supporters of the NCNP (5.2 in 1996 and 5.5 in 1997). Supporters of the ULD, which was established in March 1994 after splitting away from the ruling DLP, however, gave the lowest democracy rating to the Kim government (5.1 in 1996 and 1997).

By the same token, supporters of the ULD viewed the past authoritarian Chun Doo Hwan government as less dictatorial (3.5 in 1996 and 4.6 in 1997) than those of the DLP-NKP (3.2 in 1996 and 3.7 in 1997). Although supporters of the NCNP and the ULD both gave the Kim Young Sam government a lower democracy rating than did supporters of Kim's own party, the NCNP partisans gave the past Chun government the most dictatorial rating (2.3 in 1996 and 3.1 in 1997). Party affiliation did not much affect expectations of future democratization, save that supporters of the ruling party expected somewhat greater democratization in the future than supporters of the other parties.

Although party affiliation appears to be important in explaining different assessments of democratization, its significance is qualified by the generally low level of partisan affiliation in Korea. Only a minority of Koreans (37 percent in 1996 and 32 percent in 1997) expressed support for a particular political party. In addition, all three major parties are associated with a particular region: the DLP-NKP, Kyongsang; the NCNP, Cholla; the ULD, Chungchong. Regional identity may well be the more deep-seated factor explaining differences in perceptions of democratization (as well as other political attitudes).

Third, social and economic perceptions were identified. Neither the perceptions of social conflicts nor the degree of "life satisfaction," however, were related to the perceived level of democracy of the Kim Young Sam government or to the perceived change in democracy from the Chun to the Kim government. In contrast, one's perception of economic performance under the Kim Young Sam government was significantly related to evaluations of its level of democracy and that of the Chun government. How contemporary economic perceptions affect people's assessments of the current democratic government and the past authoritarian government will be analyzed later.

Regional background and assessments of economic performance appear to be the two most salient factors affecting perceptions of democratization. In the pages that follow, each of these two factors are carefully examined using data from the three annual surveys.

Regional Variations

Koreans tend to identify themselves on the basis of their regional origin and to cultivate personal ties and solidarity with people who share a common regional background. Regional origin is technically defined as the place where one has spent his or her youth (which usually overlaps with place of birth). Since regional origin and current residential region tend to show similar effects (with the exception of the Seoul metropolitan area), regional background here is represented by current residential region.

Koreans have experienced their new democracy differently de-pending on their regional background, which are also evident in their evaluations of the Kim Young Sam government. As can be seen in figure 1, the city of Pusan and the surrounding Kyongsang province, President Kim's native region, exhibited the highest democracy rating in 1996 and 1997 and the second highest democ-racy rating in 1995. In contrast, the city of Kwangju, the surround-ing Cholla province, and the city of Taegu/northern Kyongsang province perceive less democracy under the Kim Young Sam government than did residents of other regions. Residents of Kwangju/Cholla (the native region of Kim Dae Jung, Kim Young Sam's longtime political rival) gave the lowest democracy rating to the Kim government for 1995, 1996 and 1997, and residents of Taegu/Northern Kyongsang gave the second lowest democracy rat-ing with the exception of 1996.

Having long been excluded from the political mainstream, the people of the Kwangju/Cholla region tended to view the Kim Young Sam government as an extension of Kyongsang region's political hegemony and thus did not give Kim Young Sam credit for the existing degree of democratization. In contrast, the people of Taegu/Northern Kyongsang, the stronghold of the past regimes of Park Chung Hee, Chun Doo Hwan, and Roh Tae Woo, felt antag-onistic toward Kim Young Sam for dismantling the power bases of the military and political elites from this region.

The retrospective assessments of the Chun Doo Hwan govern-ment also showed regional variations. Residents of Kwangju/Cholla viewed that authoritarian government as much more dictatorial than did those of other regions (save for Kangwon province) because the 1980 Kwangju incident, which saw the deaths of hundreds of civilians owing to the Korean military under Chun's command. The three regions of Seoul, Inchon/Kyonggi, and Teajeon/Chungchong also gave lower democracy ratings to the Chun government. Not surprisingly, Chun Doo Hwan's native Taegu/

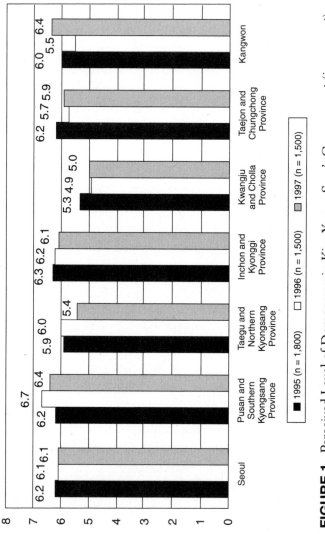

FIGURE 1 Perceived Level of Democracy in Kim Young Sam's Government (in percent)

Northern Kyongsang region gave his government the highest democracy rating of any region. Similarly, whereas residents of Kwangju/Cholla perceived a substantial increase in democracy from the Chun to the Kim government, residents of Taegu/Northern Kyongsang admitted to the least change in the level of democracy between the two governments.

All regions exhibit to one degree or another an upswing from 1996 to 1997 in the retrospective assessment of democracy in the Chun government. New political developments during 1994–95 had contributed to the collapse of the uneasy regional coalition of the ruling DLP, which could have triggered the upswing. Kim Jong Pil's breakup with President Kim and his subsequent establishment of the ULD in March 1994 alienated Kim Jong Pil's power base, Taejeon/Chungchong residents, from President Kim. The imprisonment of former presidents Chun and Roh in late 1995 under the campaign of Rectification of History also alienated their native Taegu/Northern Kyongsang regions.

However, the upswing in the Chun government's democracy rating occurred not in 1996 but in 1997. Moreover, the improvement in the retrospective assessment of the Chun government could be observed also in the Pusan/Southern Kyongsang region, Kim Young Sam's native region, and Kwangju/Cholla, where Chun is most hated. In addition, the ruling New Korea Party secured its legislative majority in the general election of April 1996. If by 1997 Koreans broadly came to have a somewhat softer view of the Chun Doo Hwan government, the reason for this attitudinal shift would appear to lie in the failures of the Kim Young Sam government, particularly after late 1996. The attempt to pass the undemocratically amended National Security Planning Agency Law and the conflict-ridden labor relations laws in December 1996, and the eruption of the Hanbo scandal in February 1997, seem to have generated considerable disenchantment among Koreans with their new

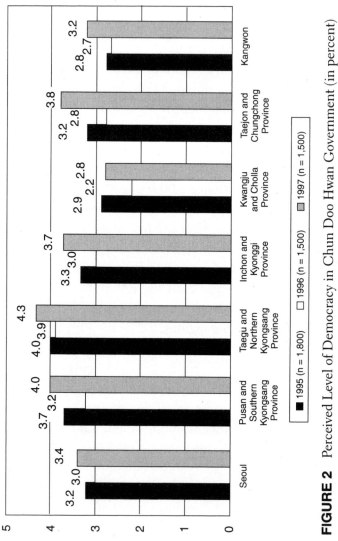

FIGURE 2 Perceived Level of Democracy in Chun Doo Hwan Government (in percent)

Legend:
- 1995 (n = 1,800)
- 1996 (n = 1,500)
- 1997 (n = 1,500)

Seoul: 3.2, 3.0, 3.4
Pusan and Southern Kyongsang Province: 3.7, 3.2, 4.0
Taegu and Northern Kyongsang Province: 4.0, 3.9, 4.3
Inchon and Kyonggi Province: 3.3, 3.0, 3.7
Kwangju and Cholla Province: 2.9, 2.2, 2.8
Taejon and Chungchong Province: 3.2, 2.8, 3.8
Kangwon: 2.8, 2.7, 3.2

democracy, despite the wave of enthusiasm that accompanied Kim Young Sam's inauguration in early 1993.

Finally, we observe that residents of Kwangju-Cholla tend to have lower expectations for democracy in the future. In 1997, however, it is the Taegu/Northern Kyongsang region that gave the lowest rating for the expected level of democracy over the next five to ten years. Overall, however, regional backgrounds did not account for significant differences in Koreans' expectations for future democracy. To the extent this implies a reduction in the influence of regionalism on political attitudes, it too seems to augur well for democratic consolidation.

Economic Performance

The relationship between economic development and democracy has been a subject of controversy in Korea. Economic development was widely considered a source of legitimation for past authoritarian regimes in Korea. At the same time, economic development is regarded to have contributed to Korea's democratic transition by increasing democratic aspirations and highlighting popular demands for democratization.

In what way and to what degree does economic development affect democratic consolidation in Korea? Affluence is considered to be an important element for sustaining democracy. Having raised its per capita national income to almost twice the level of Przeworski's threshold of $6,000 until the recent economic meltdown, Korea may be expected to sustain the finding of Przeworski and his colleagues that democracies are impregnable in affluent countries.[5]

---

5. Adam Przeworski, Michael Alvarez, Jose Antonio Cheibub, and Fernando Limongi, "What Makes Democracies Endure?" *Journal of Democracy* 7, no. 1 (January 1996): 39–55.

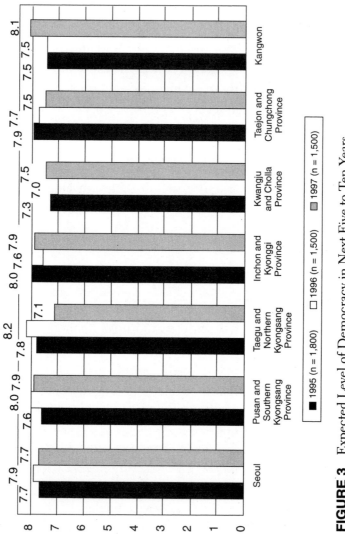

FIGURE 3 Expected Level of Democracy in Next Five to Ten Years

This expectation, however, does not mean that Koreans support their new democracy regardless of its economic performance. Koreans have become accustomed to high levels of economic growth, and successful economic performance has become an important basis for political legitimacy, even as other goals (such as social welfare, environmental protection, and liberalization) have become salient. The idea that economic development is crucial for Korea's survival is widely held among the general public as well as government officials. Maintaining economic growth thus constitutes an essential part of the government's assumed responsibility.

Koreans' perceptions of economic performance under democracy were measured with the question "How have Korea's economic conditions changed in the past several years since the Kim Young Sam government was inaugurated?" Respondents were asked to select one of five responses, ranging from "worsened substantially" to "improved greatly."

As we see in table 3, there was a dramatic change in Koreans' perceptions of the conditions of national economy during the last three years of the Kim Young Sam government. In 1995, more people viewed economic conditions as improved rather than worsened. In 1996, more people began to think their economic conditions had worsened rather than improved since the inauguration of President Kim. By 1997, perceptions of economic conditions had become overwhelmingly negative, with 85 percent of respondents saying economic conditions had worsened. Although this dramatic upswing of

TABLE 3 Perceptions of Economic Conditions under the Kim Young Sam Government (in percent)

	Worsened Substantially	Somewhat Worsened	Has Not Changed	Somewhat Improved	Improved Greatly
1995 (n = 1,800)	6.1	12.9	49.0	30.3	1.7
1996 (n = 1,500)	15.1	26.9	34.3	22.5	1.3
1997 (n = 1,500)	53.9	30.8	13.6	1.7	0.0

disenchantment preceded the economic collapse in November 1997, it reflected the downturn of the Korean economy that became noticeable in the latter half of 1996, with business bankruptcies and job losses, as well as the prolonged government indecision in dealing with large business failures including Kia Motors in 1997.

The Relationship between Economic and Political Assessments

How are the perceptions of economic performance related to political assessments of democratic progress? Koreans do view their new democracy differently depending on their perception of economic performance. Positive perceptions of national economic conditions are associated with a democratic image of contemporary and future governments and an authoritarian image of the Chun Doo Hwan government. First, the perception of economic performance under President Kim is significantly related to how Koreans rate the level of democracy under his government. People who saw economic conditions as having "worsened greatly" gave significantly lower democratization scores for Kim's era than all other groups surveyed in 1995 and 1997. Generally, Koreans who believed Kim Young Sam managed the economy poorly also judged his democratic performance poorly. Those who saw an improved economic performance under Kim Young Sam gave his government the highest average democracy rating. Interestingly, within each category of economic performance evaluation, the perceived level of democracy increased from 1995 to 1997 (see figure 4).

Second, people who viewed economic performance under Kim Young Sam negatively tended to give a more democratic (or less dictatorial) assessment of the authoritarian government of Chun Doo Hwan (see figure 5). This relationship, however, only held in 1995 and 1996, when there was considerable variation in public assessments of economic performance. As the perception of

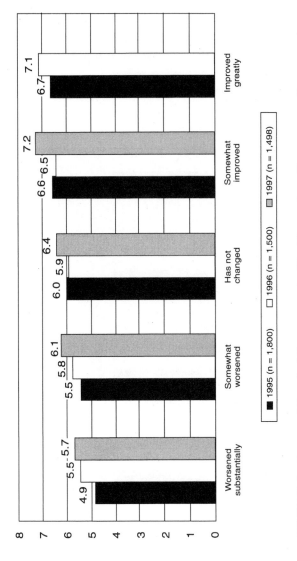

FIGURE 4 Perceived Level of Democracy in Kim Young Sam Government (in percent)

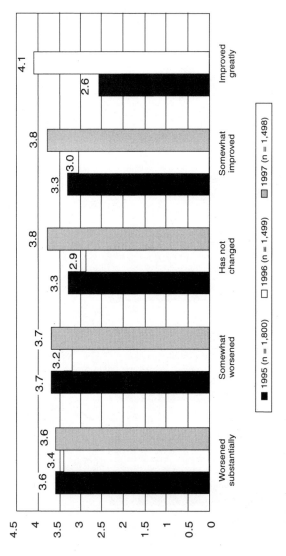

FIGURE 5 Perceived Level of Democracy in Chun Doo Hwan Government (in percent)

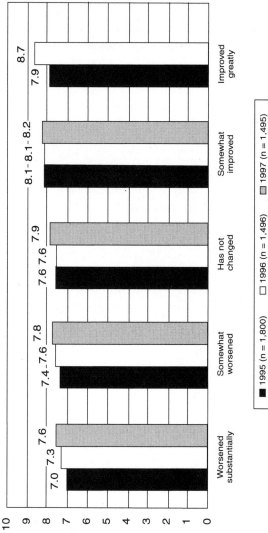

FIGURE 6 Expected Level of Democracy in Next Five to Ten Years (in percent)

economic decline became more universal in 1997, this association with the retrospective political assessment of the past authoritarian regime evaporated. In fact, by 1997, Koreans tended to consider the past authoritarian government less dictatorial than before, regardless of their different perceptions of national economic conditions. This is probably a result of the sharp rise in disappointment with the Kim Young Sam government in 1997.

Third, the perception of current economic performance under Kim Young Sam is also related to expectations of future democratization. The more positively people see current economic conditions, the more democratization people expect of the future government. As with the assessment of level of democracy under Kim Young Sam (figure 6), the expected future level of democracy rises once the perception of current economic performance is controlled for. Within each category of perceived economic performance, respondents had higher expectations for the future of democracy in 1996 and 1997 than they did in 1995.

Conclusions

This chapter makes three sets of observations. First, Koreans' popular perceptions of democratization reflected evolutionary progress. They viewed the Chun government as dictatorial, began to see the current Kim government as democratic (if not solidly democratic), and expected future governments to be more democratic. Between 1996 and 1997, a slight regression was observed in evaluations of the level of democracy at present and in the future, whereas negative assessments regarding the past authoritarian government became diluted. Koreans strongly believe that progress toward democratization is being made, however, and this is an encouraging sign for consolidating democracy in Korea.

Second, Koreans' perceptions of democracy are mediated through their regional ties. Koreans tended to view their current government as more democratic if the incumbent president came from the same region; they viewed it as less democratic if their regions were represented by leaders of opposition parties. At the same time, the past authoritarian government was perceived as less dictatorial by residents of the dictator's home region. Different perceptions of democracy by people with different regional backgrounds thus reflect the role that regionalism plays in structuring voting patterns and party affiliations in Korean politics.

Regionalism has often been suggested as a key factor limiting political development in Korea. But regionalism does not seem to be a significant barrier to democratic consolidation in Korea. Two findings are noteworthy in this regard. First, the impact of regionalism is limited. Regardless of regional affiliation, no group of Koreans considers the past dictatorial government to have been democratic. Nor does a region's isolation from political power make Koreans from that region view a new democracy as a dictatorship. For people from every region, and in each of the three years surveyed, the perceived level of democracy of the Kim Young Sam government was invariably higher than that of the Chun Doo Hwan government. Second, the expectation for greater democracy in future governments was shared broadly among all Koreans regardless of their regional backgrounds.

Third, perceptions of national economic conditions were found to affect assessments of democracy. A positive perception of the current national economic condition was associated with evaluating contemporary and future governments as more democratic. Since the survey asked about the national economic conditions under the Kim Young Sam government, the perception of economic conditions implied popular judgment of the government capacity for managing the economy. Therefore, continued economic development and the perceived good economic performance of the government seem likely to contribute to democratic consolidation in Korea by reinforcing a popular image of democracy. But this also implies that a sustained economic downturn could further erode Koreans' evaluations of their democratic regime.

Civic Mobilization
for Democratic Reform

Analysts have presented differing views on what caused South Korea's democratic transition in 1987. As far as domestic factors are concerned, there have been two different interpretations. Some observers argue that the democratic transition was chiefly—if not entirely—due to a series of elite calculations and interactions. The focus of this interpretation is June 29, 1987, when the chairman of the ruling party announced his eight-point proposal on democratic reform—the "June 29 Declaration." Whether a genuinely serious chasm existed between *duros* (hard-liners) and *blandos* (soft-liners) within the ruling bloc is still a moot question. Nonetheless, according to this explanation, ruling elites at the time predicted that the opposition would split, which explains why they agreed to adopt a set of democratic reforms, including a change to a direct presidential election system.[1] What happened in South Korea in 1987, therefore, resembled the experiences of some South European and Latin American countries where "elite dispositions, calculations, and

1. Ki Yŏng Kwŏn, "Pisa: 6–29 chŏnyaŭi kwŏnbu" (Hidden history: The ruling elite on the eve of the June 29 Declaration), *Wŏlgan Chosŏn* (Chosŏn monthly), June 1993, 197–237; Hyug-baeg Im, *Sijang, kukka, minjujuŭi: han'guk minjuhwawa chŏngch'i kyŏngje iron* (The market, the state, and democracy: Democratic transition in South Korea and theories of political economy) (Seoul, Korea: Nanam, 1994), 253–97.

pacts . . . largely determine[d] whether or not an opening [would] occur at all."[2] In other words, South Korea confirms the largely elite-centered paradigm dominant in the literature on democratic transition and consolidation.

Meanwhile, a great number of scholars inside and outside of South Korea subscribe to the view that South Korea's democratic transition was primarily mass driven and bottom up. According to this explanation, it was civil society—"the realm of organized social life that is voluntary, self-generating, (largely) self-supporting, [and] autonomous from the state"[3]—that facilitated, if not directly caused, various phases of democratization in South Korea. In particular, analysts have emphasized that student groups, labor unions, and religious organizations had waged intense antigovernment and prodemocracy struggles since the early 1970s. United under the leadership of several national umbrella organizations, these civic groups mobilized a formidable democratic alliance against the authoritarian regime in 1987.[4] The South Korean transition, therefore,

2. Guillermo O'Donnell and Philippe C. Schmitter, *Transitions from Authoritarian Rule: Tentative Conclusions about Uncertain Democracies* (Baltimore: Johns Hopkins University Press, 1986), 48; John Higley and Richard Gunther, eds., *Elites and Democratic Consolidation in Latin America and Southern Europe* (New York: Cambridge University Press, 1992), 3.

3. Larry Diamond, "Toward Democratic Consolidation," *Journal of Democracy* 5 (1994): 5.

4. Sunhyuk Kim, "Civil Society in South Korea: From Grand Democracy Movements to Petty Interest Groups?" *Journal of Northeast Asian Studies* 15 (1996): 81–97; Kyŏng Ryung Sŏng, "Han'guk chŏngch'i minjuhwaŭi sahoejŏk kiwŏn: sahoe undongronjŏk chŏpkŭn" (Social origins of South Korean democratization: A social movement approach), in Institute for Far Eastern Studies, ed., *Han'guk chŏngch'i sahoeŭi sae hŭrŭm* (New currents in South Korean politics and society) (Seoul, Korea: Nanam, 1994); Myŏng Sun Sin, "Han'gukesŏŭi simin sahoe hyŏngsŏnggwa minjuhwa kwajŏngesŏŭi yŏkhal" (The formation of civil society in South Korea and its role in democratization), in Byung-joon Ahn, ed., *Kukka, Simin sahoe, chŏngch'i minjuhwa* (The state, civil society, and political democratization) (Seoul, Korea: Hanul, 1995); Jang Jip Choi, "Han'gukŭi minjuhwa: ihaenggwa kaehyŏk" (South Korean democratization: Transition and reform), in Jang Jip Choi and Hyŏn Chin Im, eds., *Siminsahoeŭi tojŏn: han'guk*

was different from cases in southern Europe and Latin America because its civil society was not merely "resurrected" by elite-centered and top-down political liberalization.[5] Rather, South Korea's democratic transition was similar to some East European and African countries in that civic groups initiated and led the entire process of democratization by forming a prodemocracy alliance within civil society, creating a grand coalition with the opposition political party, and ultimately pressuring the authoritarian regime to yield to the "popular upsurge" from below.[6] Civic mobilization was extremely important, and the momentum for greater democracy consistently emanated from oppositional civil society, not from the state.[7]

If civil society and civic mobilization were crucial in South Korea's democratic transition, what can be said about their role in its posttransitional politics? What is the role of civic mobilization in democratic consolidation in South Korea? How has its role changed, in comparison with its role in democratic transition? The existing literature on democratic transition and consolidation generally agrees that civil society is rapidly demobilized after the transition and that therefore civic mobilization becomes significantly marginalized in the consolidational politics.[8] Is this observation valid and applicable

minjuhwawa kukka, chabon, nodong (Challenge from civil society: State, capital, and labor in South Korean democratization) (Seoul, Korea: Nanam, 1993).

5. O'Donnell and Schmitter, *Transitions from Authoritarian Rule*, chap. 5.

6. O'Donnell and Schmitter, *Transitions from Authoritarian Rule*, 53–56; Michael Bernhard, "Civil Society and Democratic Transition in East Central Europe," *Political Science Quarterly* 108 (1993): 307–26; Naomi Chazan, "Africa's Democratic Challenge: Strengthening Civil Society and the State," *World Policy Journal* 9 (1992): 279–307; Robert Fatton, Jr., "Democracy and Civil Society in Africa," *Mediterranean Quarterly* 2 (1991): 83–95; Marcia A. Weigle and Jim Butterfield, "Civil Society in Reforming Communist Regimes: The Logic of Emergence," *Comparative Politics* 25 (1992): 1–23.

7. John S. Dryzek, "Political Institution and the Dynamics of Democratization," *American Political Science Review* 90 (1996): 476.

8. Steven Fish, "Rethinking Civil Society: Russia's Fourth Transition," *Journal of Democracy* 5 (1994): 34.

to the case of South Korea? What kind of lingering impact, if any, does the high level of civic mobilization during the transition have on the subsequent politics of democratic consolidation? This chapter purports to answer those questions by analyzing and assessing the role of civic mobilization in South Korea's democratic consolidation since 1988. I first identify and examine several areas in which civic mobilization has significantly contributed to institutional reform and democratic consolidation. Then I compare the role of civic mobilization in the democratic consolidation with that in the transition. I conclude the chapter with some theoretical reflections on the continuing influence of civic mobilization on the politics of democratic consolidation in South Korea.

Civic Mobilization and Democratic Consolidation, 1988–

Since South Korea's democratic transition in 1987, there have been at least two junctures at which civil society and civic mobilization appeared to become largely peripheral, if not utterly irrelevant, to the politics of democratic consolidation. Incidentally, both times closely followed presidential elections. The reasons for the apparent marginalization of civil society and civic mobilization, however, differed significantly.

First, civil society became marginalized and fragmented immediately after the presidential elections in 1987 and the inauguration of Roh Tae Woo. Once the authoritarian regime consented to implementing a set of democratic reforms including direct presidential elections in June 1987, the gravity of the politics of democratic transition quickly switched to the founding elections (i.e., the presidential elections in December 1987 and the National Assembly elections in April 1988). As these founding elections were approaching, South Korean politics increasingly revolved around party politics, election campaigns, and electoral competitions in political society. Consequently, civil society and civic mobilization became significantly marginalized.

Furthermore, after attempting in vain to remedy the chasm between the two leading opposition presidential candidates, Kim Young Sam and Kim Dae Jung, various groups in South Korean civil society split over whom to support for the presidential elections in December 1987. Some supported Kim Young Sam, arguing that he had a greater chance of winning the elections. Others supported Kim Dae Jung because he was considered more progressive. Still others believed that the two Kims should yield to a third "people's" candidate. When the December presidential elections ended with the ruling party's victory, therefore, civic groups in South Korea were left dejected and fractured.

The second juncture at which civil society and civic mobilization seemed peripheral and irrelevant to the politics of democratic consolidation came immediately following the election and inauguration of Kim Young Sam, the first genuinely civilian South Korean president in more than three decades. Once inaugurated, especially during the first two years of his tenure, Kim designed and carried out a series of unprecedented political and socioeconomic reforms, waging intensive anticorruption campaigns, introducing the real-name bank system, legislating political reform bills, and consolidating the civilian control of the military.[9] The Kim government's policy toward civic groups, aimed at normalization with civil society, was aimed at not only progovernment or moderate groups but also radical movement groups in civil society. Kim's soaring popularity left civic groups, which had been good at criticizing

9. For a detailed description of these reforms, see "Introduction," this volume, and Victor D. Cha, "Politics and Democracy under the Kim Young Sam Government: Something Old, Something New," *Asian Survey* 33 (1993): 849–63.

unpopular governments and used to the repression of authoritarian regimes, bewildered, demobilized, and demoralized.[10] In a word, civic groups were no longer able to find a common target. Civil society and civic mobilization appeared largely irrelevant to South Korean politics. It was truly ironic that civic groups, which had weathered harsh state repression during the previous authoritarian regimes, had to endure their most serious identity crisis under a democratic government.

However, both these junctures — at which civil society and civic mobilization appeared to be seriously marginalized — were relatively brief. Overall, civil society has continued to play an important role in the politics of democratic consolidation in South Korea. Civic mobilization continued to be an essential part of reform politics in South Korea. In this section, I focus on three different areas in which civic mobilization has played an important role in promoting and facilitating South Korea's democratic reform and consolidation.

Confronting and Dealing with the Authoritarian Past

Democratic consolidation is "the process in which democracy becomes so broadly and profoundly legitimate among its citizens that it is very unlikely to break down."[11] Without a reasonably clean separation from the previous authoritarian regimes, it is nearly impossible for a new democratic regime to become "broadly and profoundly legitimate." Consequently, how to investigate and, if necessary, punish the past wrongdoings and corruption becomes crucial in either augmenting or undermining the legitimacy of a fledgling democracy. Liquidation of the authoritarian past has also

10. Mun Hong Song, "Munmin ch'unggyŏk, 'taesasaek'e ppajin chaeya" (The civilian shock: Dissident movement in "profound agony"), *Sindonga* (Tonga monthly), May 1993, 494–505.

11. Larry Diamond, "Toward Democratic Consolidation," 15.

been one of the most critical and urgent issues in the politics of democratic consolidation in South Korea. Civic mobilization has played an important role in pressuring the governments to squarely confront and deal with the authoritarian past.

During the first two years (1988–89) of his term, Roh Tae Woo, another general-turned-president elected in the 1987 presidential elections, made efforts to settle some of the old scores bequeathed by the previous Chun Doo Hwan regime. For example, the chief justice, Kim Yong Ch'ŏl, who participated in the trial of Kim Dae Jung in connection with the Kwangju uprising in 1980, was pressured to resign after a petition demanding his removal received the support of a number of members of the judiciary. Chun Kyŏng Hwan, Chun Doo Hwan's younger brother, was arrested and sentenced to a seven-year term of imprisonment for embezzlement and corruption. Eventually, Chun Doo Hwan himself, faced with multiple allegations of malfeasance, was forced to testify before the National Assembly, offer a public apology, return his wealth to the state, and go into exile in a distant Buddhist temple for two years.[12]

At the time, the impetus for a clean break with the previous authoritarian regimes came largely from political society. In the National Assembly elections in February 1988, the ruling Democratic Justice Party was deprived of majority control of the National Assembly. This *yŏso yadae* (small ruling party versus large opposition parties) composition of the National Assembly empowered the opposition to push for investigations into irregularities of past governments. Because Roh himself was one of the greatest beneficiaries of the past authoritarian regime and the successor to Chun Doo Hwan, however, there were certain limits to what he was able to do.

More serious efforts to break with the authoritarian past began in 1993 with the installation of the Kim Young Sam regime. Immediately

12. For details, see James Cotton, "From Authoritarianism to Democracy in South Korea," *Political Studies* 37 (1989): 256.

following his inauguration, Kim reshuffled the top command of the military by removing nineteen generals and admirals who had been involved either in a previous coup or in corruption. The Board of Audit and Inspection, under the leadership of a former Supreme Court judge, Yi Hoe Ch'ang, undertook rigorous investigations into illegal acts or misconduct committed by public officials in the past. The board even asked Chun Doo Hwan and Roh Tae Woo to answer questionnaires on their roles in past decisions. Chun was asked to clarify his role in the construction of a multimillion-dollar "peace dam" against possible flood attacks from North Korea before the 1988 Olympics in Seoul. Roh was asked to explain his role in the 1991 decision to buy 120 F-16 fighters from the General Dynamics Corporation instead of the F-18s from McDonnell-Douglas that had previously been decided on.

Most important, the Kim government characterized Chun's takeover of power on December 12, 1979, as "a coup-like event" and promised further investigations into the military putsch as well as the Kwangju massacre in 1980. After a year-long investigation, the government prosecutor's office announced in October 1994 that Chun and Roh had engineered a military revolt. To the chagrin of many South Koreans, however, the government declared that it would not prosecute them so as to avoid any damage to national unity. Fearing that prosecution might cause serious political unrest, the Kim government urged the nation to let history judge the December coup of 1979. In July 1995, pointing to the statute of limitations, the government announced its final decision not to pursue insurrection charges against Chun Doo Hwan and Roh Tae Woo.

This government announcement was followed by a series of protests by many civic groups that ultimately led to a national crisis. College and university professors took the initiative. On August 14, 1995, the Korea Council of Professors for Democratization (Min'gyohyŏp) released a statement criticizing the government decision and demanding a special law for prosecuting the coup leaders. About 150 professors waged protest sit-ins. Together with the People's Solidarity for Participatory Democracy (Ch'amyŏ yŏndae), the Korea Council of Professors for Democratization submitted a legal petition that the statute of limitations not apply to those involved in the May 18 massacre.

In addition, 221 Seoul National University professors released a statement calling for the enactment of a special law and an immediate reinvestigation of the May 18 insurrection in 1980. This was the third time that Seoul National University professors released antigovernment statements—the first was during the April uprising in 1960, and the second was during the June uprising in 1987. The number of professors who signed the statement exceeded the number that signed in the campaign of 1987. Many deans and senior professors also joined this time. As of August 29, 3,912 professors from eighty universities had participated in the signature campaign calling for the punishment of Chun and Roh.[13]

On September 29, 1995, under the leadership of the Korean Coalition of College Student Governments (Hanch'ongryŏn), students at many universities boycotted classes. Some professors cooperated by canceling classes in advance. This was the first nationwide class boycott since the inauguration of the Kim Young Sam regime.[14] On September 30 the streets of thirteen major cities across the country were filled with students, workers, and ordinary citizens who held massive meetings and demonstrations, calling for a special law prosecuting and punishing those involved in the May 18 Kwangju massacre of 1980.

The disclosure of Roh Tae Woo's corruption scandal by an opposition National assemblyman in October 1995 dramatically escalated the campaign for the prosecution of Chun and Roh. On

13. *Kwangju ilbo* (Kwangju daily), August 29, 1995; *Han'gyŏre sinmun* (Han'gyŏre daily), August 30, 1995.
14. *Han'gyŏre sinmun*, September 30, 1995.

November 1, three hundred members of the Preparatory Committee for the Korea Federation of Democratic Trade Unions (Minnojun) staged demonstrations in Seoul. The National Alliance for Democracy and Unification of Korea (Chŏn'guk yŏnhap), the official umbrella organization of the people's movement groups, also staged sit-ins at its office. The All-nation Emergency Committee on Enacting a Special Law for Punishing the Perpetrators of the May 18 massacre was established by 297 people's and citizens' movement groups. This committee waged signature campaigns—gaining some hundred thousand signatures—and street protests and held the People's Action Day to call for the imprisonment of Roh Tae Woo, attended by ten thousand citizens and students.[15] After the rally, thousands of students, workers, activists, and citizens waged street demonstrations throughout the main streets of Seoul. As in the June uprising of 1987, ordinary citizens, drivers, and pedestrians cheered the demonstrators on. Similar gatherings were held in Pusan, Kwangju, Taegu, Inch'ŏn, Suwŏn, Sŏngnam, Anyang, and Ch'unch'ŏn.[16]

On November 3, 1995, which is Students' Day in South Korea, at a gathering of three thousand students at Sungkyun'gwan University, the Korean Coalition of College Student Governments called for the immediate imprisonment of Roh Tae Woo and enactment of a special law for punishing those involved in the May 18 massacre.[17] Throughout November, thousands of university students waged street demonstrations in Kwangju, Pusan, Cheju, and other major cities of the country. As of November 25, 6,549 professors at eighty-nine colleges and universities had participated in the signature campaign, which had been originally launched by some

15. *Chungang ilbo* (Chungang daily), November 2, 1995.
16. *Han'gyŏre sinmun*, November 5, 1995.
17. *Chungang ilbo*, November 4, 1995.

Korea University professors. This number was far greater than that of participants in the June uprising in 1987.[18]

Yielding to the popular pressure generated by such an unprecedented level of civic mobilization, the government jailed Roh Tae Woo in mid-November on bribery charges, making him the first South Korean president to face legal action for misdeeds in office. State prosecutors interrogated thirty-six business leaders about how Roh collected the $650 million in secret funds he admitted maintaining when he was president from 1988 to 1993. Moreover, on November 24, 1995, the ruling party finally decided to enact a special law that would punish retroactively those involved in the violent suppression of the Kwangju uprising in 1980. Kim Young Sam himself ordered the ruling party to draft it, admitting that the military crackdown on the Kwangju uprising had tarnished the honor of the country and the people and damaged the nation's pride; he emphasized that a special law was necessary to deal with the responsible people. Consequently, as of late February 1996, eleven former generals, including Chun and Roh, had been arrested in connection with the crackdown. Chun and Roh were prosecuted on multiple charges of bribery, insurrection, and treason.

Chun Doo Hwan and Roh Tae Woo were eventually amnestied and released in December 1997, actions that were harshly criticized and protested by many civic groups. The arrests and imprisonments of the two former presidents on various charges of insurrection and corruption, however, served to establish a clear demarcation between the democratic present and the authoritarian past. The prosecution of former dictators, unimaginable in many other fledgling democracies in the world, unambiguously symbolized the end of the authoritarian rule and officially proclaimed the beginning of a new

18. *Han'gyŏre sinmun,* November 26, 1995.

era in which democracy has become "the only game in town."[19] In making democracy the only game in town, civic mobilization played an extremely crucial role.

Maintaining, Expanding, and Protecting Democracy

Civic mobilization has also played important roles in maintaining, expanding, and protecting democracy — in both procedural and substantive terms.

During the Roh Tae Woo regime, civic groups, having quickly recovered from their marginalization and fragmentation during the presidential elections in 1987, remobilized themselves and resumed their prodemocracy campaign with a vigor comparable to or stronger than that during the democratic transition. One important reason why civic groups could relatively rapidly resume their movement for democratic reform lay in the continuity the Roh regime had with the previous authoritarian regime. Roh himself, just another general-turned-president, was not an effective symbol of a clear break with the past. Being a close friend of Chun Doo Hwan and deeply involved in the multistaged military coup of 1979–1980 and the subsequent consolidation of the authoritarian political system, he had been groomed and eventually anointed as an official successor to Chun until the last minute, when the ruling bloc decided to yield to popular pressure by proclaiming the June 29 democratization package. Because Roh was the greatest beneficiary of the authoritarian regime, he was therefore constrained from liquidating the authoritarian past. To most of the movement groups that had led the June uprising in 1987, the Roh regime was regarded as a mere extension of authoritarian rule. Thus civic groups often pe-

19. Juan J. Linz and Alfred Stepan, *Problems of Democratic Transition and Consolidation* (Baltimore: Johns Hopkins University Press, 1996), 5.

joratively characterized Roh as "Chun with a wig" (the previous military ruler had been bald). At best, Roh's regime seemed to be a *dictablanda* (liberalized authoritarianism), and the need to continue the prodemocracy struggle appeared vital.

Furthermore, the grand party merger in 1990 served as glaring evidence that the Roh Tae Woo regime was indeed just a continuation of the past authoritarianism and that the opposition parties were unreliable. In early 1990, Roh, who had been seriously concerned about his political vulnerability in the National Assembly since his inauguration, succeeded in merging with two opposition parties: the Reunification Democratic Party led by Kim Young Sam and the New Democratic Republican Party led by Kim Jong Pil. This was similar to *trasformismo* in Italy, where, in 1876, Agostino de Pretis, the new prime minister, invited the opposition Destra Party to shift to the government majority in exchange for personal benefits, access to state patronage, and the right to local rule. The opposition parties, finding themselves marginalized from power and state spoils, agreed and "transformed" themselves from the opposition into a stable part of the governing majority.[20] A Korean-style *trasformismo* was seen by many civic groups as a frontal attack on the consolidation of democracy in their country—civic groups in some sense had no choice but to intensify their prodemocracy movement.

Throughout the politics of democratic consolidation since 1988, civic groups have also been trying hard to transform the election climate (*Son'gŏ p'ungt'o*) of South Korea. Many civic groups have joined their efforts to monitor the election process and increase

20. Frances Hagopian, "The Compromised Consolidation: The Political Class in the Brazilian Transition," in Scott Mainwaring, Guillermo O'Donnell, and J. Samuel Valenzuela, eds., *Issues in Democratic Consolidation: the New South American Democracies in Comparative Perspective* (Notre Dame, Ind.: University of Notre Dame Press, 1992), 282; Jang Jip Choi, " 'Pynŏhyŏngjuŭi'wa han'gukŭi minjujuŭi" (Transformism and South Korean democracy), *Sahoe pip'yŏng* (Social critique) 13 (1995): 187–99.

political participation. The most notable in this regard is the Citizen Movement Council for Fair Elections (Kongsŏnhyŏp), which was created in 1991 by seven civic groups. Through a number of local, National Assembly, and presidential elections, it has now grown into a prestigious nationwide organization in the movement for fair elections, made up of fifty major civic groups and encompassing all religious denominations — Protestant, Buddhist, Catholic, Wŏn Buddhist, and Confucian — and all classes.

Vowing to terminate South Korea's corrupt election practices through concerted citizen action, the Citizen Movement Council for Fair Elections has demanded the revision of unfair election laws, run report centers for unethical conduct, held hearings, sponsored policy debates, published reports comparing public promises of the candidates, distributed "selection criteria" for choosing the right candidate, disseminated information, and developed solidarity with the people's movement groups in enhancing voter participation.[21]

Meanwhile, many other civic groups that support substantive democracy have continually paid special attention to increasing the inclusiveness of South Korean democracy. In particular, the Association of Families of Political Prisoners (Min'gahyŏp), together with other social movement groups and religious organizations, waged a campaign for the release of long-term political prisoners and organized the Investigative Committee on the Fabrication of Spy Stories by the Agency for National Security Planning. This committee severely criticized the Agency for National Security Planning and the Kim Young Sam regime for suppressing opposition and civic groups by exaggerating or fabricating spy stories before almost every election. In addition, most of these civic groups have also consistently demanded the repeal of the National Security Law. To them, South Korean democracy is at best "pseudo" and highly hypocritical with-

21. CMCFE (Citizen Movement Council for Fair Elections), "Kongsŏnhyŏp chŏn'guk ponpu paltaesik" (Inaugural ceremony of the CMCFE), March 1995.

out substantially increasing the level of tolerance to different ide-
ologies and ideas.[22]

The most recent tide of civic mobilization came in late 1996.
On December 26, 1996, the ruling New Korea Party passed several
labor-related bills and a reform bill regarding the Agency for National Security Planning. These bills had been intensely debated
and contested among South Koreans. Labor unions had opposed the
proposed labor reform bills because the bills, if legislated, would
weaken labor unions and facilitate massive layoffs. Civic groups had
also disputed the proposed Agency for National Security Planning
reform bill because the bill would expand the investigative power of
the already powerful state agency. Despite these concerns and criticisms from labor unions, civic groups, and the opposition parties, the
ruling party resolved to ram the bills through the National Assembly,
at 6 A.M. December 26, clandestinely, without opposition legislators.

This railroading of the controversial bills profoundly outraged
civic groups and led to a series of antigovernment protests. Lawyers
and university professors waged sit-ins and street demonstrations, demanding the immediate nullification of the bills. Student organizations, comparing the passage of the bills to the notorious legislation
of two antidemocratic laws during the Chang Myŏn government in
1961, launched nationwide demonstrations. Labor unions characterized the Kim government as a civilian dictatorship and led a series of strikes, including a successful general strike in January 1997,
the first time since the birth of the South Korean state in 1948.
Catholic churches and groups including the National Catholic
Priests' Corps for the Realization of Justice (K'atollik chŏngŭi kuhyŏn
chŏn'guk sajedan) supported the student demonstrations and labor
strikes. Buddhist and Protestant organizations also joined in support.[23] Well into mid-March, massive demonstrations and signature

22. "Introduction," this volume.
23. *Han'gyŏre sinmun* (Han'gyŏre daily), January 14, 1997.

collection campaigns by civic groups and labor strikes destabilized the country. The government remained uncompromising, not yielding to the pressure engendered by such civic mobilization. Nevertheless, the Kim regime lost the battle because these anti-government protests greatly tarnished the regime's previous democratic image and drastically diminished Kim's popularity.

Addressing New Social Issues

The presence of civil society contributes positively to the consolidation of democracy, according to Philippe Schmitter, by providing "channels for self-expression and identification that are more proximate to individuals, hence less likely to alienate actors from the political system when making demands."[24] Civic mobilization in South Korea has played an important role in addressing and promoting social issues that had been ignored by the authoritarian regimes in the past and to some degree also by the democratic regimes since 1988, which has significantly increased ordinary citizens' political participation.

In particular, the emergence and proliferation of new social movement groups, called "citizens' movement groups," have fundamentally transformed the overall landscape of South Korean civil society. One significant political implication of the emergence and rapid expansion of the citizens' movement groups has been that more diverse issues are now being addressed by civic groups. Under the authoritarian regimes, civic groups focused their efforts chiefly on political democracy, demanding the restoration, if not the installation, of democracy. Either explicitly or implicitly, other issues were

24. Philippe C. Schmitter, "Civil Society East and West," in Larry Diamond, Marc F. Plattner, Yun-han Chu, and Hung-mao Tien, eds., *Consolidating the Third Wave Democracies: Themes and Perspectives* (Baltimore: Johns Hopkins University Press, 1997), 247.

considered marginal or petty and therefore subject to the greater cause of political democratization. Since the democratic transition in 1987, however, such "issue hegemony" has been incrementally eroded. Civic groups have raised a variety of new issues, particularly those issues neglected and underrepresented in the past.

Of the newly created civic groups in South Korea, the most salient are the environmental organizations. Although the environmental movement existed during the 1960s and the 1970s, it was spontaneous, transient, and local in nature. Moreover, the environmental movement at the time was considered marginal and a luxury, not only by the developmental state but also by many civic groups. Most civic groups concentrated on the more urgent issues of human rights, labor conditions, and political democratization. Not until the democratic transition in 1987 did the environmental movement finally begin to gain influence.

The history of the environmental movement in South Korea is inseparable from the establishment and expansion of the Korean Anti-Pollution Movement Association (Kongch'uryŏn), which was established in 1988 by merging two existing environmental organizations—the Korean Anti-Pollution Citizen Movement Council (Konghae pandae simin undong hyŏpŭihoe) and the Korean Anti-Pollution Movement Youth Council (Konghae ch'ubang undong ch'ŏngnyŏn hyŏbŭihoe). The Korean Anti-Pollution Movement Association consists of thousands of dues-paying members, including many working journalists, academics, lawyers, doctors, farmers, workers, students, Roman Catholic priests, and Protestant ministers. The leadership positions are filled with the new urban middle class. The cadres or activists who carry out the everyday duties of the Korean Anti-Pollution Movement Association are also highly educated and reform-oriented. They possess a considerable degree of expertise on environmental issues.

Since its inauguration, the Korean Anti-Pollution Movement Association has concentrated on diverse antipollution and antinuclear activities. It has organized numerous conferences, round-the-country slide shows, and picture exhibitions, pressuring the business community to spend more on pollution control as well as raising awareness among the general public. Also, alarmed by the Chernobyl disaster in 1986, the leaders of the Korean Anti-Pollution Movement Association have actively joined the debate on nuclear issues and launched a major campaign against the construction of nuclear plants in South Korea, organizing mass rallies and collecting signatures. It has published monthly newsletters such as *Survival and Peace* and *Against Nuclear Plants* to create a national consensus against nuclear power plants and to consolidate the existing local environmental movements.[25]

On April 2, 1993, with many other local environmental organizations, the Korean Anti-Pollution Movement Association created the Korea Federation for Environmental Movement [*sic*: official translation] (Hwan'gyŏngryŏn). This organization is the biggest environmental movement group in South Korean history. In its inaugural address, the Korea Federation for Environmental Movement put forward the following goals: (1) environmental movement as a daily practice; (2) environmentally sound business practices; (3) development of feasible policy alternatives; (4) consistent support for an antinuclear position; and (5) strengthened solidarity with environmental groups abroad to cope with environmental problems on a global scale. The federation has one central office and twelve regional offices. The membership includes lawyers, professors, religious leaders, medical doctors, nurses, social workers, artists, and businesspersons.

Another issue that has been vigorously explored and developed by the citizens' movement groups is economic justice. The Citizens' Coalition for Economic Justice (Kyŏngsillyŏn) was founded in July 1989 by some five hundred academics, lawyers, and church activists.

25. Su-Hoon Lee, "Transitional Politics of Korea, 1987–1992: Activation of Civil Society," *Pacific Affairs* 66 (1993): 362–63.

The educational status of the inaugural membership was quite impressive—63 percent of the total membership were college graduates or postgraduates. High levels of education were also reflected in the occupational distribution, with 27 percent being employed in white-collar occupations, 26 percent in professional occupations, and nearly 10 percent in small and medium businesses or self-employed. Fifteen and a half percent were college students. Blue-collar workers constituted only 1.7 percent. Also, in terms of age, the membership was strikingly young, with 73 percent being under forty years old and 41 percent under thirty.[26] In its inaugural statement, the Citizens' Coalition for Economic Justice emphasized that the most important socioeconomic issues in South Korea were unearned income, land speculation, maldistribution of income, and the tax system. These economic injustices, according to the statement, could not be changed by the government or politicians alone but ultimately must be solved by the organized power of the civil society. It also proclaimed that the strategy of the Citizens' Coalition for Economic Justice to achieve its goals would be to (1) organize ordinary citizens; (2) make its demands in peaceful, nonviolent, and legitimate ways; (3) seek concrete and workable alternatives; and (4) mobilize civil society on a non-class-struggle principle.[27]

The Citizens' Coalition for Economic Justice is now a national organization of more than fifteen thousand dues-paying members, with dozens of regional offices. Under the banner of "economic justice through the power of committed citizens," it has supported the independence of the central bank from government control, revision of tax laws to discourage land speculation, and regulation of the rental system in favor of the poor. Some of its major programs, including the Economic Injustice Complaint Center, Legislature

26. Lee, "Transitional Politics of Korea, 1987–1992," 364.
27. CCEJ (Citizens' Coalition for Economic Justice), "Palki sŏnŏnmun" (Inaugural statement), 1989.

Watch, and Research Institute for Economic Justice, have received wide public attention.[28] In June 1990, it began to publish a bimonthly magazine, *Kyŏngje chŏngŭi* (Economic justice), in which academic writings on issues related to economic (in)justice are published. Conducting research into dozens of policy sectors covering practically all aspects of social, economic, and political life, the Citizens' Coalition for Economic Justice has assumed a commanding position as the voice of all middle-class reformists in South Korea.

Civic Mobilization—Transition versus Consolidation

In the preceding section, focusing on three different areas, I examined the role of civic mobilization in promoting institutional reform and democratic consolidation in South Korea. As in the stage of democratic transition, civic mobilization has continued to be highly relevant and critical to the politics of democratic consolidation. Civic mobilization in South Korea today is perhaps not as dramatic and sweeping as that of the democratic transition. Yet it has contributed significantly to institutional reform and democratic consolidation in South Korea, pressuring the government to break with the authoritarian past, demanding more reform measures in various procedural and substantive dimensions of democracy, and addressing those social issues customarily neglected by the state. In this respect, the case of South Korea appears to refute a general consensus in the existing literature on democratic transition and consolidation: "Elite choices appear to predominate at the consolidation phase of newly emerging democracies."[29] In South Korea, civil society and

28. Lee, "Transitional Politics of Korea, 1987–1992," 364.
29. Sidney Tarrow, "Mass Mobilization and Regime Change: Pacts, Reform, and Popular Power in Italy (1918–1922) and Spain (1975–1978)," in Richard Gunther, P. Nikiforos Diamandouros, and Hans-Jürgen Puhle, eds., *The Politics of Democratic Consolidation: Southern Europe in Comparative Perspective* (Baltimore: Johns Hopkins University Press, 1995), 207.

civic mobilization have not become seriously marginalized in the posttransitional politics. Rather, they continue to be influential in furthering institutional reform and democratic consolidation.

In addition to its continuing relevance and influence, civic mobilization in South Korea's current democratic consolidation is similar to that of the democratic transition in at least two respects. First, civic mobilization in both phases was primarily initiated by students and intellectuals. For example, in the two most recent waves of civic mobilization in South Korea (i.e., one in 1995 leading to the prosecution of the two former presidents and the other in 1997 protesting various antidemocratic legislations), students and intellectuals were again at the forefront of mass mobilization. Initially organized and led by students, antigovernment demonstrations and protests quickly expanded to encompass religious activists, industrial workers, ordinary citizens, and so forth. Most of the civic mobilization during the democratic transition in the past followed the same pattern. This persistent pattern also corroborates and reinforces the traditional image of intelligentsia who, according to the Confucian culture prevalent in South Korea, should remain vigilant and critical of any abuse or misuse of power by the ruling regime.

Second, specific forms of mobilization remain largely unchanged. Most of the familiar forms of civic mobilization used during the transition—class boycotts by college students, signature collection campaigns, announcement of antigovernment statements, street demonstrations, protest parades, labor strikes, and so forth—have been used in the phase of democratic consolidation. In terms of the specific form of mobilization, there exists a high level of continuity between the transition and posttransition periods.

Two important differences, however, exist between the transition and consolidation phases in terms of the composition and strategies of civic mobilization. First, the composition of civic mobilization is no longer as homogeneous as that of the democratic transition. During the transition, the internal configuration of South

Korean civil society was exceedingly simple: it was dichotomized between a small number of progovernment groups, which were part of the state corporatist system, and many prodemocracy movement groups. Since the transition, however, South Korean civil society has become increasingly variegated. In particular, the emergence and rapid expansion of the citizens' movement groups have drastically changed the overall landscape of South Korean civil society. Unlike the transition, when most civic groups focused on democracy and human rights, now different civic groups are focusing on different goals and different issues. Today what is crucial is no longer an intense battle between the prodemocracy civic groups and the repressive state but the constructive competition and collaboration among different civic groups on various elements of institutional reform and democratic consolidation.

Second, in terms of goals and strategies, civic mobilization in South Korea is slowly but substantially moving out of the "conflictual engagement" that characterized the mode of interaction between civil society and the state during the authoritarian breakdown and democratic transition.[30] During the transition, the state was something to protest, something to resist, and, if at all possible, something to overthrow. But now the ultimate challenge confronted by civic groups is not simply to criticize and repel the state but to constructively provoke and engage the democratic state with concrete policy alternatives.[31] Consequently, more and more civic groups try to avoid radical images and violent methods, either implicitly or through the open support of peaceful activism. Acknowledging the legitimacy and authority of the democratic government, civic groups are also becoming more willing to abide by the existing laws and so-

30. Regarding different modes of state–civil society relations, see Michael Bratton, "Beyond the State: Civil Society and Associational Life in Africa," *World Politics* 41 (1989): 407–30.

31. Sunhyuk Kim, "State and Civil Society in South Korea's Democratic Consolidation: Is the Battle Really Over?" *Asian Survey* 37 (1997): 1135–44.

cial order, which clearly attests the fact that the "rule of law," one of the essential "arenas" of a consolidated democracy,[32] is gradually taking root in South Korean democracy.

Conclusion

Civic mobilization, which had been extremely crucial in facilitating authoritarian breakdown and democratic transition, has also been critical in the politics of democratic consolidation in South Korea since 1988. Although at some junctures civil society appeared to be marginal to the politics of democratic consolidation, these moments were relatively short. Civic mobilization has been continually important to institutional reform and democratic consolidation in South Korea—particularly in liquidating the authoritarian past; maintaining, expanding, and protecting democracy; and addressing new social issues. At least two potential perils, however, reside in the continued influence of civic mobilization on the politics of democratic consolidation that merit our special attention.

First, as I have already pointed out, civic mobilization in South Korea is gradually moving out of the previous pattern of "conflictual engagement" between civil society and the state. This change, however, is far from being irreversible. There still exist numerous and influential civic groups in South Korea that advocate the fundamental transformation of entire political, economic, and social systems. As far as these maximalist groups are concerned, the ruling regime, however hard it may try, will always remain pseudodemocratic. The only mode of interaction between civil society and the state known to them is a "conflictual engagement."

Depending on political circumstances—for example, if a democratic government proves unable or unwilling to accomplish some

32. Juan J. Linz and Alfred Stepan, *Problems of Democratic Transition and Consolidation* (Baltimore: Johns Hopkins University Press, 1996), 10–11.

of the reform goals expected—these groups can quickly dominate civil society and radicalize the populace. Radicalization and the resultant resumption of intense confrontation between civil society and the state would hinder the emergence and development of a political culture that appreciates and promotes tolerance, moderation, negotiation, consultation, bargaining, and compromise. In other words, they would hinder the evolution of a "civic culture," which is deemed essential to the daily workings of a viable democracy. Instead, the continued antagonism and confrontation between the state and civil society would foster and amplify radicalism, extremism, fundamentalism, and often violence. In the intense battle between the two opposing sides, moderation and tolerance would be looked upon as opportunism and indecisiveness. During the democratic transition, such a clear-cut distinction between "we" and "they—the enemy" greatly contributed to the unity and power of the prodemocracy alliance. But confronted with the crucial task of deepening and institutionalizing democracy, such a dichotomous view of the polity would only delay the development of a democratic political culture and may create a political environment in which governability remains elusive.

Second, the basic goal or function of civic mobilization is to bring various issues in the consolidational politics directly to the (invisible) table between the state and civil society. To a great degree, therefore, civic mobilization reflects and represents the malfunctioning or failure of political society. In contrast, direct encounter and negotiation between the state and civil society themselves can sometimes adversely affect the institutionalization and functioning of political parties. Key political issues continue to be addressed in the middle of direct, intense, and sometimes violent confrontation between the state and civic groups. Where direct confrontation between the state and civil society dominates political discussion, political parties are considered peripheral at best and irrelevant at worst. This in turn aggravates one of the chronic problems of South

Korean politics—the underdevelopment and amorphousness of political society.[33] The literature on democratic transition and consolidation agrees that democratic consolidation can seldom be successful without developing a highly institutionalized and viable party system.[34] Considering the traditionally hyperactive civil society and underdeveloped political society in South Korea, it would be unrealistic to expect an overnight eclipse of civic mobilization and an exclusive reliance on party politics. Neither would such a drastic swing of the pendulum (i.e., little civic mobilization on the one hand and superactive party activities on the other) be necessarily desirable for the consolidation of South Korean democracy. However, civic mobilization, although conducive to South Korea's democratic consolidation so far, will have to be utilized sparingly in the future, only to supplement, *not replace*, institutionalized political parties and interest groups that normally represent and intermediate social interests in most consolidated democracies in the world.

33. Byung-Kook Kim, "Parties, Elections, and the Party System: Challenges of Democratic Consolidation in Korea," 1996, ms.
34. Leonardo Morlino, "Political Parties and Democratic Consolidation in Southern Europe," in Richard Gunther, P. Nikiforos Diamandouros, and Hans-Jürgen Puhle, eds., *The Politics of Democratic Consolidation: Southern Europe in Comparative Perspective* (Baltimore: Johns Hopkins University Press, 1995), 315–17.

Asian Values, Korean Values, and Democratic Consolidation

It may seem a bit like beating a dead horse to criticize the concept of "Asian values" in the wake of the economic crisis that swept Asia in 1997 and 1998. Within the space of less than ten years, opinion has shifted dramatically on both sides of the Pacific: Western revisionists like Chalmers Johnson and James Fallows are today widely ridiculed for having argued that Asian economic and political institutions should be a model for the United States, while statesmen like Prime Minister Mahathir bin Muhammed of Malaysia have returned to a traditional kind of Third World blame-mongering in place of trumpeting the superiority of Asian cultural values. Indeed, the severity of Asia's crisis has led many Western pundits to argue that Asian institutions and practices like nepotistic credit allocation, an overly meddlesome state, and absence of a rule of law mandating transparency in financial transactions lie at the heart of the region's current problems and that economic recovery means that Asia must drop many of its distinctive practices and Westernize.

Of all Asian countries, Korea has been one of the hardest hit by the crisis, having seen both its currency and its equity markets fall by more than 50 percent. A number of Korean *chaebols* such as Ssaangyong and Halla have declared bankruptcy, and the president elected in December 1997, Kim Dae Jung, has begun a sweeping series of economic reforms. Whatever assertions were made about the relationship between Korean institutions, culture, values, and its economic and political development will have to be carefully reevaluated in light of developments over the coming years.

The purpose of this chapter is to evaluate the concept of Asian values, and particularly Korean values, as it relates to the prospects of the further consolidation of Korean democracy. My argument is twofold: first, that Asian values in general and Korean values in particular have been and are given much greater weight than they deserve in explaining the potential success or failure of democracy in Korea and, second, that although Koreans share a number of important cultural values with other Asian societies, they are distinctive in a number of ways that will create a unique set of problems and opportunities for democratic governance. Neither Asian nor Korean values explain the economic success of the region or the country, and neither constitutes an insurmountable barrier to the consolidation of democracy in South Korea—and, one ultimately hopes, throughout the Korea peninsula.

The Asian Values Argument

The idea that Asian cultural values are more hospitable to paternalistic authoritarianism of the sort practiced in Singapore, Malaysia, or Indonesia than to Western-style democracy has been put forward by politicians like former Prime Minister Lee Kwan Yew of Singapore and Mahathir bin Muhammed of Malaysia.[1] In this they have been supported by a number of Western academic ob-

---

1. See Fareed Zakaria, "A Conversation with Lee Kuan Yew," *Foreign Affairs* 73, no. 2 (March–April 1994): 109–27.

servers. Samuel Huntington has argued that there is a broad zone of "Confucian" civilization that is hostile to democracy:

> Almost no scholarly disagreement exists on the proposition that traditional Confucianism was either undemocratic or anti-democratic. . . . Harmony and cooperation were preferred over disagreement and competition. The maintenance of order and respect for hierarchy were central values.[2]

Tom Gold has argued that there is much in the Confucian political heritage that suggests a continuing pattern of authoritarian politics.[3] Tu Wei-Ming in perhaps the most thorough account enumerates areas of incompatibility between Confucian doctrine and democratic practice.[4]

The case that Asian values constitute an obstacle to democracy can be summarized succinctly. If we take Confucianism as the dominant value system in Asia, we see that it describes an ethical world in which people are born not with rights but with duties to a series of hierarchically arranged authorities, beginning with the family and extending all the way up to the state and emperor. In this world, there is no concept of the individual and individual rights; duties are not derived from rights as they are in Western liberal thought, and although there is a concept of reciprocal obligation between ruler and ruled, there is no absolute grounding of government responsibility

2. Samuel P. Huntington, "Religion and the Third Wave," *National Interest* no. 24 (summer 1991): 29–42.

3. Thomas B. Gold, "Taiwan: Still Defying the Odds," in Larry Diamond, Marc Plattner, Yun-han Chu, and Hung-mao Tien, eds., *Consolidating the Third Wave Democracies: Regional Challenges* (Baltimore: Johns Hopkins University Press, 1997).

4. Tu Wei-Ming, *Confucian Traditions in East Asian Modernity: Moral Education and Economic Culture in Japan and the Four Dragons* (Cambridge, Mass.: Harvard University Press, 1996).

either in the popular will or in the need to respect an individual's sphere of autonomy.

Apart from Confucianism, Asia's religions do not give particular support to Western democratic principles. The chief folk religions like Taoism and Shinto are animist and pantheistic. Westerners sometimes forget the importance of the transcendent monotheism of the Judaeo-Christian tradition to their political and social lives. The idea that there is an eternal realm of divine law superior to all positive law gives the individual with access to that higher law potential grounds for revolt against all forms of secular authority. It promotes both individualism and the concept of universalism.[5] The universalism is the ground not only for the Western concept of human rights that are transferable from one culture to another but for abstraction in the observation of nature and human behavior that is at the basis for both the natural and the social sciences.

The Case against Asian Values

I have argued elsewhere that the argument that Asian values constitute an insuperable barrier to democracy is mistaken, for reasons that can be summarized briefly.[6] I begin with the premise that there is a correlation between democracy and development and that for a variety of reasons wealthier societies tend to expand political participation. Since the original elaboration of the correlation by Lipset in 1959,[7] it has been analyzed intensively using data from the

5. This point is explored at length in Deepak Lal, *Unintended Consequences: The Impact of Factor Endowments, Culture, and Politics on Long-Run Economic Performance* (Cambridge, Mass.: MIT Press, 1998).

6. See my articles "Confucianism and Democracy," *Journal of Democracy* 6 (1995): 20–33, and "The Illusion of Exceptionalism," *Journal of Democracy* 8 (1997): 146–49.

7. Seymour Martin Lipset, "Some Social Requisites of Democracy: Economic Development and Political Legitimacy," *American Political Science Review* 53

Third Wave democracies formed in the 1980–90 period. With some exceptions, the correlation continues to hold up rather well. Adam Przeworski has concluded that there is not a single historical case of democracy reversal in a country that had reached a level of $6,000 per capita in 1992 parity purchasing power terms.[8]

If we presume that modernization creates conditions neither necessary nor sufficient but nonetheless helpful to the establishment of stable democracy, the burden of proof then falls on those who argue that Asian values are so exceptional as to undermine the relationship. This case has in fact been made: with a limited number of well-known exceptions, virtually all developed democracies are also countries with a Christian cultural heritage. Samuel Huntington has argued that it is that cultural heritage rather than level of development per se that is the determinant of stable democracy.[9] But the empirical record in Asia is relatively supportive of the democracy/development correlation: the first three Asian countries to industrialize—Japan, South Korea, and Taiwan—now have functioning democracies. That two of the highest per capita income entities, Singapore and Hong Kong, are not democratic tends to disconfirm the correlation (as well as the fact that the Philip-pines has been a democracy while remaining one of the region's poorer countries), though these anomalies can be explained by other factors.

(1959): 69–105; Lipset, "The Social Requisites of Democracy Revisited," *American Sociological Review* 59 (1994): 1–22; Larry Diamond, "Economic Development and Democracy Reconsidered," *American Behavioral Scientist* 15 (1992): 450–99; and Michael Coppedge, *Inequality, Democracy, and Economic Development* (Cambridge, Eng.: Cambridge University Press, 1997).

8. Adam Przeworski and Michael Alvarez, "What Makes Democracies Endure?" *Journal of Democracy* 7 (1996): 39–55.

9. Samuel P. Huntington, *The Third Wave: Democratization in the Late Twentieth Century* (Oklahoma City: University of Oklahoma Press, 1991).

The further reason to believe that Asian values are no bar to democracy is that a number of key values characteristic of many Asian societies are supportive both of a modern economy and of democratic politics. (Even if they were supportive only of economic modernization, they would still be conducive to democracy because of the link between development and democracy.) Asian religions and ethical systems are remarkably tolerant in a way that monotheistic traditions such as Judaism, Christianity, and Islam historically have not been; Confucianism, with its exam system that opens up prospects for social mobility, can be highly meritocratic; Confucianism is a highly rational ethical system and does not have the obscurantist tendencies of, say, orthodox Shiism; the Confucian emphasis on education is well adapted to the needs of a modern technological economy; and, finally, the Confucian family system provides a certain protected sphere of private life that is relatively free of state intrusion.

The second reason is that, as Amartya Sen has pointed out, Asian values are extremely heterogeneous, are themselves evolving rapidly, and can be disaggregated to suit different political needs.[10] As anyone the least bit familiar with Asia understands, Japan, Korea, China, Indonesia, Thailand, and the Philippines are all quite culturally different from one another. Indeed, multiethnic societies like Singapore and Malaysia are themselves culturally divided; Lee Kwan Yew's efforts to push Confucianism as a kind of state ideology for Singapore foundered on the resistance of the city-state's Malay population. As seen in the section on Korea below, Korean values in particular appear to be different in critical ways from virtually any other Asian state, in ways that have important implications for democratic stability. Although it is probably true that all Asian societies manifest greater respect for authority than liberal-individualist

10. Amartya Sen, in *Human Rights and Asian Values* (New York: Carnegie Council on Ethics and Public Policy, 1997).

America,[11] attitudes toward the state (which some observers characterize as a core Asian value) vary widely. Japan, Korea, and Taiwan have connected their modern bureaucracies to older statist traditions, which are lacking in countries like Indonesia and Malaysia.

Besides implying that it is hard to generalize about Asian values, cultural heterogeneity means that there are plenty of cultural supports on which to draw for defending democratic political institutions. Any old, complex cultural system like Confucianism is going to contain within it different and sometimes contradictory strands, and in any event is capable of an infinite variety of alternative interpretations. Christianity, after all, was used to defend and delegitimate both slavery and democracy; political partisans were able to pick and choose among principles to defend their particular point of view. It is safe to say that, from the Reformation onward, Christianity was *made* compatible with democracy as modern political norms evolved. Similarly with Confucianism, even though Lee Kwan Yew has argued that it supports hierarchy and benevolent authoritarianism, Taiwan's president, Lee Teng-hui, has called upon *his* Confucian scholars to find doctrinal sources of support for popular participation in politics. Most Asian societies have long since abandoned many aspects of traditional culture, from family structure to dress to politics, while choosing to retain those that have value or utility in a modern, technological world, and there is no reason to think that this process will not continue.

The strongest argument Asian authoritarianism had going for it was its ability to produce higher long-term rates of economic growth than democracy. Lee and Mahathir both argued in favor of

11. It should be pointed out, moreover, that the United States itself is considerably more antistatist than other developed countries that do not come out of the same revolutionary tradition. See Seymour Martin Lipset, *Continental Divide: The Values and Institutions of the United States and Canada* (New York and London: Routledge, 1990); and Lipset, *American Exceptionalism: A Double-Edged Sword* (New York: W. W. Norton, 1995).

technocratic states that would keep government energies focused on noncontroversial economic issues. Now that the Asian financial bubble has burst for both democratic and authoritarian governments alike, the wind has been taken out of their sails. As Robert Barro and others have shown, there is no reason to think that authoritarian regimes should produce higher rates of growth over the long run, though their short-run record has been impressive.

In my view, the most distinctive Asian values are not attitudes toward political order but those having to do with social order and, in particular, the complex of values concerning the family, gender roles, and kinship. As Asia has modernized, there has been much less social disruption than in Western societies. Although these social patterns are not irrelevant to politics, they are not determinative in any way of whether a society chooses authoritarian or democratic rule. They do, however, have large implications for the quality of life in each society and pose a set of problems and challenges distinct from those faced in the West, as seen below.

How Korea Is Similar to Other Parts of Asia

One striking feature of the Asian values debate was how little of it was based on empirical evidence. Perhaps because it was driven primarily by politicians for political purposes, grand generalizations were made and assertions of cultural difference were thrown around without an effort to establish or compare what the actual value differences were.

Values are, of course, notoriously difficult to measure and even more difficult to compare on a cross-cultural basis. This is particularly true for Asia, where the kind of polling data and opinion survey research common in the United States is not nearly as available and where the results of value surveys lend themselves to cultural misinterpretation. The most important comparative value survey is probably the World Values Survey (WVS), led by Ron Inglehart at the University of Michigan, which has data available for Korea for 1981, 1991, and 1996, as well as a number of other opinion polls carried out either by academics or by the Korea National Statistical office. In addition, relatively reliable comparative data exist on family structure, crime, and other social indicators that shed some light on how Korea differs from other Asian states and from the West.

What we find when we look at the available values data is what one would expect: Korea shares certain characteristics with other Asian societies but is also different from them in distinctive ways— ways that, I argue below, may make Korea more receptive to stable democracy than other countries in the region. This is as one would expect. Korea is, after all, a Confucian society onto whose Chinese cultural core a number of Japanese institutions and practices were grafted in the twentieth century, yet which retains an extraordinarily strong and unique culture. Indeed, despite Korea's strong ties to both China and Japan, what is most striking about Korean culture is how different it is from that of both of its immediate neighbors.

It is hard to compare Asian modernization to that of the West because it has taken place over a much more compressed period of time. The rise in per capita income that took place in the two hundred years between the late eighteenth and late twentieth centuries in the United States and Western Europe was compressed into a hundred or so for Japan and a mere forty or fifty for Korea and Taiwan. Social norms have obviously changed in all Asian societies as they developed: fertility rates have come down dramatically; joint and stem families have been replaced with nuclear ones; multigenerational households have given way to Western-style elder care arrangements as agricultural societies were transformed into industrial and even postindustrial ones.

One would expect such rapid cultural changes to have produced a great deal of social disorder as populations adjusted to dramatically different expectations over a short period of time. Nonetheless,

Japan and Korea stand out from virtually every other member of the Organization for Economic Cooperation and Development (OECD) in certain key respects. One indicator is crime. In Britain and the United States, the initial phases of industrialization were accompanied by a sharp increase in deviance through at least the 1840s. Crime rates then declined for much of the remainder of the nineteenth century, and they began to rise dramatically again all over the Western developed world beginning in approximately the 1960s (they are only now beginning to subside, in the United States at least). Japan and Korea started with low crime rates that have remained low throughout the postwar period, with certain exceptions for politically related violence in Korea (see figure 1).

Japan and Korea are distinctive in terms of the way ethical values have shifted as well. The World Values Survey asks a series of ethical questions, such as "Would you consider taking a bribe?" "Would you cheat on your taxes?" "Would you keep money that you found on the street?" and the like. The surveys for virtually all Western developed countries (with the exception of Spain) showed a distinct drop in the percentages of people answering "never" between 1981 and 1991 (see table 1), respectively.

Japan and particularly Korea stand out, in contrast, for showing increases in self-reporting of most categories of ethical behavior (see figures 2 and 3 for how responses changed in Korea and Japan, respectively). It is, of course, difficult to know exactly what to make of the large upward jump in the Korean numbers. It is conceivable that it reflects the transition to democracy in 1987 and the greater openness that that event encouraged. The first survey was taken in 1981, a tumultuous year for Korea that saw the Kwangju massacre and a severe crackdown by the regime of Chun Doo Hwan. We do not know whether the greater cynicism evident in the 1981 numbers reflects the feelings of only that year.

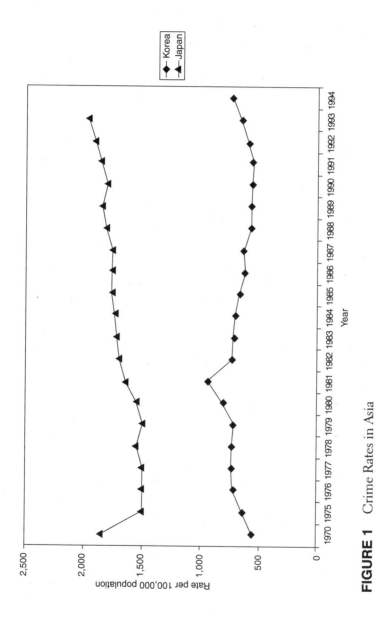

FIGURE 1 Crime Rates in Asia

TABLE 1 Change in Ethical Values, 1981–91

Change in % Responding They Would Never	United States	Federal Republic of Germany	Italy	Spain	Britain	France	Sweden	Canada
Claim false benefits	-12.7	-0.5	-17.4	3.5	-9.3	-6.1	-4.8	4.7
Avoid transportation fare	-11.2	-9.7	-14.9	8	-7.7	-3	-7.5	-2.5
Cheat on taxes	-0.1	-13.1	-17.8	9.9	-3.3	2.3	-12.2	-7.8
Buy stolen goods	-3	-10.4	-9.1	12	-4.7	13.8	-3	-3.2
Joy ride	-3	-10.4	-3	7.6	-3.1	2.6	8.8	-7.1
Use marijuana	3.6	-3.6	-7.5	11.1	-4.4	11.6	3.1	-0.2
Keep money that is not yours	-0.3	-5.5	-20.9	6.3	-8	-10.7	-7.1	-8.8
Lie in own interest	0.4	-11.6	-18.8	7.4	-7.4	-8.9	1.2	8
Commit adultery	4.3	-10.2	-11.6	3	3	16.2	8.6	-5.7
Have sex w/ underage	-1.9	-11.7	-16.7	3.1	3.1	1.2	2	-9.8
Accept bribe	-1.5	-2.6	10.4	4	-5.6	16.7	0.4	-3.3

Korea: Would you ever do the following?

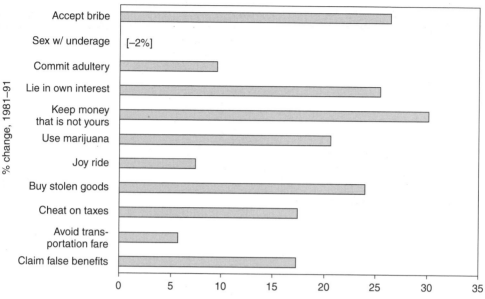

FIGURE 2 Mores in Korea

Asian exceptionalism is apparent, finally, in the data on family structure.[12] As noted earlier, family structure has changed dramatically in Korea and other modernizing Asian countries as various extended family systems are replaced with nuclear ones. The number of three-generation households dropped from 22.1 percent of all households in 1970 to 12.2 percent in 1990, and the average size of a household went from 5.2 persons to 3.7 in that same period.[13] In

12. Other parts of Asia run counter to European patterns of modernization. In peninsular Malaysia and Indonesia, divorce rates have fallen sharply in tandem with economic modernization. See Gavin W. Jones, "Modernization and Divorce: Contrasting Trends in Islamic Southeast Asia and the West," *Population and Development Review* 23 (1997): 95–114.

13. Republic of Korea, National Statistical Office, *Social Indicators in Korea* 1995, p. 228. On changes in Korean family structure, see Yeonoak Baik and Jin Young Chung, "Family Policy in Korea," *Journal of Family and Economic Issues* 17 (1996): 93–112.

Would you ever do the following?

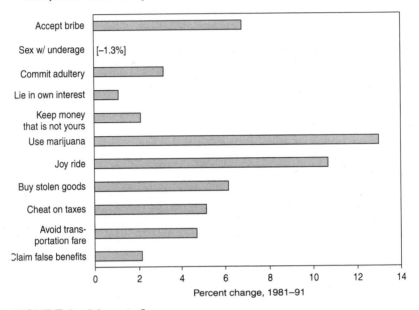

FIGURE 3 Mores in Japan

contrast, modernization has had very different effects on family structure in Asia than in Europe and North America. In the latter areas, economic modernization broke down larger extended families but did not stop there: both Japan and Korea have shown highly stable nuclear family structures in a period when divorce rates went through the roof in most Western developed countries (see figure 4). (As a point of comparison, the U.S. crude divorce rate moved from 2.6 to 4.7 between 1950 and 1990, and the British rate went from .69 to 2.9 in this same period.) Along with a low divorce rate goes an extremely small illegitimacy rate; the problem of poor, mother-headed families that is so pronounced in the United States is all but unknown in either Korea or Japan.

In the United States and other parts of the West, family breakdown and the social problems associated with it (poverty, illegitimacy, crime, etc.) have been driven by shifts in technology, which

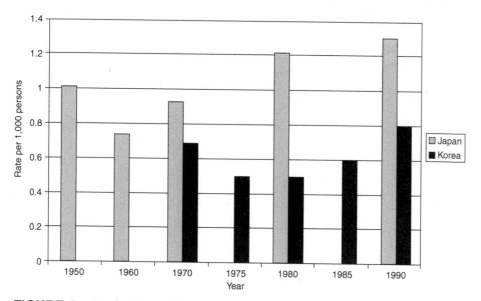

FIGURE 4   Crude Divorce Rates in Japan and Korea

by changing the nature of work have permitted women to enter the workforce in large numbers and to control their reproductive cycles.[14] The cases of Korea and Japan show, however, that technology alone is not sufficient to explain the shift in family structure. Japan has reached a level of development comparable to those of Europe and North America, with Korea lagging behind by perhaps fifteen years, and yet for a variety of cultural reasons has retained a higher degree of social order.

The reason for this difference, in my view, has a great deal to do with the role of women in Western as opposed to Asian societies. While female labor force participation is reasonably high in both Korea, Japan, and other parts of Asia, women tend to stop working

14. This is a point I have argued in *The End of Order* (London: Social Market Foundation, 1997), p. 311, and in my book, *The Great Disruption* (New York: Free Press, 1999).

when they get married and tend to return to labor markets, if ever, only when their children are grown. This tendency is reinforced by labor laws in Japan and Korea that discriminate against women in the workplace and make it much more difficult for them to earn an income sufficient to support themselves and their children over a lifetime.[15] In one international survey where respondents were asked to agree with the statement that "Men should work outside the home and women should stay home," the highest numbers expressing agreement were found in Japan and Korea (30.6 and 35.9 percent, respectively).[16] I would argue that the one characteristic of Asian values that differentiates them most dramatically from Western ones has to do not with attitudes toward economic life or politics but with gender relations and the family.

How Korean Values Are Distinctive

Although Koreans share a core of values with other Asians, they also differ markedly from other Asian societies—and particularly from East Asia's oldest and most developed democracy, Japan—in ways that would seem to have some implications for the quality of democratic politics there. These differences can be summed up as follows: Koreans seem to prize social order less, and are more willing to engage in social and political struggle, than other Asians.

15. On Korea, see Insook Han Park and Lee-Jay Cho, "Confucianism and the Korean Family," *Journal of Comparative Family Studies* 26 (1995): 117–33; and Hyoung Cho, "The Position of Women in the Korean Work Force," in Eui-Young Yu and Earl H. Philips, eds., *Korean Women in Transition* (Los Angeles: Center for Korean-American and Korean Studies, 1987). On Japan, see Eiko Shinotsuka, "Women Workers in Japan: Past, Present, Future," in Joyce Gelb and Marian Lief Palley, eds., *Women of Japan and Korea* (Philadelphia: Temple University Press, 1994), pp. 95–199.

16. Shinotsuka, "Women Workers," in Gelb and Palley, *Women of Japan and Korea*, p. 102.

In a way, this conclusion should be obvious to anyone aware of recent Korean history. Korea has Asia's best-organized and most powerful trade union movement, one that played an important role in bringing down the military dictatorship in 1987 and that has succeeded in extracting large yearly wage increases from Korean employers over the past decade that have pushed labor costs up more than 600 percent. Korea also has Asia's most vocal and in many ways most radical student protest movement, one that also played a key political role during the 1987 events.

Surveys of Asian values, such as that of David Hitchcock, show that overall Asians prize social order much more than Americans.[17] This appears to be least true in Korea, however. Take, for example, the willingness to engage in various forms of political protest (see table 2, based on Gallup data, for young people aged eighteen to twenty-nine from Europe, Japan, and Korea). In all but one category, young Koreans score higher in willingness to protest than do young Japanese; indeed, they score higher than young Europeans in all but two categories.[18] A clear generational shift is at work here since the table shows that, for respondents aged fifty and up, Koreans are generally less willing to partake in protest than their European or Japanese counterparts, particularly the more serious forms. The willingness to protest sometimes shades over into an outright cynicism about the law; in another survey, 25–32 percent of the sample expressed a disregard for the law.[19]

The lesser value accorded to social order by Koreans is also borne out in a poll taken by the *Far Eastern Economic Review* of its readers. Koreans placed "greater emphasis on personal achievement,

---

17. David Hitchcock, *Factors Affecting East Asian Views of the United States: The Search for Common Ground* (Washington, D.C.: CSIS, 1997), p. 73.

18. Data in figure 6 are taken from Aie-Rie Lee, "Culture Shift and Popular Protest in South Korea," *Comparative Political Studies* 26 (1993): 63–80.

19. Aie-Rie Lee, "Values, Government Performance, and Protest in South Korea," *Asian Affairs* 18 (1992): 240–53.

TABLE 2   Willingness to Engage in Protest

	AGES 18–29			AGES 50 AND UP		
	Europe	Japan	Korea	Europe	Japan	Korea
Sign a petition	42	54	58	32	23	36
Join in boycotts	44	54	55	17	44	31
Attend lawful demonstrations	44	36	51	23	22	13
Join unofficial strikes	32	25	23	7	8	4
Occupy buildings	27	9	17	6	3	1

achieving financial success and individual rights," and "less on or-derly society, respect for authority, self-reliance and accountability."[20] It is a bit hard to know what to make of some of the data in table 3 since the Koreans, who work an average of forty-seven hours a week,[21] claim that hard work is not a value in their culture; one would think that an interest in order and self-expression would be inversely cor-related, but they are not for the Korean responses.

A large literature has by now concluded that social trust levels are important for the proper functioning of democratic institutions. Trust in political and other large institutions underpins the legiti-macy of the regime and facilitates the work of leadership; trust in fel-low citizens is important to the formation of civil society and self-organizing social groups.

The World Values Survey shows Korean trust levels to be ap-proximately comparable to those of a number of Catholic developed countries in Europe, slightly below Japan, and considerably below that of the United States and a number of European Protestant countries (see figure 5). Although Japan's relatively low trust score

20. *Far Eastern Economic Review*, August 1, 1996.
21. This is down from over fifty hours a week during the high-growth period. See Republic of Korea, National Statistical Office, *Social Indicators in Korea 1995*, p. 76.

TABLE 3 Values Survey

The Values That Count in My Culture	Highly Valued	Less Valued
Honesty	Singapore, Philippines, Malaysia	Korea, Taiwan
Hard work	Singapore, Philippines, Hong Kong	Japan, Korea
Helping others	Thailand, Indonesia, Philippines	Korea
Respect for learning	Singapore, Philippines	Australia
Harmony	Indonesia, Malaysia	Australia, Western expatriates
Self-reliance	Singapore, Philippines, Malaysia	Korea
Orderly society	Singapore, Philippines, Malaysia	Korea
Freedom of expression	Australia, Philippines, Western expatriates	Singapore, Taiwan
Respect for authority	Philippines, Singapore, Malaysia, Indonesia	Korea, Japan, Western expatriates

seems anomalous, the WVS findings are roughly consistent with the view that familism and regionalism continue to be relatively strong factors in Korean culture, as they are in parts of Latin Catholic Europe and Latin America, limiting the radius of trust to smaller groups. It is of course hard to capture this type of distribution of social trust in survey data since the questions posed are usually fairly vague, such as "Do you generally trust other people?" One society may actually have a higher stock of social trust than another but concentrated exclusively in kinship groups, which such a poll would be unable to pick up. Trusting "other people" may also have different connotations in different cultures. A poll cited by Rose and Shin show a very different result for Korea, with 77 percent of respondents answering that they trusted "most people" (comparative figures were

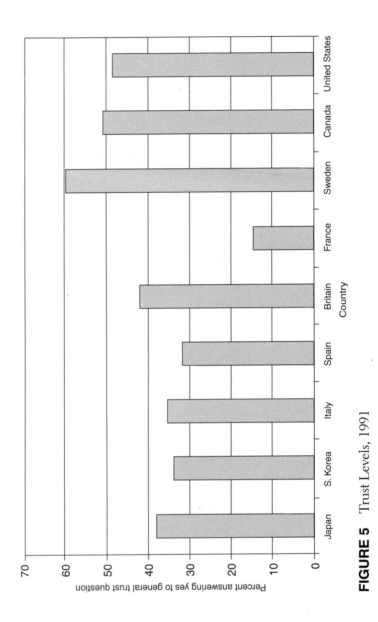

FIGURE 5 Trust Levels, 1991

available only for the Czech Republic and Russia, where Korea scored substantially higher than either of the other former communist states in virtually all trust categories).[22]

Whatever the levels of social trust compared with other societies, public trust levels in Korea appear to be improving over the past two decades. This would seem a natural development given the shift from military authoritarianism to democratic government in this period. In Korea, 77 percent of respondents said they approved of the present regime in 1997, compared with 17 percent who said they approved of the previous one.[23] Forty-one percent of Korean respondents said they felt "people like me" can have more influence on government in the present than they could under the previous regime, compared to 29 and 23 percent for the Czech Republic and the Russian Federation, two other countries that made the transition to democracy in this same period.[24]

This increase in public trust of political institutions is accompanied by apparent increases in participation in civil society. In the WVS data, Korea stands out among OECD countries for the large increases in respondents saying that they participated in organizations of various sorts (see figure 6). By contrast, developed countries in North America and Europe show no particular pattern in overall group memberships; although certain groups such as trade unions see fairly consistent membership declines, their place is taken by other organizations in areas such as education or culture.

It should be noted that increased participation in organizations of various sorts does not necessarily correlate with higher degrees of generalized social trust, nor does it imply that social cleavages are necessarily reduced. Many people join organizations

22. Richard Rose and Doh C. Shin, "Discerning Qualities of Democracy in Korea and Post-Communist Countries," unpublished paper, 1997.
23. Ibid., figure 1.
24. Ibid., table 1.

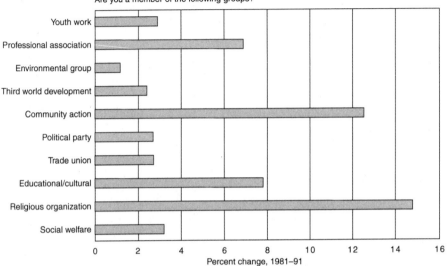

FIGURE 6   Participation in Groups in Korea

for self-interested reasons that may or may not make them more likely to trust and cooperate with others outside that organization. Many groups have mutually contradictory or antagonistic purposes; some forms of increased group memberships such as increased trade unionism can lay the groundwork for greater social conflict. In the Korean case, the largest percentage increase in organizational membership was for religious groups. It is not clear whether this is somehow correlated with the increase in self-reported ethical behavior noted earlier, and it is further not clear what political consequences greater church membership would have on politics.

Korean Values and Korean Democracy

The question remains, how do Korean values relate to the prospects for democratic consolidation in that country? And do its differences from Japan and other Asian countries make it a more or less likely candidate for enduring democracy?

The principal issue has to do with the consequences of Korea's relatively low levels of trust, and the greater propensity for social conflict, on democratic practice. Obviously, no society is free of social conflicts; indeed, democracy exists in order to organize and reconcile the claims of the different interests and passions within a political community. What is necessary for democratic stability is consensus on the basic rules of the democratic game, within which lesser conflicts can be adjudicated. On this score, it would seem that there is relatively little nostalgia for nondemocratic alternatives in Korea. As noted above, a large majority of the country prefers the current to the previous regime. Despite the current wave of nostalgia for the high-growth days of Park Chung Hee, only 15 and 19 percent of those polled agree that the country would be better off under either army rule or under the rule of a strongman (see table 4).[25]

I have argued elsewhere that Korea has a relatively low level of generalized social trust between people who do not belong to common families, kinship groups, or other small-scale social structures, an assertion that is generally borne out by the data presented above.[26] In this respect, Korean culture is closer to that of traditional China than Japan, and the problems of inadequate trust should resemble those of the former country. There is no ready counterpart in Korean culture to the Japanese concept of *amae*, the unwillingness to take advantage of other people's weaknesses, that is important in establishing bonds of mutual dependence in Japanese society.[27] Many observers have consequently argued that Korean

25. Ibid., figure 2.

26. See Francis Fukuyama, *Trust: The Social Virtues and the Creation of Prosperity* (New York: Free Press, 1995), pp. 127–45.

27. For a discussion of this point, see Fukuyama, *Trust*, p. 135.

TABLE 4 Preferences in Type of Rule

Would the Country Be Better Off if Governed By (% agreeing)	Korea	Czech Rep.	Russia
Army rule	15	3	12
Strongman	19	14	32
Communist regime	0	11	35

culture is more individualistic and Western than that of Japan.[28] Although this perception is in many ways accurate, true Western-style individualism is less prevalent than a certain kind of small-group solidarity within what Koreans call the *uri*, or we-group, defined by family, friends, neighbors, classmates, military academy graduating class, and the like.[29]

The relatively narrow radius of trust defined by the *uri* is similar to that of China, where the radius of trust is often restricted to kinship and regional ties, and in many Latin Catholic countries in southern Europe and Latin America, where both business and politics are organized along familistic lines. As noted earlier, Korea's general trust levels as measured by the WVS are comparable to those of Latin Europe, where democracy has been firmly established in all countries since at least the mid-1970s. A small radius of trust is therefore in no way incompatible with democratic institutions.

The problems created by a small radius of trust have rather to do with the quality of governance within a democracy. Strongly familistic societies tend to develop a two-tier system of ethical values, with higher standards of behavior reserved for relations within the family

28. Byong-Nak Song, *Rise of the Korean Economy* (Hong Kong: Oxford University Press, 1990), p. 199.

29. See Diane Hoffman, "Culture, Self, and 'Uri': Anti-Americanism in Contemporary South Korea," *Journal of Northeast Asian Studies* (1993): 3–20; and Yun-Shik Chang, "The Personalist Ethic and the Market in Korea," *Journal for the Comparative Study of Society and History* 33 (1991): 106–29.

or other types of personal relations and lower ones for public life. One consequence is a relatively low level of civic obligation and hence a greater propensity for political corruption. Political corruption has, of course, been a serious problem plaguing any number of Latin Catholic countries from Italy to Mexico and Brazil. Corruption produces economic inefficiency and, from the standpoint of democratic order, increases citizen cynicism over the political system.

Korea has, of course, been rocked by a number of high-profile corruption scandals over the past decade, including the conviction of former president Roh Tae Woo for collecting a $600 million slush fund. Korea, however, is by no means exceptional in Asia for its levels of corruption. It ranks as number twenty-seven on Transparency International's 1996 corruption perception index, below Singapore, Japan, Hong Kong, and Malaysia but ahead of Thailand, the Philippines, China, and Indonesia.[30] Indeed, one remarkable characteristic of the Park Chung Hee period was its relatively low levels of corruption. Corruption is a function both of inadequate institutional controls on the abuse of power and of cultural factors such as a lack of civic responsibility on the part of officials and political leaders. In Korea's case, it is difficult to disentangle the two: the large role played by the Korean state in economic matters invites abuse and provides little by way of institutional constraints on power; in contrast, the culture supports (or perhaps more properly, does not sanction) certain forms of official corruption even when formal laws and institutions exist. Clearly, however, allegations of corruption coming out of the slush fund, Hanbo Steel, and other cases have seriously tarnished the image of a large part of Korea's political elite.

The historical sources of the relatively low levels of trust in Korean society are complex. Although Korea has displayed a high degree of social order, that order has often been achieved through hierarchical, authoritarian methods to a higher degree than in

---

30. Information taken from the Transparency International web page.

neighboring Japan and probably to a greater extent than in non-communist Chinese societies such as Taiwan, Hong Kong, and Singapore. Korea went directly from traditional monarchy to Japanese colonial rule to military dictatorship, which lasted up until 1987, and it is understandable that the harshness of these various forms of authoritarian rule produced strong opposition forces such as the country's military trade union and student protest movements. Many of the steps undertaken by postwar authoritarian governments—the suppression of union activities, the failure to create basic welfare-state protections like old age and health care benefits, and the brutal suppression of the Kwangju uprising in 1981—all detracted from the general fund of social trust in ways that have persisted under the post-1987 democratic regime.

Beyond these obvious and relatively recent sources of social distrust are longer-term cultural patterns of hierarchy and authority. By all accounts, class structure in premodern Korea was more rigid than its Japanese and Chinese counterparts. The gulf between *Yangban* and *Chonmin* was large and for all practical purposes unbridgeable, and the history of dynastic Korea is marked by periodic peasant uprisings. The samurai class that led Japan's economic development after the Meiji restoration behaved in many respects like the English aristocracy during the British industrial revolution, tolerating intermarriage with the merchant class while suffusing the new business elites with its own *bushido* ethic.[31] The same tended to be less true of high-status Koreans during Korea's period of industrialization, evident in the relatively high rates of intermarriage among the offspring of the founders of the country's largest *chaebols*.[32]

31. On social mobility in Yi dynasty Korea, see Quee-Young Kim, "Korea's Confucian Heritage and Social Change," *Journal of Developing Societies* 4 (1988): 255–69.

32. Choong Soon Kim, *The Culture of Korean Industry: An Ethnography of Poongsan Corporation* (Tucson: University of Arizona Press, 1992), p. 77. See also Fukuyama, *Trust*, p. 133.

Class cleavages and sharply hierarchical authority persist under the current democratic regime, most notably in the internal structure of large Korean corporations. Most Korean *chaebols* are much more hierarchical than the Japanese *zaibatsu* or postwar *keiretsu* on which they were modeled, though practice varies from one group to another.[33] Management authority remains, for the most part, centralized in the hands of the CEO or his family and extends downward in a traditional hub-and-spoke system rather than in the more decentralized manner of a large, professionally managed American firm.[34] The Korean *chaebols* have never practiced corporate paternalism, like extensive in-company welfare and support services, to the extent of Japan.

The consequences of this authoritarian business culture are manifest in labor-management relations, which given the current economic crisis will probably be the most significant source of social conflict and perhaps even instability over the next few years. The militancy of Korea's trade union movement was evident in the 1996–97 showdown between the unions on the one hand and the employers and the government party on the other, a confrontation in which neither side acquitted themselves well. The unions, for their part, which had been responsible for driving Korean labor costs up to perhaps 70 percent of Japan's by 1996, were uncompromising in the face of employer demands for greater flexibility in wages and hiring. The government, facing intransigence from both the unions and the opposition party, forced through new labor legislation in a special early-morning session to which only its members had been invited and used the occasion to pass new national security legislation that many observers feared would give the government new powers to restrict individual rights.

33. Some *chaebols* like Hyundai have a much greater reputation for internal authoritarianism than others like Samsung or Ssangyong.
34. Fukuyama, *Trust*, pp. 134–35.

The economic crisis that Korea now faces will increase the stress of class conflict by increasing unemployment, wage declines, and bankruptcies dramatically. There are, of course, mitigating circumstances. The very severity of the crisis may create a sense of national solidarity and lead the contending parties to cooperate where they might not be inclined to in normal times. The election of Kim Dae Jung as president in December 1997 may also have a meliorating effect; although he has been strongly supportive of labor's positions in the past, he also understands the need to appease international markets and investors and may be better positioned to ask sacrifices of the trade unions than the government party's candidate would have been.

There is, however, an important upside to the all-too-evident divisions within Korean society. To any Western observer, Korean politics looks much more recognizable than does Japanese democracy, despite the latter's age and degree of institutionalization. What seems strangest about Japan is the fact that the different social actors are so reticent in asserting their interests against various forms of authority. The interests of workers are somehow smothered in a system of corporate unions and lifetime employment, while the long-ruling LDP is run on a personalistic basis that amalgamates a wide variety of frequently contradictory societal interests (e.g, rice farmers and industrialists). (Of course, American political parties, such the Democrats under FDR, also consolidate highly disparate interests, but politics is still organized under more ideological lines than in Japan.) Korean interest groups, in contrast, are not reluctant to challenge authority and do so at times violently; workers and managers dislike each other and fight vigorously for bigger pieces of the pie. In an authoritarian political system, this might be a formula for instability. But to the extent that Korea's interest groups begin using democratic political mechanisms to advance their interests, Korean politics might well develop along more European lines, where the development of societal interest groups occurs hand in glove with a broadening of political participation and the growth of distinctive political parties representing those interests. One of the unfortunate things that Korea has imported from Japan is the concept of a broad, all-embracing majority party that will remain in power for extended periods of time instead of alternating in power with smaller but more focused parties. Whether the election of Kim Dae Jung will halt this trend and force a multiparty system based not on personalities but on underlying societal interests remains to be seen.

Conclusion

From the above, it should be clear that neither Asian values nor Korean values have had much of an effect on the prospects for democracy in Korea. Asian values are not meaningless: in the sphere of social relations they have an important impact on gender relations and hence on the family, public order, and a host of important social indicators. But, politically, it is not clear that they constitute a barrier to democratization that is sufficiently strong to overcome the functional requirements for political participation generated by a modernizing society. The correlation between democracy and development remains intact; although there are probably a host of ways that having a Christian culture helps in the establishment of stable democracy, a Confucian culture is no bar.

In contrast to Japan but similar to China, Korean culture tends to favor kinship and other small groups at the expense of broader social trust. Authority tends to be stronger and more hierarchical, and social conflict, closer to the surface. As long as a general consensus concerning the democratic political system exists—and there is ample evidence that it does—this narrow radius of trust constitutes no particular obstacle to democracy and may in fact enhance the long-run prospects for genuine multiparty contestation among important societal interests. By contrast, a narrow radius of trust increases problems of governance by lowering the sense of civic obligation and laying the groundwork for political corruption.

APPENDIX

Conference Agenda

HOOVER INSTITUTION
CONFERENCE

INSTITUTIONAL REFORM
AND
DEMOCRATIC CONSOLIDATION
IN KOREA

Larry J. Diamond
Thomas H. Henriksen
Doh C. Shin
CONFERENCE DIRECTORS

JANUARY 8–9, 1998

STAUFFER AUDITORIUM
HOOVER INSTITUTION
STANFORD UNIVERSITY
STANFORD, CALIFORNIA

COSPONSORED BY THE KOREA FOUNDATION AND THE HOOVER INSTITUTION

Thursday, January 8, 1998

8:15 A.M.	CONTINENTAL BREAKFAST	

Hoover Staff Lounge

8:45 A.M. OPENING REMARKS

John Raisian, *Director, Hoover Institution*

8:55 A.M. INTRODUCTION

Thomas H. Henriksen, *Associate Director, Hoover Institution*

9:00 A.M. Panel I: TRANSFORMING THE POLITICAL
SYSTEM

Larry J. Diamond, chair, *Hoover Institution*

Hoon Jaung, *Chung-Ang University*
Political Parties and Electoral Politics

Chan W. Park, *Duke University*
Legislative Reforms and Executive-Legislative Relations

Thomas B. Gold, discussant, *University of California at Berkeley*

10:30 A.M. BREAK
Hoover Staff Lounge

10:45 A.M.

Larry J. Diamond, chair, *Hoover Institution*

Kyoung-Ryung Seong, *Hallym University*
Local Government Autonomy and Decentralization

David W. Brady, discussant, *Hoover Institution*

12:00 NOON LUNCH
Hoover Staff Lounge

1:30 P.M.   Panel II: REFORMING POLITICAL INSTITUTIONS

Chae-Jin Lee, chair, *Claremont-McKenna College*

Young-Jo Lee, *Kyung Hee University*
President Kim Young Sam's Model of Democratic Reforms

Mun Gu Kang, *Kyungnam University*
Military and Civilian Rule

Robert Scalapino, discussant, *University of California at Berkeley*

3:00 P.M.   REFRESHMENTS
               Hoover Staff Lounge

3:15 P.M.   Panel III: REFORMING SOCIETAL INSTITUTIONS

Robert J. Myers, chair, *Hoover Institution*

Eun Mee Kim, *Ewha Woman's University*
Business Conglomerates: The Chaebol

Seung-Mock Yang, *Seoul National University*
The News Media

Henry S. Rowen, discussant, *Hoover Institution*

6:30 P.M.   RECEPTION
               Stanford Faculty Club

7:00 P.M.   WELCOME

John Raisian, *Director, Hoover Institution*

               ADDRESS
Francis Fukuyama, *George Mason University*
Asian Values, Korean Values, and Democratic Consolidation

7:45 P.M.   DINNER

Friday, January 9, 1998

8:30 A.M.   CONTINENTAL BREAKFAST
                 Hoover Staff Lounge

9:00 A.M.   Panel IV: CULTIVATING DEMOCRATIC CITIZENS

Hong Yung Lee, chair, *University of California at Berkeley*

Doh C. Shin, *University of Illinois at Springfield*
The Evolution of Popular Support for Democracy during the Kim
Young Sam Regime

Sook-Jong Lee, *Sejong Institute*
Mass Participation in Old and New Politics

Abraham Lowenthal, discussant, *University of Southern California*

10:15 A.M.   BREAK
                 Hoover Staff Lounge

10:30 A.M.

Sunhyuk Kim, *University of Southern California*
Civic Mobilization for Democratic Reform

Larry J. Diamond, discussant, *Hoover Institution*

11:45 A.M.   CONCLUDING REMARKS

Thomas H. Henriksen, *Hoover Institution*

12:00 NOON   FAREWELL LUNCHEON
                 Hoover Staff Lounge

Index

Abdollahian, Mark Andrew, 33
Act Relating to Registration of Periodicals, 155
adopted son dilemma, 122
Against Nuclear Plants newsletter, 296
Agency for National Security Planning, 38, 292, 293
All-nation Emergency Committee on Enacting a Special Law for Punishing the Perpetrators of the May 18 Massacre, 288
amae (Japanese value), 327
ANSP (Agency for National Security Planning), 10–11
anticorruption laws, 13–14
APEC (Asia Pacific Economic Cooperation), 202
Articles 15 and 16 (Local Autonomy Act), 133
Asia Motors, 215
Asian crime rates, 314, 315
Asian financial crisis. *See* economic crisis
Asian values: change in ethical (1981–91), 316; of Confucian culture, 299, 307–8, 310, 311; democratic transition and, 308–12; distinctive between Korean and, 320–26; Japanese mores and, 318; Korean mores and, 317; overview of, 305–6; paternalistic authoritarianism and, 306–8; on role

of women, 319–20; similarity between Korean and, 312–20. *See also* culture; Korean values
Association of Families of Political Prisoners, 292
authoritarian rule: confronting and dealing with past, 284–90; Confucian political heritage and, 307–8; international survey on, 328; popular support for, 244–45. *See also* democracies; Korean democracy; reform authoritarianism

banking regulation reforms, 206–8, 228. *See also* Korean financial sector; Korean labor system reform
Basic Press Act (1980), 6, 8, 153, 155
Beck, Peter M., 199
BIP (Bureau of Information Policy), 156
blandos (soft-liners), 279
blitzkreig tactics, 115
blitzkrieg dilemma, 122–23
blitzkrieg strategy, 114–16
Board of Audit and Inspection, 286
Brazil, 56–57
Broadcast Act (1987), 155, 157
bushido ethic, 330

CATV (cable television), 158
Central Election Management Committee, 12

economic crisis: impact on Korea by, 305–6; impact on Korean class conflict, 332; as institutional reform opportunity, 200–202; Korea as symbol of Asian, 2

Economic Injustice Complaint Center, 297

economic performance: democratic consolidation and, 28–29; enterprise reform implications for, 219–21; failure of *chaebol* reform and, 190–95; under Kim Young Sam, 67–68; Kim Young Sam's reforms/outcomes for, 105; labor system reform and, 223–24; mass perceptions of democracy and, 269–72; political assessments and, 272–76

elections: of fourteenth/fifteenth assemblies, 78; Latin American runoff, 64; measuring representativeness/governability of, 61–62; 1997 Kim Dae Jung, 3, 16–17; party split during thirteenth assembly, 78; regional voting index in presidential, 51; runoff, 64; voter shares in presidential, 52–53

election system: as democratic consolidation element, 44–46; impact on democracy by reforms in, 12–13, 292; proportionality of Korean (1988–96), 48; reform of double-ballot system of, 62–64

eleventh assembly, 76, 81

elite behavior, 38. *See also* civic mobilization; popular support

embedded reformism: *chaebol* policies: goals/implementations, 172–90; *chaebol* policies chronology, 196–97; *chaebol* policy failures, 190–95; coalition heterogeneity and, 113–14; context of, 99–112; described, 98–99; goals of financial, 107; instrumental legitimization problem and, 116–17; limits of, 121–25; *pactismo* and *decretismo* strategies for, 103, 121; "paradox of success" of, 124; problem of autocratic

presidency and, 119–21; problem of blitzkrieg approach to, 114–16; rise and fall of, 104–12; scope, level, and sequence of, 117–19; strong authoritarian legacies prior to, 99–101; weak political society/fragmented civil society context of, 101–4. *See also* institutional reforms; Kim Young Sam; Korean financial sector

environmental movement, 295–96

EPB (Economic Planning Board), 173

ethical behavior values, 314, 316

executive branch: autonomy of National Assembly from, 13, 26–27, 93–95; governability and party share held by, 54–55; legislative oversight of, 90–93; legislative proposals drafted by, 85; reform politics and autocratic, 119–21; under Sixth Republic constitution, 6–7; veto power of, 87–88. *See also* government; legislative-executive relations

External Auditors Committee, 189

Fabian approach, 114–16

Fair Trade Act revisions (1992 and 1994), 173, 175–76, 179–80

Fallows, James, 305

family structure, 317–18

Far Eastern Economic Review, 321

Federation of Korean Industries, 182–83

female status, 319–20

fifteenth assembly, 78

Fifth Republic: assembly sessions of, 81; Basic Press Law of, 6, 8; budget modifications during, 88; DJP legislative seats during, 78; eleventh and twelfth assemblies of, 76; government branches under, 10; June 29 declaration adopted by, 5–6; legislative-executive relations under, 75–77; media suppression under, 153–54; National Assembly law under, 75, 76; *songyok* (unwritten taboos) of, 92; use of com-

mittee system during, 83. *See also* Republic of Korea
financial sector. *See* Korean financial sector
Financial Supervisory Committee, 210
first-past-the-post (FPTA) system, 49
First Republic (1948), 149
fiscal control, 88–89. *See also* legislative-executive relations
Five-Year New Economy Plan (1993), 106
FKI (Federation of Korean Industries), 178–81
FM radio stations, 157
fourteenth assembly, 78, 80, 83
Fourth Republic, 152
Fourth Revision of Fair Trade Act (1994), 173, 176
fractionalization index (political parties), 54
freedom of speech, 92–93
FTC (Fair Trade Commission), 179–80, 218
Fukuyama, Francis, 36

Gallup Korea poll (1995), 110
Gallup Korea polls (1994, 1996, 1997), 249
General Dynamics Corporation, 286
German electoral reform model, 63
GNP (Grand National Party), 210
Gold, Tom, 307
governability: conceptual map of representativeness and, 61; criterion for, 52–55; as democratic criteria, 46; effective number of political parties and, 52–54; stability and, 55–57, 59–60; undivided government and, 52
government: corruption scandals of Korean, 68–69, 91, 112, 124, 267, 329; divided, 52, 78; division of administrative tasks between, 136; hierarchical structure of Korean, 133n.11; intergovernmental conflicts/challenges, 142–45; regionalism, 136–42;

strengthening relationship of parties and, 66; structure of Korean local, 137n.17; tasks of central, 135n.14; taxing constraints placed on local, 134. *See also* centralism; executive branch; local government; National Assembly
government bills, 84–88
governorships, 138, 139, 141n.21
Graduate School of International Studies (Yonsei University), 199
Grand National Party, 27
"Great Compromise" (1998), 187n.22

Halla, 305
Hana Hoe Club, 10
Hanahoe (Society of One), 106
Hanbo Steel Corporation scandal (1997), 91, 112, 124, 267, 329
Hankyoreh Shinmun newspaper, 164
Hitchcock, David, 321
"How Koreans Squander Press Freedom" (Halvorsen), 169–70
human rights concept, 308
Huntington, Samuel, 307
Hyundai, 185, 188, 191, 192, 218

IMF (International Monetary Fund): brokered deal for banking/labor reforms by, 227, 228, 230; *chaebol* reform pushed by, 172, 184–90, 202, 204–5, 227–29; labor market reform advocated by, 224–25; position on banking reform by, 210–11; rescue package to Korea from, 2, 3n.4, 68, 184, 204
Inchon/Kyonggi province, 265–69
Inglehart, Ron, 313
institutional barriers to electoral strength, 48–49
institutional reforms: chronology of major, 5–15, 16–18; direction of electoral, 62–64; direction of, 60–66; economic crisis as opportunity for, 200–202; future of, 66–71; halt to (1996), 15; legislative, 73–83; of

by, 5–6; legislative oversight of executive branch by, 90–93; organizational features of, 80–83; party makeup of Sixth Republic, 79–80; protests against railroading of bills in, 293–94; Public Official's Ethics Act revised by, 9–10; real estate market transaction reforms by, 13–14; reforms laws of Sixth Republic, 10–15; Sixth Republic opposition parties in, 156; state control over, 70; treatment of government bills by, 84–88; under Fifth Republic constitution, 75, 76; under Sixth Republic constitution, 6, 74–77; use of committee system by, 82–83; *yeoso yadae* composition of, 26, 39–40, 285. *See also* executive branch; legislative-executive relations

National Assembly law (Fifth Republic), 75, 76

National Assembly law (Sixth Republic), 6, 76–77

National Catholic Priests' Corps for the Realization of Justice, 293

National Council of New Politics, 27

National Security Act: demands for repeal of, 292–93; recommended reform of, 40–41; revision of, 155

National Security Planning Agency Law, 267

NCNP (National Congress for New Politics), 51, 109, 111, 210, 218, 263, 264

NDRP (New Democratic Republican Party), 101

New Five-Year Economic Development Plan (1993), 173, 175

New Korea Party, 70, 87

New Zealand electoral reform, 63

NKP (New Korea Party), 59, 111, 263, 293

NMCK (National Mayors Conference of Korea), 144

Northern League (Italy), 67

ODI (overseas direct investment, 1994–96), 177

O'Donnell, Guillermo, 19, 65, 120, 238

OECD (Organization for Economic Cooperation and Development), 1, 314, 325

Office of Legislation and Budget, 83

pactismo reform strategy, 103, 121

Park, Chan Wook, 30

Park Chung Hee, 9, 151, 152, 200, 327, 329

"peace dam" (1988), 286

People's Action Day, 288

People's Solidarity for Participatory Democracy, 287

Periodicals Act, 155

Plattner, M. F., 147

political elites, 22–23. *See also* civic mobilization

political institutions: democratic consolidation and choice of, 26–28; structural weakness of, 202–4. *See also* institutional reforms

political parties: as democratic consolidation element, 44–46; fractionalization index of, 54; governability and effective number of, 52–54; institutional reform of, 64–66; as legislative reform factor, 77–83; mergers/splits among Korean, 58–59; popular support for, 108–11; representativeness and electoral support of, 50–51; three-party merger under Roh administration, 101. *See also* government

political society: defining, 101n.4; embedded reformism and, 101–4; impact of media on, 164–67; Kim Young Sam's reforms/outcomes for, 105. *See also* civil society

political support, 236. *See also* popular support

popular support: apportioning dissatisfaction and, 251; for authoritarian rule, 245; character of Korean, 244–47; conceptualization of,